B.C.

WITHOUT FORM AND VOID

A Study of the Meaning of Genesis 1.2.

Arthur C. Custance,

M.A., Ph.D., F.R.A.I.

Brockville, Canada, 1970

Acknowledgments

The number of people who have helped me in this study is considerable. My very special thanks are due to Dr. John R. Howitt of Toronto and Mr. W. Dennis Burrowes of Victoria, both in Canada; and to Mr. Gerald L. Gooden of California (U.S.A.), to Mr. A. G. Tilney in England, and above all to Miss Evelyn M. White, the Sec-Treas. of the Doorway Papers (also published by the author) and who did almost all the typing of the manuscript.

Published by
Arthur C. Custance
Canada 1970

DOORWAY PAPERS
Box 291, Brockville,
Ontario, Canada.

Dedicated to two, Lillian and Evelyn,
who have sacrificed very much
over many years,
to make this study possible.

TABLE OF CONTENTS

* * *

2 בְּרֵאשִׁ֖ית בָּרָ֣א אֱלֹהִ֑ים אֵ֥ת הַשָּׁמַ֖יִם וְאֵ֥ת הָאָֽרֶץ: וְהָאָ֗רֶץ הָיְתָ֥ה אֱ
תֹ֙הוּ֙ וָבֹ֔הוּ וְחֹ֖שֶׁךְ עַל־פְּנֵ֣י תְה֑וֹם וְר֣וּחַ אֱלֹהִ֔ים מְרַחֶ֖פֶת עַל־פְּנֵ֥י
הַמָּֽיִם:

3 וַיֹּ֥אמֶר אֱלֹהִ֖ים יְהִ֣י א֑וֹר וַֽיְהִי־אֽוֹר: וַיַּ֧רְא אֱלֹהִ֛ים אֶת־הָא֖וֹר
4
5 כִּי־ט֑וֹב וַיַּבְדֵּ֣ל אֱלֹהִ֔ים בֵּ֥ין הָא֖וֹר וּבֵ֥ין הַחֹֽשֶׁךְ: וַיִּקְרָ֨א אֱלֹהִ֤ים ׀ לָאוֹר֙
י֔וֹם וְלַחֹ֖שֶׁךְ קָ֣רָא לָ֑יְלָה וַֽיְהִי־עֶ֥רֶב וַֽיְהִי־בֹ֖קֶר י֥וֹם אֶחָֽד:

6 וַיֹּ֣אמֶר אֱלֹהִ֔ים יְהִ֥י רָקִ֖יעַ בְּת֣וֹךְ הַמָּ֑יִם וִיהִ֣י מַבְדִּ֔יל בֵּ֥ין מַ֖יִם
7 לָמָֽיִם: וַיַּ֣עַשׂ אֱלֹהִים֮ אֶת־הָרָקִיעַ֒ וַיַּבְדֵּ֗ל בֵּ֤ין הַמַּ֙יִם֙ אֲשֶׁר֙ מִתַּ֣חַת
8 לָרָקִ֔יעַ וּבֵ֣ין הַמַּ֔יִם אֲשֶׁ֖ר מֵעַ֣ל לָרָקִ֑יעַ וַֽיְהִי־כֵֽן: וַיִּקְרָ֧א אֱלֹהִ֛ים
לָֽרָקִ֖יעַ שָׁמָ֑יִם וַֽיְהִי־עֶ֥רֶב וַֽיְהִי־בֹ֖קֶר י֥וֹם שֵׁנִֽי:

9 וַיֹּ֣אמֶר אֱלֹהִ֗ים יִקָּו֨וּ הַמַּ֜יִם מִתַּ֤חַת הַשָּׁמַ֙יִם֙ אֶל־מָק֣וֹם אֶחָ֔ד וְתֵרָאֶ֖ה
10 הַיַּבָּשָׁ֑ה וַֽיְהִי־כֵֽן: וַיִּקְרָ֨א אֱלֹהִ֤ים ׀ לַיַּבָּשָׁה֙ אֶ֔רֶץ וּלְמִקְוֵ֥ה הַמַּ֖יִם
11 קָרָ֣א יַמִּ֑ים וַיַּ֥רְא אֱלֹהִ֖ים כִּי־טֽוֹב: וַיֹּ֣אמֶר אֱלֹהִ֗ים תַּֽדְשֵׁ֤א הָאָ֙רֶץ֙
דֶּ֗שֶׁא עֵ֚שֶׂב מַזְרִ֣יעַ זֶ֔רַע עֵ֣ץ פְּרִ֞י עֹ֤שֶׂה פְּרִי֙ לְמִינ֔וֹ אֲשֶׁ֥ר זַרְעוֹ־ב֖וֹ
12 עַל־הָאָ֑רֶץ וַֽיְהִי־כֵֽן: וַתּוֹצֵ֨א הָאָ֜רֶץ דֶּ֠שֶׁא עֵ֣שֶׂב מַזְרִ֤יעַ זֶ֙רַע֙ לְמִינֵ֔הוּ
וְעֵ֧ץ עֹֽשֶׂה־פְּרִ֛י אֲשֶׁ֥ר זַרְעוֹ־ב֖וֹ לְמִינֵ֑הוּ וַיַּ֥רְא אֱלֹהִ֖ים כִּי־טֽוֹב:
13 וַֽיְהִי־עֶ֥רֶב וַֽיְהִי־בֹ֖קֶר י֥וֹם שְׁלִישִֽׁי:

14 וַיֹּ֣אמֶר אֱלֹהִ֗ים יְהִ֤י מְאֹרֹת֙ בִּרְקִ֣יעַ הַשָּׁמַ֔יִם לְהַבְדִּ֕יל בֵּ֥ין הַיּ֖וֹם וּבֵ֣ין
15 הַלָּ֑יְלָה וְהָי֤וּ לְאֹתֹת֙ וּלְמ֣וֹעֲדִ֔ים וּלְיָמִ֖ים וְשָׁנִֽים: וְהָי֤וּ לִמְאוֹרֹת֙
16 בִּרְקִ֣יעַ הַשָּׁמַ֔יִם לְהָאִ֖יר עַל־הָאָ֑רֶץ וַֽיְהִי־כֵֽן: וַיַּ֣עַשׂ אֱלֹהִ֔ים אֶת־שְׁנֵ֥י
הַמְּאֹרֹ֖ת הַגְּדֹלִ֑ים אֶת־הַמָּא֤וֹר הַגָּדֹל֙ לְמֶמְשֶׁ֣לֶת הַיּ֔וֹם וְאֶת־הַמָּא֤וֹר
17 הַקָּטֹן֙ לְמֶמְשֶׁ֣לֶת הַלַּ֔יְלָה וְאֵ֖ת הַכּוֹכָבִֽים: וַיִּתֵּ֥ן אֹתָ֛ם אֱלֹהִ֖ים בִּרְקִ֣יעַ
18 הַשָּׁמָ֑יִם לְהָאִ֖יר עַל־הָאָֽרֶץ: וְלִמְשֹׁל֙ בַּיּ֣וֹם וּבַלַּ֔יְלָה וּֽלְהַבְדִּ֔יל בֵּ֥ין
19 הָא֖וֹר וּבֵ֣ין הַחֹ֑שֶׁךְ וַיַּ֥רְא אֱלֹהִ֖ים כִּי־טֽוֹב: וַֽיְהִי־עֶ֥רֶב וַֽיְהִי־בֹ֖קֶר
י֥וֹם רְבִיעִֽי:

20 וַיֹּאמֶר אֱלֹהִים יִשְׁרְצוּ הַמַּיִם שֶׁרֶץ נֶפֶשׁ חַיָּה וְעוֹף יְעוֹפֵף עַל־
21 הָאָרֶץ עַל־פְּנֵי רְקִיעַ הַשָּׁמָיִם׃ וַיִּבְרָא אֱלֹהִים אֶת־הַתַּנִּינִם הַגְּדֹלִים
וְאֵת כָּל־נֶפֶשׁ הַחַיָּה ׀ הָרֹמֶשֶׂת אֲשֶׁר שָׁרְצוּ הַמַּיִם לְמִינֵהֶם וְאֵת
22 כָּל־עוֹף כָּנָף לְמִינֵהוּ וַיַּרְא אֱלֹהִים כִּי־טוֹב׃ וַיְבָרֶךְ אֹתָם אֱלֹהִים
לֵאמֹר פְּרוּ וּרְבוּ וּמִלְאוּ אֶת־הַמַּיִם בַּיַּמִּים וְהָעוֹף יִרֶב בָּאָרֶץ׃
23 וַיְהִי־עֶרֶב וַיְהִי־בֹקֶר יוֹם חֲמִישִׁי׃

24 וַיֹּאמֶר אֱלֹהִים תּוֹצֵא הָאָרֶץ נֶפֶשׁ חַיָּה לְמִינָהּ בְּהֵמָה וָרֶמֶשׂ וְחַיְתוֹ־
25 אֶרֶץ לְמִינָהּ וַיְהִי־כֵן׃ וַיַּעַשׂ אֱלֹהִים אֶת־חַיַּת הָאָרֶץ לְמִינָהּ וְאֶת־
הַבְּהֵמָה לְמִינָהּ וְאֵת כָּל־רֶמֶשׂ הָאֲדָמָה לְמִינֵהוּ וַיַּרְא אֱלֹהִים כִּי־
26 טוֹב׃ וַיֹּאמֶר אֱלֹהִים נַעֲשֶׂה אָדָם בְּצַלְמֵנוּ כִּדְמוּתֵנוּ וְיִרְדּוּ בִדְגַת הַיָּם
וּבְעוֹף הַשָּׁמַיִם וּבַבְּהֵמָה וּבְכָל־הָאָרֶץ וּבְכָל־הָרֶמֶשׂ הָרֹמֵשׂ עַל־
27 הָאָרֶץ׃ וַיִּבְרָא אֱלֹהִים ׀ אֶת־הָאָדָם בְּצַלְמוֹ בְּצֶלֶם אֱלֹהִים בָּרָא אֹתוֹ
28 זָכָר וּנְקֵבָה בָּרָא אֹתָם׃ וַיְבָרֶךְ אֹתָם אֱלֹהִים וַיֹּאמֶר לָהֶם אֱלֹהִים פְּרוּ
וּרְבוּ וּמִלְאוּ אֶת־הָאָרֶץ וְכִבְשֻׁהָ וּרְדוּ בִּדְגַת הַיָּם וּבְעוֹף הַשָּׁמַיִם
29 וּבְכָל־חַיָּה הָרֹמֶשֶׂת עַל־הָאָרֶץ׃ וַיֹּאמֶר אֱלֹהִים הִנֵּה נָתַתִּי לָכֶם אֶת־
כָּל־עֵשֶׂב ׀ זֹרֵעַ זֶרַע אֲשֶׁר עַל־פְּנֵי כָל־הָאָרֶץ וְאֶת־כָּל־הָעֵץ אֲשֶׁר־בּוֹ
30 פְרִי־עֵץ זֹרֵעַ זָרַע לָכֶם יִהְיֶה לְאָכְלָה׃ וּלְכָל־חַיַּת הָאָרֶץ וּלְכָל־
עוֹף הַשָּׁמַיִם וּלְכֹל ׀ רוֹמֵשׂ עַל־הָאָרֶץ אֲשֶׁר־בּוֹ נֶפֶשׁ חַיָּה אֶת־כָּל־
31 יֶרֶק עֵשֶׂב לְאָכְלָה וַיְהִי־כֵן׃ וַיַּרְא אֱלֹהִים אֶת־כָּל־אֲשֶׁר עָשָׂה
וְהִנֵּה־טוֹב מְאֹד וַיְהִי־עֶרֶב וַיְהִי־בֹקֶר יוֹם הַשִּׁשִּׁי׃

GENESIS ONE (Greek: Septuagint)

ΕΝ ΑΡΧΗ ἐποίησεν ὁ θεὸς τὸν οὐρανὸν καὶ τὴν γῆν. 2 ἡ δὲ γῆ
ἦν ἀόρατος καὶ ἀκατασκεύαστος, καὶ σκότος ἐπάνω τῆς ἀβύσσου· καὶ
πνεῦμα θεοῦ ἐπεφέρετο ἐπάνω τοῦ ὕδατος. 3 καὶ εἶπεν ὁ θεος Γενηθήτω φῶς· καὶ ἐγένετο φῶς. 4 καὶ ἴδεν ὁ θεὸς τὸ φῶς ὅτι καλόν·
καὶ διεχώρισεν ὁ θεὸς ἀνὰ μέσον τοῦ φωτὸς καὶ ἀνὰ μέσον τοῦ σκό-
τους. 5 καὶ ἐκάλεσεν ὁ θεὸς τὸ φῶς ἡμέραν, καὶ τὸ σκότος ἐκάλεσεν
νύκτα. καὶ ἐγένετο ἑσπέρα καὶ ἐγένετο πρωί, ἡμέρα μία. 6 Καὶ
εἶπεν ὁ θεός Γενηθήτω στερέωμα ἐν μέσῳ τοῦ ὕδατος, καὶ ἔστω δια-
χωρίζον ἀνὰ μέσον ὕδατος καὶ ὕδατος· καὶ ἐγένετο οὕτως. 7 καὶ ἐποίησεν ὁ θεὸς τὸ στερέωμα· καὶ διεχώρισεν ὁ θεὸς ἀνὰ μέσον τοῦ ὕδατος
ὃ ἦν ὑποκάτω τοῦ στερεώματος, καὶ ἀνα μέσον τοῦ ὕδατος τοῦ ἐπάνω
τοῦ στερεώματος. 8 καὶ ἐκάλεσεν ὁ θεὸς τὸ στερέωμα οὐρανόν· καὶ
ἴδεν ὁ θεὸς ὅτι καλόν. καὶ ἐγένετο ἑσπέρα καὶ ἐγένετο πρωί, ἡμέρα
δευτέρα. 9 Καὶ εἶπεν ὁ θεός Συναχθήτω τὸ ὕδωρ τὸ ὑποκάτω τοῦ
οὐρανοῦ εἰς συναγωγὴν μίαν, καὶ ὀφθήτω ἡ ξηρά· καὶ ἐγένετο οὕτως.
καὶ συνήχθη τὸ ὕδωρ τὸ ὑποκάτω τοῦ οὐρανοῦ εἰς τὰς συναγωγὰς αὐτῶν,
καὶ ὤφθη ἡ ξηρά. 10 καὶ ἐκάλεσεν ὁ θεὸς τὴν ξηρὰν γῆν, καὶ τὰ συστέ-
ματα τῶν ὑδάτων ἐκάλεσεν θαλάσσας· καὶ ἴδεν ὁ θεὸς ὅτι καλόν. 11 καὶ
εἶπεν ὁ θεός Βλαστησάτω ἡ γῆ βοτάνην χόρτου, σπεῖρον σπέρμα κατὰ
γένος καὶ καθ' ὁμοιότητα, καὶ ξύλον κάρπιμον ποιοῦν καρπόν, οὗ τὸ
σπέρμα αὐτοῦ ἐν αὐτῷ κατὰ γένος εἰς ὁμοιότητα ἐπὶ τῆς γῆς· καὶ
ἐγένετο οὕτως. 12 καὶ ἐξήνεγκεν ἡ γῆ βοτάνην χόρτου, σπεῖρον σπέρμα
κατὰ γένος καὶ καθ' ὁμοιότητα, καὶ ξύλον κάρπιμον ποιοῦν καρπόν, οὗ τὸ
σπέρμα αὐτοῦ ἐν αὐτῷ κατὰ γένος ἐπὶ τῆς γῆς. καὶ ἴδεν ὁ θεὸς ὅτι
καλόν. 13 καὶ ἐγένετο § ἑσπέρα καὶ ἐγένετο πρωί, ἡμέρα τρίτη. 14 Καὶ
εἶπεν ὁ θεός Γενηθήτωσαν φωστῆρες ἐν τῷ στερεώματι τοῦ οὐρανοῦ εἰς
φαῦσιν τῆς γῆς, καὶ ἄρχειν τῆς ἡμέρας καὶ τῆς νυκτὸς καὶ διαχωρίζειν ¶
ἀνὰ μέσον τῆς ἡμέρας καὶ ἀνὰ μέσον τῆς νυκτός· καὶ ἔστωσαν εἰς σημεῖα
καὶ εἰς καιροὺς καὶ εἰς ἡμέρας καὶ εἰς ἐνιαυτούς· 15 καὶ ἔστωσαν εἰς φαῦσιν
ἐν τῷ στερεώματι τοῦ οὐρανοῦ, ὥστε φαίνειν ἐπὶ τῆς γῆς. καὶ ἐγένετο
οὕτως. 16 καὶ ἐποίησεν ὁ θεὸς τοὺς δύο φωστῆρας τοὺς μεγάλους, τὸν
φωστῆρα τὸν μέγαν εἰς ἀρχὰς τῆς ἡμέρας καὶ τὸν φωστῆρα τὸν ἐλάσσω
εἰς ἀρχὰς τῆς νυκτός, καὶ τοὺς ἀστέρας. 17 καὶ ἔθετο αὐτοὺς ὁ θεὸς ἐν
τῷ στερεώματι τοῦ οὐρανοῦ, ὥστε φαίνειν ἐπὶ τῆς γῆς, 18 καὶ ἄρχειν τῆς
ἡμέρας καὶ τῆς νυκτός, καὶ διαχωρίζειν ἀνὰ μέσον τοῦ φωτὸς καὶ ἀνὰ
μέσον τοῦ σκότους· καὶ ἴδεν ὁ θεὸς ὅτι καλόν. 19 καὶ ἐγένετο ἑσπέρα
καὶ ἐγένετο πρωί, ἡμέρα τετάρτη.¶ 20 Καὶ εἶπεν ὁ θεός Ἐξαγαγέτω
τὰ ὕδατα ἑρπετὰ ψυχῶν ζωσῶν καὶ πετεινὰ πετόμεν[α] ἐπὶ τῆς γῆς κατὰ
τὸ στερέωμ[α τοῦ] οὐρανοῦ· καὶ ἐγένετο οὕτως. 21 καὶ ἐποίησεν ὁ θεὸς
τὰ κήτη [τὰ με]γάλα καὶ πᾶσαν ψυχὴν [ζῴων ἑρπε]τῶν, ἃ ἐξήγαγεν [τὰ
ὕδατα κατὰ γένη αὐτῶν], καὶ πᾶν πετεινὸν πτ[ερωτὸν] κατὰ γένος· καὶ
ἴδεν ὁ [θεὸς ὅτι καλά]. 22 καὶ ηὐλόγησεν αὐτὰ ὁ θ[εὸς λέγων] Αὐξάνεσθε
καὶ πληθ[ύνεσθε, καὶ] πληρώσατε τὰ ὕδατα [ἐν ταῖς θα]λάσσαις, καὶ τὰ
πετε[ινὰ πληθυ]νέσθωσαν ἐπὶ τῆς [γῆς. 23 καὶ ἐγέ]νετο ἑσπέρα καὶ ἐγ[έ-
νετο πρωί], ἡμέρα πέμπτη. 24 Καὶ εἶπεν ὁ θεός Ἐξαγαγ[έτω ἡ γῆ
ψυχὴν] ζῶσαν κατὰ γένος, [τετράποδα] καὶ ἑρπετὰ καὶ θηρί[α τῆς γῆς
κατὰ] γένος, καὶ ἐγένετο [οὕτως]. 25 καὶ ἐποίησεν ὁ θεὸς τὰ [θηρία τῆς

γῆς] κατὰ γένος καὶ τὰ κτ[ήνη κατὰ γέ]νος καὶ πάντα τὰ ἑρπ[ετὰ τῆς γῆς]
κατὰ γένος αὐτῶν· καὶ ἴδεν ὁ θεὸς ὅτι καλά. § 26 καὶ εἶπεν ὁ θεός Ποιήσω-
μεν ἄνθρωπον κατ' εἰκόνα ἡμετέραν καὶ καθ' ὁμοίωσιν· καὶ ἀρχέτωσαν τῶν
ἰχθύων τῆς θαλάσσης καὶ τῶν πετεινῶν τοῦ οὐρανοῦ καὶ τῶν κτηνῶν
καὶ πάσης τῆς γῆς καὶ πάντων τῶν ἑρπετῶν τῶν ἑρπόντων ἐπὶ τῆς γῆς.
27 καὶ ἐποίησεν ὁ θεὸς τὸν ἄνθρωπον, κατ' εἰκόνα θεοῦ ἐποίησεν αὐτόν·
ἄρσεν καὶ θῆλυ ἐποίησεν αὐτούς. 28 καὶ ηὐλόγησεν αὐτοὺς ὁ θεὸς λέγων
Αὐξάνεσθε καὶ πληθύνεσθε, καὶ πληρώσατε τὴν γῆν καὶ κατακυριεύσατε
αὐτῆς, καὶ ἄρχετε τῶν ἰχθύων τῆς θαλάσσης καὶ τῶν πετεινῶν τοῦ οὐρανοῦ καὶ πάντων τῶν κτηνῶν καὶ πάσης τῆς γῆς καὶ πάντων τῶν ἑρπετῶν
τῶν ἑρπόντων ἐπὶ τῆς γῆς. 29 καὶ εἶπεν ὁ θεός Ἰδοὺ δέδωκα ὑμῖν πᾶν
χόρτον σπόριμον σπεῖρον σπέρμα, ὅ ἐστιν ἐπάνω πάσης τῆς γῆς· καὶ πᾶν
ξύλον, ὃ ἔχει ἐν ἑαυτῷ καρπὸν σπέρματος σπορίμου· [ὑ]μῖν ἔσται εἰς
βρῶσιν, 30 καὶ πᾶσι [τοῖ]ς θηρίοις τῆς γῆς καὶ πᾶσι [τοῖ]ς πετεινοῖς τοῦ
οὐρανοῦ [καὶ π]αντὶ ἑρπετῷ τῷ ἕρπον[τι ἐπὶ τῆς] γῆς, ὃ ἔχει ἐν ἑαυτῷ
[ψυχὴ]ν ζωῆς· καὶ πάντα χόρ[τον χλ]ωρὸν εἰς βρῶσιν. καὶ [ἐγένετ]ο
οὕτως. 31 [καὶ ἴδεν ὁ] θεὸς τὰ πάντα ὅσα ἐποίη[σεν, καὶ] ἰδοὺ καλὰ
λίαν. καὶ ἐγέ[νετο ἑσ]πέρα καὶ ἐγένετο πρωί, [ἡμέρα ἕ]κτη.

* * *

GENESIS ONE (Latin: the Vulgate)

Vss.1-2. In principio creavit Deus coelum et terram. Terra autem erat inanis et vccua, et tenebrae erant super faciem abyssi; et Spiritus Dei ferebatur super aquas.

Vss.3-5. Dixitque Deus: Fiat lux. Et facta est lux. Et vidit Deus lucem quod esset bona: et divisit lucem a tenebris. Appellavitque lucem Diem, et tenebras Noctem: factumque est vespere et mane, dies unus.

Vss.6-8. Dixit quoque Deus: Fiat firmamentum in medio aquarum: et dividat aquas ab aquis. Et fecit Deus firmamentum, divisitque aquas, quae erant sub firmamento, ab his quae erant super firmamentum. Et factum est ita. Vocavitque Deus firmamentum, Coelum: et factum est vespere et mane, dies secundus.

Vss.9-13. Dixit vero Deus: Congregentur aquae, quae sub coela sunt, in locum: et appareat arida. Et factum est its. Et vocavit Deus aridam, Terram, congregationesque aquarum appellavit Maris. Et vidit Deus quod esset bonum. Et ait: Germinet terra herbam virentem et facientem semen, et lignum pomiferum faciens fructum juxta genus suum, cujus semen in semetipso sit super terram. Et factum est ita. Et protulit terra herbam virentem, et facientem semen juxta genus suum, lignumque faciens fructum, et habens unumquodque sementem secundum speciem suam. Et vidit Deus quod esset bonum. Et factum est vespere et mane, dies tertius.

Vss.14-19. Dixit autem Deus: Fiant luminaria in firmamento coeli, et dividant diem ac noctem, et sint in signa et tempora, et dies et annos: ut luceant in firmamento coeli, et illuminent terram. Et factum est ita. Fecitque Deus duo liminaria magna, luminare majus, ut praeesset diei: et luminare minus, ut praeesset nocti: et stellas. Et posuit eas in firmamento coeli, ut lucerent super terram, et praeessent diei ac nocti, et dividerent lucem ac tenebras. Et vidit Deus quod esset bonum. Et factum est vespere et mane, dies quartus.

Vss.20-23. Dixit etiam Deus: Producant aquae reptile animae viventis, et volatile super terram sub firmamento coeli. Creavitque Deus cete grandia, et omnem animam viventem atque motabilem, quam produxerant aquae in species suas, et omne volatile secundum genus suum. Et vidit Deus quod esset bonum. Benedixitque eis, dicens: Crescite, et multiplicamini, et re-

lete aquas maris: avesque multiplicentur super terram. Et factum est vespere et mane, dies quintus.

Vss. 24-31. *Dixit quoque Deus: Producat terra animam viventem in genere suo, jumenta, et reptilia, et bestias terrae secundum species suas. Factumque est ita. Et fecit Deus bestias terrae juxta species suas, et jumenta, et omne reptile terrae in genere suo. Et vidit Deus quod esset bonum. Et ait: Faciamus Hominem ad imaginem et similitudinem nostram: et praesit piscibus maris, et volatilibus coeli, et bestiis, universaeque terrae, omnique reptili, quod movetur in terra. Et creavit Deus hominem ad imaginem suam: ad imaginem Dei creavit illum: masculum et feminam creavit eos. Benedixitque illis Deus, et ait: Crescite, et multiplicamini, et replete terram et subjicite eam, et dominamini piscibus maris, et volatilibus coeli, et universis animantibus, quae moventur super terram. Dixitque Deus: Ecce dedi vobis omnem herbam afferentem semen super terram, et universa ligna quae habent in semetipsis sementem generis sui, ut sint vobis in escam: et cunctis animantibus terrae, omnique volucri coeli, et universis quae moventur in terra, et in quibus est anima vivens, ut habeant ad vescendum. Et factum est ita. Viditque Deus cuncta quae fecerat: et erant valde bona. Et factum est vespere et mane, dies sextus.*

* * *

GENESIS ONE (An English Translation)

Vss.1-2. In the beginning God created the heaven and the earth. But the earth had become a ruin and a desolation; and darkness was upon the face of the deep. And the spirit of God hovered over the face of the waters.

Vss.3-5. And God said, Let it become light: and it became light. And God saw the light that it was good: and God divided the light from the darkness. And God called the light Day, and the darkness He called Night. And the evening and the morning became one day.

Vss.6-8. And God said, Let there come to be a firmament in the midst of the waters, and let it divide the waters from the waters. And God appointed the firmament and divided the waters which were under the firmament from the waters which were above the firmament: and it came to be so. And God called the firmament Heaven. And the evening and the morning became the second day.

Vss.9-13. And God said, Let the waters under the heaven be gathered together unto one place, and let the dry land appear: and it became so. And God called the dry land Earth; and the gathering together of the waters called He Seas: and God saw that it was good. And God said, Let the earth bring forth grass, the herb yielding seed, and the fruit tree yielding fruit akin to itself, whose seed is in itself, upon the earth: and it became so. And the earth brought forth grass, and herb yielding seed akin to itself, and the tree yielding fruit, whose seed was in itself, after its kind: and God saw that it was good. And the evening and the morning became the third day.

Vss.14-19. And God said, Let there come to be lights in the firmament of the heaven to divide the day from the night; and let them come to be for signs, and for seasons, and for days, and years: and let them come to be for lights in the firmament of the heaven to give light upon the earth: and it became so. And God appointed two great lights; the greater light to rule the day, and the lesser light to rule the night: He appointed the stars also. And God set them in the firmament of the heaven to give light upon the earth and to rule over the day and over the night, and to divide the light from the darkness:

and God saw that it was good. And the evening and the morning became the fourth day.

Vss. 20-23. And God said, Let the waters bring forth abundantly the moving creature that hath life, and fowl that may fly above the earth in the open firmament of heaven. And God created great whales, and every living creature that moveth which the waters brought forth abundantly, akin to themselves, and every winged fowl after its kind: and God saw that it was good. And God blessed them, saying, Be fruitful, and multiply, and fill the waters in the seas, and let fowl multiply in the earth. And the evening and the morning became the fifth day.

Vss. 24-25. And God said, Let the earth bring forth living creatures breeding true to themselves, cattle and creeping things and the wild creatures of the earth, also breeding true to themselves. And this came to pass. And God appointed the wild things of the earth, breeding true to themselves, and the cattle similarly, and likewise everything that creepeth upon the earth. And God saw that it was good.

Vss. 26-31. And God said, Let us appoint man in our image, after our likeness: and let them have dominion over the fish of the sea and over the fowl of the air, and over the cattle and over all the earth, and over every creeping thing that creepeth upon the earth. So God created man in His own image, in the image of God created He him: male and female created He them. And God blessed them, and God said unto them, Be fruitful, and multiply, and fill the earth, and subdue it: and have dominion over the fish of the sea, and over the fowl of the air, and over every living thing that moveth upon the earth. And God said, Behold, I have given you every herb bearing seed which is upon the face of all the earth, and every tree, in the which is the fruit of a tree yielding seed; to you it shall become food. And to every beast of the earth, and to every fowl of the air, and to every thing that creepeth upon the earth, wherein there is life, I have given every green herb for food: and it came to be so. And God saw every thing that He had appointed, and, behold, it was very good. And the evening and the morning became the sixth day.

* * *

1

INTRODUCTION.

בְּרֵאשִׁית בָּרָא אֱלֹהִים אֵת הַשָּׁמַיִם וְאֵת הָאָרֶץ:
וְהָאָרֶץ הָיְתָה תֹהוּ וָבֹהוּ וְחֹשֶׁךְ עַל-פְּנֵי תְהוֹם.

"In the beginning God created the heavens and the earth. And the earth was without form and void, and darkness was on the face of the deep."

"And the earth was without form..." or "But the earth had become a ruin...". Which is the more correct translation? It could make a tremendous difference.

The first two verses of Genesis chapter one have been translated in essentially the same way in virtually every English Version from that authorized in 1611 by James I (no mean Hebrew scholar himself!) to those 'modern idiom' versions which seem to have been appearing with ever increasing frequency in recent years. One might therefore reasonably suppose that the rendering from the Hebrew into English of this particular passage is a perfectly straightforward matter without any ambiguity whatever. Not a few modern writers would like us to think so.

Unfortunately, this is not really the case. Some difference of opinion about the precise meaning of the original has existed for centuries. A substantial number of Hebrew scholars have held that the wording of verse 2 may be translated in a way which gives the reader a fundamentally different impression as to its meaning. And even the relationship between verse 1 and verse 2 is a matter of continuing debate because this relationship hinges very largely upon how verse 2 is translated.

Although this disagreement *has* existed for a very long time, I cannot find that anyone has really set out to review the whole issue with the thoroughness it deserves. Analysis of verse 2 shows that both the words themselves, as well as the order in which they are set forth (a matter of considerable importance in Hebrew), have been chosen with particular care; and each qualifying term is illuminated elsewhere in Scripture in a way which seems to show that this verse, far from being a mere continuation of what precedes it, may be intended to describe a somewhat later period of the earth's history which subsequent revelation takes as an important reference point. It is far more than merely a poetically worded picture of a world in the making. Indeed, no Hebrew manuscript that I am aware of ever presents this portion of Genesis in that literary form which is reserved for poetry throughout the rest of the Old Testament. This may be drama, but it is written as prose, not poetry. Were it merely a poetic statement, it need not be taken too seriously as a precise description of the early history of our earth, but considered as prose its correct interpretation is a matter of much greater importance.

The importance of establishing its intended meaning does not stem from the fact that if it is interpreted in one particular way it can then be used to resolve certain apparent conflicts between the Mosaic cosmogony and modern geological theory. Its importance stems from the fact that it is a foundation statement; and the foundation statements of any belief system are the more critical as they lie nearer the base of its structure. An error at the *end* of a long line of reasoning may be very undesirable but it is much less dangerous than an error at the beginning. And in the first three chapters of Genesis we have the basic facts upon which are erected the whole theological superstructure of the Christian faith. Uncertainty here, or misinterpretation, is likely to have repercussions throughout the whole of the rest of the system of belief.

Essentially, there are two possible interpretations of Gen. 1.2. Either it is a chaos which marks the *first* stage of God's creative activity, or it is a chaos which resulted from some catastrophic event marring what had formerly been an orderly and beautiful world. Not infrequently it is argued that it cannot be a picture of a "destroyed" earth because there is no geological evidence for such an event on a global scale. But the fundamental question at issue here is not the absence or otherwise of geological evidence for such an event.

The real question is, "What does the text really mean?" For it is a well recognized fact that when some particular idea is unpopular and runs counter to the current orthodoxy of the times, it will be widely held that it cannot be true because of lack of evidence in its facour. But when current opinion veers around for some quite unforseen reason until the originally unfavourable idea comes to be looked upon with less disfavour, it suddenly turns out, unexpectedly, that there *is* evidence to support it, evidence *that is obviously in its favour!* This happened with the theory of Continental Drift, for example, which after being popularized by Wegener, Du Toit, Taylor, and others, fell into strong disfavour because the mechanism was lacking. But now it has come right back and appears as a very useful theory indeed. We should not be too anxious if the text as it stands turns out to mean something which conflicts with present geological orthodoxy. The same thing may happen here.

To repeat, therefore, the question at issue in this study is not "What is the geological evidence?" but "What does the passage really mean?" In short, if we are once sure what some particular passage is saying, we should not allow science to determine for us - and I speak as a scientist - what we may believe in Scripture; nor are we to allow a clear statement of Scripture to determine what the scientist may observe in his laboratory. Demonstrable fact in the one cannot ultimately conflict with demonstrable fact in the other, though interpretations often do. Where a conflict of evidence seems to exist, we must search for some means of reconciliation: failing this, we need not abandon either piece of evidence if we are reasonably sure of both, but only wait for further light. Contradictory things sometimes equally turn out to be true, and in the past it has not infrequently happened that further light has shown such contradiction to be more apparent than real. Invariably Scripture has been vindicated where it often seemed most obviously in error. The light of Archaeology has consistently demonstrated this.

So the basic issue to be resolved here, as I see it, is the precise intention of this verse: and the most likely way to succeed in this enquiry is not to be guided by a branch of science (Geology) that is still comparatively young and far from precise, but by examining the rules which have governed the writing of Hebrew and by studying carefully the statements of Scripture elsewhere whenever they shed light. Other linguistic evidence (as, for example, from cognate languages) may be used to advantage to provide background information, though such evidence is seldom conclusive. In any case, the best commentary on Scripture is Scripture itself, and it is upon

Scripture that we have to depend ultimately for light on Hebrew usage. It seems to me of secondary importance to determine to what extent the meaning we derive from the passage can be squared with current geological doctrine, even though it is reasonable enough to attempt a reconciliation where possible. But such reconciliation must always be held with reserve, for the current scientific view with which harmony might thus be achieved may itself fail to survive an increase in our knowledge of the earth's past history. Modern theories of cosmogony and of earth history are very much in a state of flux and the certainties of yesterday (a steady-state universe, for example) are no longer the certainties of today. This, in a nutshell, is my feeling about the means whereby to determine the correct translation of Gen. 1.2.

But I also think that the issue needs resolving, if at all possible, because it has increasingly become a fertile source of provocation for all sorts of hard feelings and pontifical pronouncements on the part of both its adherents and its opponents. Some will surely appear in this book! The subject has become emotionally charged and, as a consequence, it is difficult to evaluate it without becoming involved in the crossfire. There is no middle ground any longer. One must apparently accept all the accretions and assigned implications if one expresses any opinion that favours either view. It is no longer possible, or at any rate it has become increasingly difficult, to isolate the fundamental issue of the precise meaning of the Hebrew original from all the superstructures that have been built upon particular interpretations of it. And the quite erroneous opinion that the view adopted in this volume originated only with the challenge of modern Geology dies very hard indeed.

The term, "Gap Theory", has become an epithet of dissaprobation in many quarters. It is widely supposed that only pinheads and nitwits give any serious thought to the matter any more. We are assured that the interpretation has not an ounce of weight in its favour from the linguistic point of view.... It is linguistic nonsense "as every Hebrew scholar knows", or so says the voice of one authority. Or to quote the views of a more recent author, an organic chemist, who dismisses a question that has engaged some of the best Hebrew scholars with complete assurance by stating categorically that the thesis is "unscriptural, unreasonable, and unscientific". So one might wonder if it is worth a moment's notice.

But history shows that as soon as "all authorities are agreed", this is when there is greatest need for caution. Majority opinion is important.... but never decisive. We accept majority rule in government not because the majority is most likely to be right but because if they are *wrong* they are not likely to be so dangerously wrong as the *minority* would be. It is a safety device - not a guarantee of infallibility.

Unfortunately, human beings accept authority rather easily. It saves having to think for oneself.... We find it more convenient to quote an authority than to become one: and such is human nature that if we quote authorities with sufficient force or frequency, we become an authority merely be the doing of it! As George Eliot said, it is possible for a man to appear so learned by his quotes that the appearance becomes a proof of what he believes. Quotation marks provide a reinforcement for an observation which lessens (or seems to lessen) the more important requirement that it be the truth. So authoritarianism spawns itself. Tremendous vocal support can be given through the medium of the printed word to statements made by genuine authorities who have been misinterpreted or misrepresented or misunderstood by lesser authorities, or to statements which the original authors have themselves since abandoned. The printed word is powerful in its persuasiveness! Things get repeated so frequently in the literature that they begin to achieve the status of unchallengeable and inspired truths. The cliche that the Hebrew word בָּרָא (bara) means "to create out of nothing" and that it is used only of divine activity, is a case in point. Both parts of the statement are demonstrably false. As to the first, we know that Scripture says of Adam that he was created out of the dust of the ground, not *ex nihilo* And as to the second, a Young's Concordance will soon show the English reader that the supposed rule is not true in this regard either. The fact is that the Hebrew word may indeed mean creation *ex nihilo*.... and probably does in Gen. 1.1. But it is not something that inheres in the word itself. And the word is only limited to divine activity in one particular verbal form (the Kal), while in its other forms it is used of human activity. To say that in these 'other' cases it does not mean "to create" is not the issue. The statement, so often made without qualification, is that the verb is never used except of divine activity. And this is simply not true.

Now, in order to avoid misunderstanding, I must repeat something which I said earlier, namely, that the question of whether Genesis, Chapter one, can be squared with modern geological theory is of secondary importance. I do not for one moment say it is quite un-important. It is important. But the more important thing is, undoubtedly, to determine what Genesis says. Other issues are secondary. My own conclusions as to the meaning of Gen. 1.2 does not accord with that reflected in almost every version published in the last fifty or sixty years. This might seem sufficient reason for discounting it. But it is well to keep the door of inquiry open anyhow, and this is really all that one can hope to achieve by such a study as this. And I think it can be demonstrated that in some respects at least, current generally accepted views are not altogether correct.

This book is not written therefore for anyone who, for example, has already decided that the correct and only reasonable rendering of הָיְתָה in Gen. 1.2 is as the simple copulative "was" and who as a consequence has no interest in any further light which may be available on the subject. It is written for those who still have an open mind and who do not expect in such questions as these to achieve absolute certainty where we are dealing with an ancient language whose grammar and syntax we still do not understand completely. It is written for those who would like to know something of what is to be said on both sides. There is no question that virtually all the usual authorities quoted at the present time, if they are not against my rendering, at least have not seen fit to recommend it as a preferred alternative, though some certainly admit it. But this need not deter one, because these same authorities contradict themselves in certain critical ways. Keil refuses to recognize the possibility of "became" for "was" in Gen. 1.2 but suggests it for "was" in Gen. 3.20 where the same word occurs in precisely the same form. And in some cases they later changed their minds on the matter, as Delitzsch seems to have done, and as Dillman expressly did, for example. And other authorities like S. R. Driver, unhesitatingly acknowledged the scholarship of contemporaries such as Pusey who held precisely the views I hold and for the same linguistic reasons.

Some writers, of course, are impatient and cannot be bothered to examine the question with sufficient thoroughness. If one has not actually examined the occurrences of the verb הָיָה that are listed for illustrative purposes in the best lexicons of the Hebrew language, one can say with some show of self-confidence, as one well-known writer has, "the verb הָיְתָה is sometimes used to mean 'became' if the context demands it, but the verb as it stands is 'was' as anyone who has studied Hebrew will testify".[1] This has the appearance of a profoundly learned observation, but is in fact quite incorrect. It is so easily proven false that one wonders what is happening to Christian scholarship.

Some hold that the meaning of Gen. 1.2 is obvious. Such writers dismiss the complexity of the problem in a paragraph and then propose to return to "the simple study" of the meaning of the passage. Such writers seem to hold the view that the matter can be safely left to the ordinary reader's good sound common sense. The obvious meaning is obviously the true meaning.

Many years ago, J. Harris wrote:[2]

> "When it is objected that the decision of the question might safely be left to any unbiased mind on a perusal of the English version of the text, the objector is evidently calculating on the effect likely to be produced on the 'unbiased' mind by the mere juxtaposition of the opening verses, and by the conjunction *and* given to the Hebrew particle *waw*, which commences the second verse. His, however, is an appeal not to his knowledge but to his ignorance. It is to take advantage, not of his judgment, but of his lack of it. For unless, by an act of marvellous intuition, he could infer the Hebrew original from the English rendering, he may, for aught he knows to the contrary, be pronouncing on the meaning of a faulty translation. So that the question to be first decided relates to the correct rendering of the original."

This was written in 1874.

Some have held that linguistically it is not possible to determine with certainty how the passage should be translated and that therefore one must decide the issue exegetically. They then propose that "contextual support" for any other view than that commonly accepted is entirely lacking. But this begs the question altogether. The context of so many passages is nothing more than the bias of the reader. To argue that "context" supports one's own views in such a case is merely to say that one's particular interpretation of the context supports one's own particular bias. Moreover, it is difficult to see how a context could be established for what is only the second sentence in a book covering such a vast span of time and subject matter as the Bible does.

To me, this issue is important, and after studying the problem for some thirty years and after reading everything I could lay my hands on *pro* and *con* and after accumulating in my own library some 300 commentaries on Genesis, the earliest being dated 1670, I am persuaded that there is, on the basis of the evidence, far more reason to translate Gen. 1.2 as "But the earth had become a ruin and a desolation, etc." than there is for any of the conventional translations in our modern versions. This persuasion rests upon an examination of the evidence itself not only in the light of commentaries and lexicons but of other related works on linguistics, of some of the better known ancient versions in languages other than English - such as the Targum of Onkelos, the Book of Jasher, the Septuagint, the Vulgate, and of the voluminous works of the early Church Fathers (of which I have the 40 volume Scribner edition), as well as upon the writings of the Medieval Scholars.

I used to enjoy argument, but I no longer do. Whatever the impression to the contrary which my particular style of writing may give, I have not set down these conclusions merely to provoke a battle with those who will disagree. I am prepared to leave the matter to sort itself out with time, in the firm belief that the truth will ultimately become apparent. Some wrong conclusions will be manifest enough to those better qualified than I: no claims to finality are made. After some years in scientific research where one always has the privilege at all times of the sharp criticisms of one's colleagues, it has seemed to me that more value would be attached to a work which honestly and genuinely sought to note the weaknesses (as well as the strengths) of the position favoured by the author. Perhaps in an underhand kind of way, one may hope to lessen the force of the contrary evidence by admitting its validity! Sometimes a note of sarcasm has crept in. This is not the best weapon as I know only too well - but it can add spice to an otherwise rather indigestible menu. Occasionally it has been necessary to repudiate or ignore a favourable line of argument which others have felt important. But this has usually been done only where the evidence is of an ambiguous nature. For example, the command given to Noah, after the old order had been destroyed by the Flood, was to "replenish" the earth. The same command was given centuries earlier to Adam (Gen. 1.28). One could argue that the implications of the second occasion should properly apply to the first also, thus allowing one to assume a similar situation - namely, an old, old order destroyed, an emptied world in need of *re*-filling. Perhaps.... Yet the Hebrew word מָלֵא *(malah)* does not really mean to re-fill, but only to fill. There are other such instances. The evidence is not, to my mind, decisive enough and has not been considered worthy of inclusion. The case is strong in its own right and needs no doubtful assists. A series of appendices provides background evidence (in some quantity) without disrupting the flow of the argument in the text itself.

So these, then, are the principles upon which this volume has been written. We hope only by opening out fresh views that we may contribute light to minds of greater precision who may thus be enabled to hit upon the exact truth.

POSTSCRIPT:

One further matter which I consider of some importance before proceeding to this study. There are not available to me any libraries of the kind which would hold volumes particularly relevant to the issue involved here. Some of the Jewish literature, for example, is not obtainable for study, and I lack a few of the older commentaries of such scholars as Keil, for example. As far as possible, I have purchased copies of everything I could locate in Europe, in England, and in the United States. Sometimes a particularly desirable work has been advertised in some catalogue but sold before my order reached the agent. At other times I have been more than ordinarily fortunate....

On the whole, my own research library forms an enviable collection. Nevertheless, I am still limited to secondary sources in some important areas, besides being very limited indeed with respect to the reading of works in other languages - such as German. I greatly dislike quoting second-hand but it has been unavoidable at times. The reader will quickly discern where this has occurred, but I have made every attempt to make it apparent. By far the greater part of this volume, however, is based on first hand verification. The loan facilities (by mail) of libraries such as that of the University of Toronto have been used to advantage but many theological colleges whose holdings would have proved most valuable do not have such facilities.

And, lastly, translations from Hebrew, Greek, or Latin are my own unless otherwise stated. The Italians have a proverb: *tradittore traditture*, 'to translate is to betray'. I may now and then have betrayed the original, albeit unintentionally. But some freedom in the use of idiom is essential, and in my rendering of the Latin quotations, for example, I may have taken liberties which a purist will not like. But the original is also given in any case - and I do not believe any injustice has been done to the excerpts.

Chapter 1.

A LONG-HELD VIEW.

It is a rare thing nowadays to find in a scholarly work on Genesis any acknowledgment of the fact that there is evidence of a discontinuity between the first two verses of Chapter One and that this was ever recognized by commentators until modern Geology arose to challenge the Mosaic cosmogony.

The usual view is that when geologists "proved" the earth to be billions of years old, conservative biblical students suddenly discovered a way of salvaging the Mosaic account by introducing a gap of unknown duration between these two verses. This is supposed to have solved the problem of time by an expeditious interpretation previously unrecognized. This convenient little device was attributed by many to Chalmers of the middle of the last cnetury, and popularized among "fundamentalists" by Scofield in the first quarter of the present century. Both the impetus which brought it to general notice and the company it kept in its heyday combined to make it doubly suspected among conservative scholars and totally ignored by liberal ones.

However, D. F. Payne of the University of Sheffield, England, in a paper published recently by Tyndale Press entitled, *Genesis One Reconsidered*,[3] makes this brief aside at the appropriate place: "The 'gap' theory itself, as a matter of exegesis, *antedated* (my emphasis) the scientific challenge, but the latter gave it a new impetus". Granted then that the view did antedate the modern geological challenge, by how long did it do so? Just how far back can one trace this now rather unpopular view and how explicit are the earlier references? And on what grounds was it held prior to the general acceptance of the views of Laplace, Hutton, and Lyell? If its antecedence can be established with any certainty, one then has to find some other reason than the threat of Geology for its having arisen.

The view was undoubtedly held by early commentators without any evidence that it was being presented as an "answer" to some suspected challenge to the veracity of Scripture. It must therefore have arisen either because a careful study of the original text of Scripture itself had given intimations of it, or perhaps due to some ancient tradition about the after-effects of the catastrophe itself, such after-effects as might well have been observed by early man before the new order had effectively buried the evidences of the old. For man must have been created soon enough after the event to observe at least *some* of the evidence which time has since eroded away. There *is* evidence of a tremendous and comparatively recent geological catastrophe still to be observed even today in certain parts of the world. There are numerous instances of mammoths and other animals which were by some agency killed *en masse* and instantly buried together, the preyed upon with the predator, while apparently still in the prime of life. Such animal cemetries have frequently been reported in northern latitudes: in Siberia, for example. And similar indications may well have existed in former years in much lower latitudes where early man could have come across them and pondered their meaning. Such evidences of destruction, even if it occurred before the creation of Man, must surely have set men's minds to wondering what had been the cause. There is no reason to suppose that early man was any less observant than his modern descendants, or any less curious about the cause of such mass destruction of living forms.

At any rate, here in broad outline is the situation in so far as ancient and modern literature reflects some knowledge of such an event. This outline will be explored in detail subsequently - but a summary review may help to establish the general picture. And it will show that it is indeed a long-held view.

We are in no position at present to determine precisely how the

Jewish commentators made the discovery, but their early literature (the Midrash for example) reveals that they had some intimation of an early pre-Adamic catastrophe affecting the whole earth. Similarly, clear evidence appears in the oldest extant Version of the Hebrew Scriptures (the Targum of Onkelos) and some intimation may be seen in the "punctuation marks" of the Massoretic text of Genesis Chapter One. Early Jewish writers subsequently built up some abstruse arguments about God's dealings with Israel on the basis of this belief and it would seem that Paul in his Epistle to the Corinthians is at one point making indirect reference to this traditional background.

A few of the early Church Fathers accepted this interpretation and based some of their doctrines upon it. It is true that both they and their Jewish antecedents used arguments which to us seem at times to have no force whatever, but this is not the issue. The truth is, as we shall see, that the idea of a once ordered world having been brought to ruin as a consequence of divine judgment just prior to the creation of Adam, was apparently quite widespread. It was not *debated:* it was merely held by some and not by others. Those who held it referred to it and built up arguments upon it without apparently feeling the need to apologize for believing as they did, nor for explaining the grounds for their faith.

During succeeding centuries not a few scholars kept the view alive, and medieval scholars wrote about it at some length - often using phraseology which gives their work a remarkably modern ring.

The *Book of Jasher*, Alcuin's version, seems clearly to assume it - even though the document itself has a questionable pedigree. It *certainly* antedates modern Geology in any case.

And for the past two hundred years many translators and commentators have maintained the view and elaborated upon it at length.

In short, it is *not* a recent interpretation of the text of Gen. 1.1 and 1.2, but an ancient one long antedating modern geological views. Indeed - it could be as old as the writing of Gen. 1.2 itself! Some of the ancient Sumerian and Babylonian fragments that, when pieced together, give us a general view of their cosmogony, seem to lend support to it as a very ancient belief. It is perfectly true that these epics and legends are full of fantasy and absurdity if read at their face value - but it is not absolutely certain that the writers themselves *intended* them to be taken precisely at face value. It may have been for teaching purposes. The use of animation as a mnemonic aid is recognized widely today, and scientific textbooks for schools and colleges adopt this technique of teaching without requiring us to believe, for example, that metallic elements do actually "marry"! Such a simile is employed in metallurgical literature because it aptly conveys what seems to be happening when one metal unites with another. The Sumerians and Babylonians may have animated their cosmogonies for the same reason, while they themselves actually held much more down-to-earth views on the matter. We should not assume that their thinking was altogether childish. At any rate, there are evidences in these ancient texts that they looked upon the earth's very early history as having been one in which things had in some way and at one particular point in time "gone wrong". And this sense of catastrophe is not limited to a recollection of the Fall of man. It seems to refer to something prior to it. It was on a cosmic scale. Since there are reverberations of these catastrophic events even as far away as China, it is possible that the earliest writers had knowledge of things which we now discern only very dimly if at all, and that this knowledge was generally shared by mankind prior to the dispersion of Genesis 11. See Appendix XXI.

It is surprising that this almost unbroken thread of testimony to a view that is now widely held to be of recent origin should have been consistently ignored or unrecognized for so long. Admittedly it is at times evanescent and occasionally ambiguous, and admittedly the fanciful methods of interpreting Scripture adopted by the Jewish Commentators and often emulated by the early Church Fathers do not exactly encourage one to seek for solid factual information in their writings, yet at other times they are quite explicit in their presentations. At any rate, whatever use or abuse they may have made of the information they had, there can really be no doubt that they *DID* have information of this sort, and this information seems never to have been entirely lost sight of from New Testament times to the present.

It is worth exploring all the strands we have, for in one way or another they each tend to contribute light to the total picture. Yet it must be emphasized once again, after saying all this, that while it is valuable to be able to correct a false impression about the antiquity of this view, it really proves nothing about the correctness or otherwise of the view espoused. The only way this can be done is by a study of the text itself.... which is undertaken in the chapters which follow: the present objective is a lesser one, a historical sketch.

Now after or during the Babylonian Captivity, the Jewish people gradually accumulated the comments and explanations of their best known teachers about the Old Testament for some 1500 years - or well on into the Christian era. This body of traditional teaching was gathered together into the Midrash which thus became the oldest pre-Christian exposition of the Old Testament. It was already the basis of rabbinical teaching in the time of our Lord and must have been quite familiar to Paul.

According to the Revised Edition of Chambers's Encyclopedia published in 1860, under the heading "Genesis", the view which was then being popularized by Buckland and others to the effect that an interval of unknown duration was to be interposed between Gen. 1. 1 and 1. 2 was already to be found in the Midrash. In his great work, *The Legends of the Jews*, Louis Ginsberg has put into continuous narrative a precis of their legends, as far as possible in the original phrases and terms. In Volume 1 which covers the period from the Creation to Jacob, he has this excerpt on Genesis 1:[4]

> "Nor is this world inhabited by man the first of things earthly created by God. He made several other worlds before ours, but He destroyed them all, because He was pleased with none until He created ours."

Clearly this reflects the tradition underlying the translation which appears in the Targum of Onkelos to be noted below.

Furthermore, in the Massoretic Text in which the Jewish scholars tried to incorporate enough "indicators" to guide the reader as to correct punctuation there is one small mark which is technically known as *Rebhia*, which is classified as a "disjunctive accent" intended to notify the reader that he should pause before proceeding to the next verse. In short, this mark indicates a "break" in the text. Such a mark appears at the end of Genesis 1. 1. This mark has been noted by several scholars including Luther.[5] It is one indication among others, that the initial *waw* (ו) which introduces verse 2 should be rendered "but" rather than "and", a dis-junctive rather than a con-junctive.

Another piece of substantiating evidence is to be found in the Targum of Onkelos, the earliest of the Aramaic Versions of the Old Testament written by Hebrew Scholars. According to the Babylonian Talmud, Onkelos was a proselyte, the son of a man named Calonicas, and although he *was* the composer of the Targum which bears his name, he is held actually to have received it from Rabbi Eliezer and Rabbi Yehoshua, both of whom lived towards the end of the first and the beginning of the second century A. D. However, since in the Jerusalem Talmud the very same thing is related by the same authorities (and almost in the same words) of the proselyte Aquila of

Pontes, whose Greek version of the Bible was used by the Greek-speaking Jews down to the time of Justinian, it is sometimes argued that Onkelos is but another name for Aquila. Aquila Ponticus was a relative of the Emperor Hadrian, living in the second century B.C. Thus even if Onkelos is not yet completely identified, the Targum attributed to him must still be placed early in the second century B.C. As his translation into Aramaic of Gen.1.2, Onkelos has the following:

וְאַרְעָא הֲוָת צְדְיָא׃ *w'aretsah hawath tsadh'ya.*

In this passage, the verb הוה is compounded with the Aramaic verb צדא which appears here as a passive participle of a verb which itself means "to cut" or "to lay waste". We have here, therefore, a rendering "and the earth was laid waste", an interpretation of the original Hebrew of Gen. 1.2 which leaves little room for doubt that Onkelos understood this to mean that something had occurred between verse 1 and verse 2 to reduce the earth to this desolated condition. It reflects Ginsberg's Jewish legend.

Akiba ben Joseph was an influential Jewish rabbi who was president of the School Bene Barek near Saffa. He laid the basis for the Mishna. When Barcochebas rebelled against the Romans, Akiba joined him and was captured. He was executed in 135 A.D. The ancient work known as *The Book of Light* or *Sefer Hazzohar*, sometimes simply *Zohar*, was traditionally ascribed to one of Akiba's disciples, a certain Simeon ben Jochai. In this work, which thus represents an opinion held towards the end of the first century and the early part of the second, there is a comment on Gen. 2.4-6 which, though difficult to follow, reads thus:[6]

> "These are the generations (ie., this is the history of....) of heaven and earth.... Now wherever there is written the word 'these' (אֵלֶה) the previous words are put aside. And these are the generations of the destruction which is signified in verse 2 of chapter 1. The earth was Tohu and Bohu. These indeed are the worlds of which it is said that the blessed God created them *and destroyed them*, and, *on that account*, the earth was desolate and empty."

Here, then, we have a comment which in the time of our Lord was held widely enough that Paul might very well have known about it. In which case we may better understand the background of his words in writing to the Corinthians (II Cor. 4.6) where he said, "God

Who commanded the light to shine out of darkness hath shined into our hearts, to give the light of the knowledge of the glory of God in the face of Christ Jesus".

Now very few will deny that in this passage Paul is referring back to Gen. 1.3, "And God said, Let there be light". What is not absolutely certain is how far one can press the analogy. Personally, I believe it makes excellent sense to assume here that Paul had in mind an interpretation of these first three verses of Genesis 1 which sees the situation as a ruin about to be restored by God's creative power, commencing with the giving of light where all was formerly darkness. This *is*, after all, precisely the position that the unredeemed soul is in. The analogy is most pointed and reasonable. And if we once allow that this is what was in Paul's mind, then we must surely also admit that Paul, speaking by inspiration, set his seal upon the truth of the interpretation of Gen. 1.2 for which we are here contending; and the more ancient tradition which lies behind the words of Akiba and the rendering of Onkelos receive a measure of confirmation.

In his *Rabbinical Commentary on Genesis*,[7] Paul Isaac Hershon has this somewhat obscure quotation which reinforces Paul's analogy:

> "'And the earth was desolate and void'. The earth will be desolate, for the shekinah will depart at the destruction of the Temple, and hence it is said: 'And the Spirit of God hovered upon the face of the water': which intimates to us that even although we be in exile (after the destruction of the Temple) yet the Torah shall not depart from us; and therefore it is added: 'And God said, Let there be light'. This shows us that after the captivity God will again enlighten us, and send us the Messiah....".

Admittedly, this mode of interpretation is strange to us, but there is really no doubt what is intended. The Promised Land with its capital city epitomized by the Temple, was once the place of God's Shekinah glory. But now it has been destroyed and made empty, as Jer. 4.24 f. predicted. Nevertheless, it was not destroyed permanently, for the Spirit of God still hovers over the place of His former 'glory', though for the present it *is* destroyed and made empty. In due time, just as God's Spirit hovered over the destroyed earth with a promise of new life to come upon it, so will He restore the Land and the Temple and renew His glory by the presence of His Messiah Who shall come.

There is little question that the whole hope of restoration underlying this passage from the rabbinical commentary is based on a view of Genesis which sees in verse 3 a similar case of restoration after judgment. And the belief that this restorative process began in the first case with a command that the light shine out of the darkness, and that this will again occur when a new Light shines unto Israel is surely the Jewish background of Paul's words to the Christian believers in Corinth.

I believe, moreover, that there may be one further evidence in the New Testament of this view in (appropriately) the Epistle to the Hebrews. Here in Heb. 11.3 the writer makes this significant observation: "Through faith we understand that the worlds were framed by the word of God". The significant thing about this statement in the present context is that the word rendered 'framed' is the Greek verb *katartidzo* (καταρτιζω) which although it is rendered 'to perfect' in seven cases in the New Testament (Matt. 21.16; Lu. 6.40; I Cor. 1.10; II Cor. 13.11; I Thess. 3.10; Heb. 13.21; and I Pet. 5.10), is more strictly a word meaning 'to repair' or 'to restore'. In Matt. 4.21 and Mark 1.19 it is used of repairing or mending nets. Liddell and Scott give the meaning in Classical Greek as 'adjust', or 'put in order again', or 'restore'. Even Young in his Concordance at these references (above) where the word is rendered 'to perfect' adds that its meaning is 'to fit thoroughly' or 'to adjust'. And in Classical Greek the word was used by Herodotus (5.106) to mean 'to put in order again', and (5.28) 'to settle by acting as mediator', and so 'to reform'; while Polybius uses it of repairing a ship, or setting a broken bone. Thayer says of its use in I Pet. 5.10 that it has the meaning of 'making one what he ought to be'.[8] This could, of course, mean nothing more than the 'maturing' of the individual with no necessary implication of a process of mending his ways. However, Thayer also adds at the same place, as an illustration of its use in an ethical sense, Gal. 6.1 where it is used 'of those who have been restored to harmony'. So that we understand by faith how the worlds were *restored* and made fit for man by the Word of God.

Now, any one of these pointers taken alone might carry little weight. But put together they seem to require that we recognize the real possibility that a view of Gen. 1.1 and 1.2 which many today feel strained and improbable may in fact have been generally taken for granted in our Lord's day and during the first century or so of the present era. In no case does the view seem to have been 'defended', and this could be either because it was so widely accepted - or because it did not seem to have any great significance. There are many today who feel that this catastrophic event was a significant turning point in the thread of God's self-revelation and that this is reflected in the recurrent New Testament phrase "since the foundation of the world", a phrase which they believe should rather be rendered "since the *disruption* of the world". I also, at one time, felt well satisfied that this is a more correct translation, but I have come to feel that the grounds for it are not altogether satisfactory from the linguistic point of view. Since a good argument is not strengthened by a weak link, I have not appealed to this possibility as part of the 'evidence', but careful consideration of some of the *pros* and *cons* will be found in Appendix XII.

In any case, the view was never thereafter entirely lost, even though it was sometimes presented only in the form of an opinion that such a gap did exist, a time interval of unknown duration between the initial creation and the work of the six days which began in verse 3.

Origen, for example, who lived from 186 to about 254 A.D., and to whom the original languages of the Bible were very familiar, has this to say in his great work, *De Principiis*, at Gen. 1.1: [9]

> "It is certain that the present firmament is not spoken of in this verse, nor the present dry land, but rather that heaven and earth from which this present heaven and earth that we now see afterwards borrowed their names."

And that he saw verse 2 as a description of a "casting down" of the original is borne out quite clearly by his subsequent observation that the condition resulted from a "disruption" which is best described, he suggests, by the Latin verb *dejicere*, 'to throw down'.

In the course of time, attempts were made - not unnaturally - to fill in the details of the event which led up to the devastation described. Since all such effects were presumed to be moral judgments and since man had not yet been created, the angels were blamed. Somewhere around 650 A.D., the English poet Caedmon (who died about 680) wrote about Genesis and the creation,[10] and presented the view that man had really been introduced in order to replace the angels which had conducted their dominion over the earth so ruinously. Fallen angels were responsible for the catastrophe. Whether the poems attributed to Caedmon were really his is a moot point, but *someone* in the seventh century knew about this tradition. According to Bede, these poems were supposed to have resulted from a dream in which an angel told Caedmon to sing and write about the Creation. This he finally did, though at first reluctantly, producing works dealing with the creation of the world, the origin of man, and the whole history of Genesis. All the 'poems' or songs thus attributed to Caedmon were first published by Francis Junius in 1665 from a manuscript now in the Bodleian Library, Oxford. At present of the whole series on Genesis, Exodus, Daniel, and Christ and Satan, it is generally conceded that only the one on Genesis is really Caedmon's work, and even this has perhaps been transmitted to us in an interpolated and modified form. At any rate, the basic idea regarding the destruction of the old world seems to have been known to him, and subsequent modifications of his original text do not alter the fact that in Bede's time (674 - 735 A.D.) this view was known and discussed whether by Caedmon himself or by those who took it upon themselves to modify his works. The earliest manuscript we now have is of the 10th century and it gives no indication (by signature) of its authorship, but the substance of it agrees well with what is attributed to Caedmon.

This work, which is a commentary on the first 22 chapters of Genesis with one small missing segment near the beginning, was written in verse but is rendered as prose by Mason in his translation. Caedmon is not as specific as one would wish but his view in brief is that the created order which preceded the present heaven (and earth?) system was ruled over by Angels. In his own words:

> "These angelic hosts were wont to feel joy and rapture, transcendent bliss in the presence of their creator; then their beautitude was measureless. Glorious ministers magnified their Lord, spoke his praise with zeal, lauded the Master of their being, and were excellently happy in the majesty of God. They had no knowledge of working evil or wickedness, but dwelt in innocence forever with their Lord: from the beginning they wrought in heaven nothing but righteousness and truth, until a Prince of Angels through pride strayed into sin: then they would consult their own advantage no longer, but turned away from God's loving kindness.
>
> "They had vast arrogance in that by the might of their multitudes they sought to wrest from the Lord the celestial mansions. Then there fell upon them, grieviously, the envy, presumption, and pride of the Angel who first began to carry out the evil plot, to weave it and promote it, when he boasted by word - as he thirsted for conflict - that he wished to own the home and high throne of the heavenly kingdom of the north".

So the Lord cast them "that had committed a dire sin" (line 46) into a specially created "joyless house of punishment", banishing them from heaven (line 68). "Then, as formerly, true peace existed (once more) in heaven, fair amity: for the Lord was dear to all, the Sovereign to his servants" (line 79 and 80). But the 'heavenly seats' of these rebellious creatures were now vacant. So (line 92 f.):

> "Our Lord bethought him, in meditative mood how he might again people, with a better race, his high creation, the noble seats and glory crowned abodes which the haughty rebels had left vacant high in heaven. Therefore Holy God willed by his plenteous power that under the circle of the firmament of the earth should be established with sky above and wide water, a world-creation (ie., as opposed to a heavenly one) in a place of the foes whom in their apostasy he hurled from bliss".

The poet then describes how "this broad earth stood.... idle and useless, alien even to God himself" (line 105) until God looked upon it in its joylessness and darkness, and then "created heaven and earth" (line 114). It is thus not too easy to see how he views these events in their precise temporal relationship, for he first describes how this "broad earth" existed in its uselessness and then some ten lines later he describes God's remedial action in creating not merely heaven but earth also. Perhaps he really means creating order on the earth rather than actually creating the globe itself.

At any rate, there existed an order of created beings prior to all this who, though living in heaven, had failed to fulfill their appointed role in the economy of God. And then there existed an earth in shrouded darkness and in a chaotic state which God later turned into a habitation for an order of created beings destined to replace the fallen angels. Admittedly not a very clear account, but at least one which makes it apparent that a created order existed long before Day One of the Creation Week.

The purpose of the ordering of this alienated world was to provide a home for this new race. But whether the earth's "state of alienation" from God (as Caedmon evidently views Gen. 1.1 and 2) was in any way the direct consequence of the fall of the Angels, he does not make clear. Perhaps he thought it was obvious.

According to Erich Sauer,[11] King Edgar of England (943 - 975) adopted the same view. This man was an unusually gifted individual and it was largely due to his enthusiastic co-operation with Dunstan, the then Archbishop of Canterbury, that Monasticism was revived in England. The evils which in time arose from these institutions should not allow us to overlook the fact that in an age which was indeed dark they kept alive and carried over from antiquity the learning and lore which in due time became the starting point for the Renaissance. It was certainly in part due to the learning which this king himself evidently enjoyed that royal patronage was so gladly given to the revival of the only schools known to that age. I have no precise information on what he actually said on the present issue, but evidently his opinion was shared quite widely by his contemporaries.

Hugo St. Victor (1097 - 1141) was a Flemish scholar and a member of the Augustinian Monastery of St. Victor and later Prior of the monastery in Paris. He wrote:[12]

> *"Fortassis jam satis est de his hactenus disputasse, si hoc solum adjecerimus quanto tempore mundus in hac confusione, priusquam ejus dispositio inchoaretur, perstiterit. Nam quod illa priam rerum omnum materia, in principio tempros vel potius cum ipso tempore exorta sit, constat ex eo quod dictum est: in principio creavit Deus coelum et terram. Quandiu autem in hac informitate sine confusione permanserit, scriptura manifeste non ostendit."*

> ie. "Perhaps enough has already been debated about these matters thus far, if we add only this, 'how long did the world remain in this disorder before the regular re-ordering (dispositio) of it was taken in hand? For the fact that the first substance of all things arose at the very beginning of time - or rather, with time itself - is settled by the statement that, 'In the beginning God created the heavens and the earth'. But how long it continued in this state of confusion, Scripture does not clearly show".

In this remark Hugo is certainly not saying, specifically, that he sees the disordered state of the world in Gen. 1.2 as the result of a catastrophe of some kind. He could mean merely that it began this way and, as here visualized, was only awaiting the ordering hand of God to make it into a Cosmos. What is, I think, *quite* clear is that he did not equate the work of the first day with the act of creation. A period of time of unknown duration intervened between Gen. 1.1 and 1.2. This is all he intends: but it is this admission which we wish to underscore.

Two centuries later, Thomas Aquinas (1226 - 1274) reiterated this view when he wrote:[13]

Sed melior videtur dicendum quod creatio fuerit aute omnen diem...

ie. "but it seems better to maintain (the view) that the creation was prior to any of the days (literally, before any day)."

St. Thomas evidently considered that the first day was not to be equated with the time of creation itself. This first day came later: he does not suggest how much later.

In somewhat indefinite statements like this, only one thing stands out clearly. The writers would not have agreed with Ussher that Creation occurred 4000 B.C. They might very probably have assented to his chronology as applied to the creation of *Adam* but they would have set the creation of the Universe (the heavens and the earth) further back in time by some unstated amount. Gen. 1.2 does NOT represent the condition of things immediately after the initial creation.... but some time later. None of these writers ventured to suggest just how long the interval had been. The idea of an earth so old that the period of man's history pales into insignificance when viewed merely in chronological terms was probably not in their thoughts. One has the impression rather that they saw this interval merely as an interval.... not as a period perhaps vastly greater than all the time that has elapsed since. My point here is merely to emphasize that we cannot make any more of these witnesses than to say that they did believe there was a break in the creative processes between Gen. 1.1 and 1.2. They may have seen it as of quite a short duration.

At any rate, it is clear that the creative process did not proceed smoothly and unbrokenly from Gen. 1.1 to Adam. With the passage of time, the question of a discontinuity became crystallized more concretely and was discussed in greater detail. Thus Dionysius Petavius (1583 - 1652), A French Roman Catholic Jesuit Theologian who was first Professor of Philosophy at Bourges and later Professor of Theology at Paris, wrote:[14]

"Quod intervallum quantum fuerit, nulla divinatio posset assequi. Neque vero mundi corpora illa, quae prima omnium extitisse docui, aquam et terram, arbitror eodem, in quem lucis ortus incidit, fabricata esse die; ut quibusdam placet, haud satis firma ratione."

ie., "The question of 'How great an interval there was', it

is not possible except by inspiration to attain knowledge of. Nor, indeed, do I judge those basic components of earth and water, which I have taught originated first of all, to have been fabricated the same day on which had occurred the appearance of daylight, as it pleases certain persons (to believe), but by no means with sound enough reason."

That is to say, Petavius did not agree with some who asserted, without sufficient reason, that the basic elements out of which land and water were later made came into being on the same day that the land and water themselves actually did. These basic elements were made long before the actual creation of water and land, though no man can know how long ago apart from revelation, and that revelation is not to be found in Scripture.

And even more specific was the most learned of all medieval commentators on Genesis, Pererius (1535 - 1610) who wrote:[15]

"Licet ante primum diem, coelum et elementa facta sint secundum substantiam, tamen non fuerit perfecta et omnino consummata, nisi spatio illorum sex dierum: tunc enim datus est illis ornatus, complementum, et perfectio. Quanto autem tempore status ille mundi tenebrosus duraverit, hoc est, utrum plus an minus quam unus dies continere solet, nec mihi compertum est, nec opinor cuiquam mortalium nisi cui divinitus id esse patefactum."

ie., "Even though before the first day, the heavens and the elements were made subsequent to the substance (ie., basic essence of creative activity) nevertheless they were not perfected and completely furnished until the period of the six days: for then was given to them (their) furnishing, (their) fulfillment (filling up), and (their) completion. However, just jow long that darkened state of the world lasted, ie., whether it lasted more than one day or less than one day, this is not clear to me, nor (I hold) is it clear to any other mortal man unless to one to whom it has been divinely made so."

This statement, suffering as it does to modern eyes from the complexity of sentence structure characteristic of the age in which it was written, nevertheless once more confirms the view stated by others quoted above that before the six days began and after the initial substance of the world had been created, an interval of time of unknown duration intervened - during which the world was in a darkened state. It would appear that by this time the view of such a darkened world as being also a *destroyed* world was beginning to be lost sight of, the poet Caedmon being the last writer, as far as I have been able to discover, who viewed the situation in the light of a divine judgment upon a previously ordered system. Yet this concept was not entirely lost for in due time we begin to meet it once again in more and more specific terms, especially by Roman Catholic scholars on the Continent.

According to Bernard Ramm,[16] the subject received its first scientific treatment by J. G. Rosenmuller (1736 - 1815) in his *Antiquissima Tellures Historica* published in 1776, a treatise which formed the basis of the theological works of Bohme. At any rate, it seems to have been sufficiently broadly recognized to influence Alcuin in his edition of *The Book of Jasher* which although it may very well be a forgery was at least issued somewhere towards the end of the 18th century. Alcuin renders the counterpart of Gen. 1.2 (which in his version appears, however, as verse 5) as follows: "So that the face of nature *was formed a second time*".[17] From 1763 to 1781, the Orientals Scholar and Biblical Critic, Professor Johann August Dathe of Leipzig published his great six-volume work on the Books of the Old Testament and he translated Gen. 1.2: "Afterwards the earth became *(facta erat)* a waste and a desolation". He comments on this passage as follows:[18]

> *"Vau ante* היה *non potest verti per ET, nam refertur ad vs. 1 ubi narratum fuit, terram acque coelum a Deo esse creatam. Jam pergit vs. 2 de terram eam incertum quo tempore, insignam subiisse mutationem. Igitur vau per postea et explicandum, uti saepe: eg. Num. 5.23 et Deut. 1.19."*

> ie., "*Waw* (ו) before 'the earth' cannot be translated 'AND', for it would then refer back to verse 1, where the narrative has 'the earth and heaven were created by God'. Whereas verse 2 proceeds to tell how that the earth, at some uncertain time, had undergone some remarkable change. Therefore *waw* stands for 'afterwards' and is so to be interpreted, as it so often is - for example in Num. 5. 23 and Deut. 1. 19".

In these two passages there are two clauses which begin with and they are translated "and.... and...." in the English. But as Dathe quite properly observes, the second might more sensibly have been rendered ".... then afterwards....".

And so with this long thread of continuous reference to and recognition of the special relationship between Gen. 1.1 and 1.2, we finally arrive at the period when modern Geology began to formulate those principles of interpretation of the earth's past history which so seriously challenged the more confined (though possibly unnecessary) limits imposed upon biblical chronology by Ussher and many others. And this challenge, far from calling forth an otherwise unknown interpretation of Genesis as an emergency measure, had rather the effect of suddenly casting this ancient view into a new light and making manifest its great significance. I do not think it would be altogether incorrect to state that this is in reality just one more instance where the Bible has again shown itself to be ahead of the times - even where the original writers may not have been aware of the ultimate significance of their own words. Only inspiration could account for such a circumstance.

In 1785, James Hutton (1726 - 1797) published in Edinburgh his *Theory of the Earth*, in which the issue as to the real age of the earth was spelled out in such a way as to make the matter clearly one of "scientific knowledge based on strict observation" and not merely a philosophical treatise. It marked the beginning of a war between chronologists, the secular and the biblical, between those who were demanding enormous periods of time of inconceivable magnitude and those who, assuming that the first of the creative days also marked the origin of the earth, held the process to have occupied a few thousand years at most.

Inevitably, the conservatives saw the issue as fundamental to the whole structure of faith and were ready to give battle at once in defence of their interpretation of Scripture. But there were some who, being aware of the "long-held view" which we have traced thus far, suddenly perceived that there really need be no conflict at all.

One of the first of these, perhaps not unnaturally, was a countryman of Hutton's, a clergyman named Dr. Thomas Chalmers of the Scottish Church engaged in lecturing at St. Andrews, a man keenly interested in the developing sciences of his day, particularly in connection with various earths of importance to the chemist. In 1804 he wrote:[19]

> "There is a prejudice against the speculations of the geologist, which I am anxious to remove. It has been alleged

that geology, by referring the origin of the globe to a higher antiquity than is assigned to it by the writings of Moses, undermines our faith in the inspiration of the Bible, and in all the animating prospects of the immortality which it unfolds. This is a false alarm. The writings of Moses do not fix the antiquity of the globe."

Ten years later, in 1814,[20] Dr. Chalmers produced his more elaborate scheme of reconciliation between the Divine and the geologic records in an *Examination of Cuvier's Theory of the Earth.* This paper presented the view that between the first act of creation which evoked out of the previous nothing the matter of the heavens and earth, and the first act of the first day's work recorded in Genesis, periods of vast duration may have intervened. He held that though in the previous period the earth may have been "a fair residence of life", it had become a desolation: and that although the sun, moon, and stars continued their existence, "in relation to our planet" their light had somehow become obscured.

Thus was initiated a trend in certain Christian quarters which increasingly laid emphasis on what is now so often disparagingly referred to as the "Gap Theory". In an age when men were more concerned than they are today about the importance of confidence in Scripture as the true basis for Christian morality, it is not unnatural that a view of such respectable antiquity should at once be seized upon and explored to the fullest. British and Continental scholars studied the question with a keeness and thoroughness it had never received before. Exegetical and linguistic grounds *pro* and *con* were explored and argued at great length. And some of the very best Hebrew scholars of the day not merely accepted it as probable but elaborated upon it, delving not only into the "fact" itself, but into its causes both physical and spiritual.

The most famous of these early protagonists in England was perhaps Dr. William Buckland who in 1836 contributed a paper in the Bridgewater Treatises. Here in summary is his view:[21]

"The word 'beginning' as applied by Moses expresses an undefined period of time, which was antecedent to the last great change that affected the surface of the earth, and to the creation of its present animal and vegetable inhabitants, during which period of time a long series of operations may have been going on: which, as they are wholly unconnected with the history of the human race, are passed over in silence by the sacred historian whose real concern was barely to state that the matter of the Universe is not eternal and self-existent, but was originally created by the power of the Almighty....

"The first verse of Genesis seems explicitly to assert the creation of the Universe, the heavens, including the sidereal systems and the earth, more especially our own planet, as the subsequent scene of the operations of the six days about to be described.....

"Millions of millions of years may have occupied the indefinite interval, between the beginning in which God created the heavens and the earth and the evening or commencement of the first day of the Mosaic narrative....

"We have in verse 2 a distinct mention of the earth and waters as already existing and involved in the darkness. Their condition is also described as a state of confusion and emptiness *(tohu va bohu)*, words which are usually interpreted by the vague and indefinite Greek term *chaos*, and which may be geologically considered as designating the wreck and ruins of a former world."

In 1847 J. Harris published a work in London entitled,[22] *The Pre-Adamite Earth.* In this work he sets forth a number of reasons why he believed Gen. 1.1 must be set apart from the work of the six days. He wrote:

"Now, that the originating act, described in the first verse, was not meant to be included in the account of the six Adamic days, is evident from the following considerations: first, the creation of the second, third, fourth, fifth and sixth days begins with the formula 'And God said'. It is only natural, therefore, to conclude that the creation of the first day begins with the third verse where the said formula first occurs, 'And God said, Let there be light'. But if so, it follows that the act described in the first verse, and the state of the earth spoken of in the second verse, must both have belonged to a period anterior to the first day."

I think there is much force in this argument. Verse 2 may be the record of a situation which not merely arose only some time after the initial creation, but a situation which may also have persisted for some time after it arose. And thus in 1853 Professor J. H. Kurtz of the University of Dorpat wrote that[23]

> ". . . . between the first and second, and between the second and third verses of the biblical history of creation, revelation leaves two great white pages on which human science may write what it will in order to fill up the blanks of natural history which revelation omitted to supply itself as not being its office."

Much has seemed to depend, in the minds of many writers then and today, upon whether in the second verse the verb הָיְתָה should be translated "was" or "became". In the next chapter this matter is dealt with from the linguistic point of view, but it seems proper here to note what some of these earlier commentators said and to what extent their arguments for an interval here depended upon the translation of this verb one way or the other.

Kurtz himself did not apparently feel it proper to render Gen. 1.2 "but the earth *became* a desolation" as Dathe had done. Nevertheless he did favour the view that verse 2 described a ruin and not a first stage in the creative process. Thus he wrote:[24]

> "The theory that a devastation of the earth took place between the primary creation of heaven and earth, and the fashioning of the earth during the six days, which devastation had made a restitution and a new creation necessary, cannot be proved from Genesis 1: but neither does the whole chapter contain anything which would exclude it."

He then remarks that part of this uncertainty arises from the fact that Scripture does not say *how* it happened or *how* long it lasted, nor what followed afterwards or what evolutions and revolutions took place before the state of things was reached which is described in verse 2.[25] However, in his *History of the Old Covenant*, published in 1859, he committed himself more fully.[26] In the Introduction to this work he presents the view that "the state of the earth described in verse 2 was connected with the fall of the angels who kept not their first estate (Jude 6)". He continues:

> "This view is very old, though not exactly known to the Fathers, who generally asserted that mankind were created to fill the gap left by the fall of the angels. Many of them thought that the race was to increase until the number of the redeemed should equal the number of the fallen angels."

As to his view of the events of the first creation, he wrote:[27]

> "The organisms of the primeval world are not the animals and plants of the Mosaic economy, neither are they those of historical times: while those of the biblical narrative are those which natural history at present makes us acquainted with. Thus the supposed contradiction is removed. The types buried in the rocks.... were not created for *man* and have not been his contemporaries on earth. *Long before* he appeared they had become extinct or were shut up in their rocky graves.... Beyond doubt, *the fossils of the rocks cannot represent those organisms whose creation the Bible relates*"(emphasis his).

In his *New Commentary on Genesis*, Delitzsch carefully considers the wording of Gen. 1.2.[28] He is not decided as to the *precise* intent of the author but is reasonably sure that there is no justification for "assuming that the chaos was the consequence of a derangement connected with the fall of the angels and that the six days' creation was the restoration of a new world from the ruin of an old".[29] He expresses the feeling that the relation in which verse 1 stands to verse 2 is not at all clear.[30] In considering verse 2 he observes that the word *tohu* comes from the verbal root *tahah* (תָּהָה) in Hebrew (which = תְּהָא in Aramaic) meaning "to be desolate", "confounded", and as a noun therefore signifying "desolation". *Bohu* is from a verbal root which means 'to be closed' or 'deaf' or 'stupid', and as a noun implies unconsciousness or lifelessness. He adds:[31]

> "The sound as well as the meaning of the pair of words is awe-inspiring; the earth according to its substratum was a desolate and dead mass, in a word a chaos."

I think he is perfectly right in noting that Dillman held the view that[32]

> ".... a created chaos is a nonentity. If once the notion of an Almighty God is so far developed that He is also conceived of as the author of matter, the application of chaos in the doctrine of creation must consequently cease. For such a God will not first create the matter and then the form, but both together."

Delitzsch adds his own comment to Dillman: "Certainly the

account does not *expressly* (my emphasis) say that God created chaos". But surely if we render *Hayetha* as "was", we cannot but read this meaning into the text. The force of this was fully recognized by Delitzsch who nevertheless, while he had to reject the alternative rendering of "had become", emphasizes that the verb *hayethah* here "is no mere *erat*;"[33] ie., cannot simply be taken to mean "was" in the English copulative sense. Yet he feels that there is no justification whatever to adopt what he calls "the restitution hypothesis" which assumes that "the Chaos was the consequence of a derangement connected with the fall of the angels and that the six days' creation was the restoration of a new world from the ruin of the old".[34]

But during the next decade Delitzsch was much in correspondence with Kurtz about the matter, and in the end he made a complete about-face and wholeheartedly adopted the concept of a rebellion in heaven and a judgment brought upon the earth as a consequence prior to the creation of Adam. Thus while he still did not propose that *hayethah* should be rendered "became", he admitted that this is really what had happened. It is a curious circumstance in Delitzsch's case, for when he came to deal with the origin of the name Jehovah he asserted not only that the verb הָיָה lay at the root of it but that it does not signify εἶναι ('to be') but γιγνέσθαι ('to become')![35]

Delitzsch now believed that the cause of the judgment was that the "Prince of the Angels would not continue in the truth and therefore the earth was consumed".[36] So he finally concluded that:[37]

> "There is much for and nothing against the supposition that the *tohu wa bohu* is the *rudis indigestaque moles* into which God brought this earth which He had first created good, after the fall of Satan to whom it had been assigned as a habitation."

In his *System of Biblical Psychology* he expressed the view that man (in Adam) was created to be guardian *(ut custodiret)* of a world which was now in constant danger of being taken over once again to its ruin by a power which was not material yet was self-conscious, as he put it, and must therefore be angelic.[38] This angelic Being (and his followers) was once part of that still unfallen order of beings who[39]

> ".... were created before the creation of our corporeal world. The creation of the angels is thus included in the summary statement of Gen. 1. 1.... and the more particular

narrative (1.2) takes its point of departure at a time when the angels were already created."

He then pointed out that this was no new idea. It was held by such Church Fathers as Gregory of Nyssa, Basilios, Gregory of Nazianzen, and others, and was taught by Josephus Philoponius in his seven volume work on the creation. Delitzsch felt that the very choice of the words תֹהוּ וָבֹהוּ reinforces the idea of judgment. Thus he wrote:[40]

"How we are to apprehend this condition, occurs to us when we reflect that *tohu* in every case, where it has not the general meaning of wasteness, of emptiness, of nothingness, betokens a condition of desolation by judgment of God (Isa. 24.10) and especially fiery judgment (as in Isa. 34.9-11 and Jer. 4.23-26)."

Subsequently, Delitzsch has a footnote in which he refers to a certain Mr. R. Rocholl who porposed some questions to him, and he replied to these questions by saying substantially what we have extracted above from his work. Referring to this correspondence, he remarked:[41]

"The above will show, as far as it is here permitted, to what result further enquiry has led me since the second edition of my *Genesis*, and after manifold correspondence with Kurtz (one of his critics - ACC).... The Mosaic history of creation proceeded from revelation; and since knowledge of salvation, and generally, knowledge of the truth, has endured subsequent to Moses for a period of thirty centuries, we are certainly in a position to read things which transcended the intelligence of Moses, *between the lines* of the Mosaic history of creation" (emphasis mine).

Delitzsch may have exceeded the bounds of strict scholarship and allowed his imagination too much free play. Yet Delitzsch was also a great Hebrew scholar, and it is therefore noteworthy that he did base his views, in part, on linguistic evidence, evidence be it noted which in earlier editions of his Commentary he had denied but which he later embraced. Thus he wrote subsequently:[42]

"The writer of Gen. 1.2 taking his position on this side of 'the beginning' continues in verse 2 'and the earth was a desolation and a ruin'. The preterite, with the subject prefixed is the usual way of introducing a subsequent history and so the beginning of it. The הָיְתָה ('was') is *more than the expression of the copula ERAT*; the earth, as it came directly into being through God's creative power OR (and we do not here yet decide on this) as God's six days' creative operation found it *already existing* was a תֹהוּ וָבֹהוּ, a desolation and a ruin."

Now the important point to notice next is that Delitzsch adopted the *second* supposition and admits, as we have already seen, that there is "much for and nothing against" the supposition that this is indeed a picture of an earth brought into a chaotic state.[43] And so Delitzsch then notes that had the writer intended to connect verse 2 with verse 1, "the form וַתְּהִי must have stood in the place of הָיְתָה."

In a somewhat similar manner, Fr. H. Ruesch, Professor of Catholic Theology in the University of Bonn, while not agreeing that 'was' in Gen. 1.2 may be translated 'became', nevertheless holds that this is really what happened. He did not agree with Delitzsch's views about a spiritual rebellion as the cause but he did believe some element of judgment had led to the earth's desolation and to the destruction of its original order of life. Thus he wrote:[44]

> "In other words, the Six Days treats not of the first formation of the earth and of the first creation of organized beings but of a *re-formation* of the earth; and a re-creation of organized beings, for which reason this has been called the theory of restitution."

So he concludes later,[45] "If, therefore, we ask first whether this theory is exegetically admissible, I answer unhesitatingly in the affirmative".

Bishop Gleig added one argument in support of this view which others had not considered. He wrote:[46]

> "Moses records the history of the earth only in its present state. He affirms, indeed, that it was created, and that it was 'without form and void', when the Spirit of God began to move on the face of the fluid mass, but he does not say how long that mass had been in the state of chaos nor whether it was or was not the wreck of some former system which had been inhabited by living creatures of different kinds from

those which occupy the present.

"We read in various places of Scripture of a New Heavens and a New Earth to succeed the present earth and visible heavens, after they shall again be reduced to chaos by a general conflagration, and there is nothing in the books of Moses positively affirming that there was not an *old earth and old heavens*, or in other words a former earth and heaven.... There is nothing in the sacred narrative forbidding us to suppose that they are ruins of a former earth deposited in the chaotic mass out of which Moses informs us that God formed the present system. How long it continued in such a chaotic state it is in vain to inquire."

This is not, of course, very satisfactory. It is too vague and is based entirely on negative evidence. His argument is that since we are *not* told we may not make this assumption, therefore we obviously may! The Bishop might have found positive warrant in II Pet.3.5,6 which some believe applies more appropriately to the event under discussion than it does to the Flood of Noah's day. But as time went on and writers used their imagination more and more, it must have seemed to many that the issue had ultimately to be settled on lingusitic rather than exegetical grounds. Only linguistic evidence could really give a firm answer, although unfortunately even this has not been decisive.

However, among those who approached the problem from this angle was the famous Dr. E. B. Pusey of Oxford University whose work on Daniel provided him with an opportunity to give a summary statement of his own views on the matter. First of all, he deals strictly with the questions of grammar and syntax, and writes:[47]

"The substantive verb not being used in Hebrew as mere copula, had Moses intended to say that the earth 'was waste and desolate' when God created it, the idiom for this would have been וְהָאָרֶץ תֹּהוּ וָבֹהוּ omitting the verb - just as it is omitted in the following phrase 'and darkness upon the face of the deep'. The insertion of the verb הָיְתָה has no force at all unless it be used to express what was the condition of the earth in some time past previous to the rest of the narrative, but in no connection at all with what preceded. Such a connection might have been expressed by וַתְּהִי הָאָרֶץ or by the omission of the verb. Moses was directed to choose just that idiom which expresses a past time, anterior to what follows but in no connection of time whatever with what precedes.

"Yet on the other hand, the *waw* by which verse 2 is united with verse 1 shows that verse 1 does not stand as a mere summary of what follows."

Thus Pusey concludes that we have

".... nothing to connect the time spoken of in verse 2 with the first declaration 'in the beginning God created....' What intervened between 'In the beginning' and the remodelling of our habitation does not concern us....".

Now Pusey was a careful - though complex - writer. He made no attempt therefore to "fill in" where Scripture has "left out". As he wrote:[48]

"I have confined myself to the statement that any length of time which might seem eventually to be required by the facts of Geology need not trouble the believer, even on this ground - that Scripture said nothing whatever about time. Where, then, nothing was said on the one side, there could obviously be no contradiction on the other. I did not say that this mode of speech *impels* (us to the meaning of) a vast gap - perhaps ages in length - between the first verse and the second. I only said that since the two verses stand in no connection with each other, it *admits* of a long geological history. It was not my business to enter upon the claims of geology. I was only an interpreter of the sacred record, and, in view of that record, I said 'the claims of geology do not even touch upon Theology'."

He then continues later:

"There are cases in which words, arranged as they are here (the subject being placed before the verb הָיָה and joined with the preceding sentence by 'and') form a parenthesis. But then the context makes it quite clear.... The only other alternative is that הָיְתָה being in the past tense, relates to a past time, and that *that* past time is unconnected with the time of the previous verse. For had Moses intended to connect it, he would have used the common form וַתְּהִי. No one can doubt that the words 'and darkness (was) on the face of the deep' expresses a condition contemporary with that of the earth as *tohu wa bohu;* no one can doubt that the words 'and the Spirit of God (was) brooding on the face of the waters' expresses *continuous* action co-existing with that state of things. No one doubts of course that the word 'and God said' denotes an action of God which followed immediately thereon.

"Since these denote time, contemporary and subsequent, as little doubt can there be that the word הָיְתָה expresses time upon which that contemporary condition and action depend and by which they are determined. Relative time is the very force of the participle,* but then it must be contemporary with time expressed already; which time is here expressed by the word הָיְתָה. Had Moses' object been merely to express past time, the natural construction would have been to omit the הָיְתָה, just as the verb is omitted in the words which follow וְחֹשֶׁךְ עַל־פְּנֵי תְהוֹם. The continuity of the narrative implies that הָיְתָה denotes time, and if so, then every one admits it is *time subsequent to and unconnected with* the words 'In the beginning God created'. They express simply a past condition of the earth at the beginning of the six days of creation; they express *nothing* as to the relation of that condition with the creation of heaven and earth 'in the beginning'. They are simply the beginning of a new statement or record.

"And this is, for the most part, the object of this collocation. This collocation is the more remarkable in that the word הָיָה is used, which there is no occasion to be so employed. But everyone knows also that not only in the case of the substantive verb but in the case of other words as well, the idiom chiefly adopted in a narrative to DETACH what follows from what precedes, is that which is here employed, viz., the placing of the subject first and then the past verb."

While it has become a custom to challenge the Hebrew scholarship of anyone who supports the "Gap Theory", and while it has thus be-

---

* *Referring to the Spirit of God 'brooding' on the face of of the waters.*

come possible to get away with such pontifical statements as "no Hebrew scholar supports this view" (!),[49] there never has been any question as to the scholarship of Pusey who nevertheless *did* support it. And if there were any question, it would be sufficient for most people who know the meaning of the word "scholar" to note that S. R. Driver unhesitatingly recognized Pusey as an authority. It is doubtful if Driver has an equal as a Hebraist - certainly not, I venture to say, in the matter of the use of the Hebrew verb. And Pusey himself notes that Delitzsch, who in earlier editions had argued against his own view, "subsequently embraced it".[50] It is also worth noting that another scholar of equal stature with Delitzsch, namely, August Dillman, likewise wrote against the view and subsequently changed his mind - on lingusitic grounds alone. In his *Commentary on Genesis* published in 1897, Dillman renders Gen. 1.2, "But* then was the earth waste, etc.", and he expresses the view that "became" would be incorrect.[51] However, before the two volume work was actually published he had changed his mind, for on page x under *Corrigenda*, he notes that the above rendering should be altered to read: "But then the earth became....", and a later *Corrigendum* refers to page 57 in Vol. 1 of the Commentary reiterating that here, too, the text ought to have read, "but the earth became waste....". It was not a matter of indifference to Dillman, therefore, but of sufficient importance to justify two *Corrigendum* notices. S. R. Driver resisted this translation to the end - even, as we shall see, at the price of a certain inconsistency. But Driver *did* admit in his *The Book of Genesis* that it was "exegetically admissible".#[52] Yet Skinner, in his *Critical and Exegetical Commentary on Genesis*

**His use of the disjunctive here agrees with the LXX, Vulgate, etc.*

#*It should be understood also, that Driver had a very great respect for Dillman's scholarship. In the Preface to his* Treatise on the Use of the Tenses in Hebrew, *Driver says: "The Commentaries of Dillman are exceedingly complete and valuable, their author being distinguished both for calm and sober judgment and for sound scholarship".*

in *The International Critical Commentary*, says simply: "This view that verse 1 describes an earlier creation of heaven and earth, which were reduced to chaos and then re-fashioned, needs no refutation"![53] It is all the more surprising that Skinner should commit himself to such an out-of-hand rebuttal when he says a little later:[54]

> "The weird effect of the language (of verse 2) is very important.... The exact meaning of this alliterative phrase *tohu wa bohu* is difficult to make out.... But our safest guide is perhaps Jeremiah's vision of chaos-come-again, which is simply that of a darkened and devastated earth, from which life and order have fled."

It seems to me that Skinner merely needed to follow out his own reasoning to its logical conclusion to reach precisely the position Driver reached on exegetical grounds - viz., that the view espoused in this volume *is* "admissible", to say the very least. Indeed, on Skinner's own argument it is not merely admissible but highly probable!

It is well to remember that a substantial number of other Hebrew scholars have adopted this view on the linguistic evidence: Martin Anstey, Alfred Edersheim (to whom Hebrew was almost a native language), H. Browne, G. V. Garland, N. Snaith (who seems to me to *favour* "became" for "was"), T. Jollie Smith, A. I. McCaul, R. Jameison, and many others.* In the Transactions of the Victoria Institute two papers appeared in 1946 on the issue, one by P. W. Heward in favour and the other by F. F. Bruce against it.[55] Only by reading these two papers can one assess which is the more scholarly. Personally, I believe both contribute equally to the debate. But it is some indication of the extent to which prejudice can cloud over better judgment that one writer, in referring to these two valuable papers, says that Bruce's paper is scholarly but his opponent's is "full of special pleading and much padding".[56] Needless to say, this writer did not favour the "Gap Theory". Unfortunately, this attitude is reflected in many current works nowadays, a situation which makes it difficult for the newcomer to assess the matter fairly or even to be inclined to review the evidence on both sides *at all*.

---

* *For excerpts from these and other sources, see Appendix I.*

In Chapter V we shall examine some of these contrary opinions with care and it will become apparent then, I believe, how large a place emotion has played in the views expressed and how very little first hand examination of the facts of the case seems to be in evidence. But not all who reject the "Gap Theory" are as openly indifferent to the grounds upon which it is based. Edward J. Young has written a valuable monograph entitled, *Studies in Genesis One*, in which, though he rejects the concept of an earth under judgment, yet finds good linguistic grounds to believe that in the narrative of Genesis 1 there exists an interval between Gen. 1.1 and 1.2 of unknown duration. He holds that Gen. 1.2 begins a *new* narrative entirely; and that there are *two* narratives in Chapter one, the first being wrapped up in verse 1, the second in verses 2-31. Thus he writes:[57]

> "The first act in forming the *present* world (my emphasis) was God's speaking. The verb וַיֹּאמֶר is introduced by *waw* consecutive, but it should now be clear that וַיֹּאמֶר is not the second verb in a series introduced by בָּרָא of verse 1. Verse 1 is a narrative complete in itself. Verses 2-31 likewise constitute a narrative complete in itself."

In short, Young's picture is that we have a self-contained and complete statement in verse 1, "in the beginning God created, etc.". Then the narrative re-commences as a kind of second chapter with the words, "And God said, Let there be light", and *when* God said this, "the earth was (at that time) without form and void, and darkness was on the face of the deep, and the Spirit of God was hovering over the waters". The phrases of verse 2 are thus made secondary to, and in explanation of, the circumstances which prevailed when God spoke for the first time in verse 3. The idea is an interesting one, but Young feels that it requires one to believe the descriptive terms of verse 2 have no undertones of judgment in them.[58] With this point we shall deal at greater length subsequently, but at the moment it is only important to note that the break between verse 1 and verse 2 is frankly recognized.

And as to the length of the intervening period before the earth was made habitable, Young has this to say:[59]

> "On this construction we are not told how long this threefold condition (of formlessness, void, and darkness) had been in existence, whether for years or merely for moments. Nor is the creation (ie., cause?) of it (ie., of the situation in

Gen. 1.2) explicitly stated."

Young believes it not unreasonable to assume that this was in fact the originally created condition of the earth: "Verse 2 then states the condition of the earth as it was when created and until God began to form from it the present world". He repeats this three pages later: "Verse 2 describes the earth as it came from the hands of the Creator and as it existed at the time when God commanded the light to shine forth".

While this essay of Professor Young's is a pleasure to read for its most moderate tone in dealing with the views of those with whom he disagrees and for its unashamed acceptance of the Scripture as the Word of God, it must be said that the argument that verse 2 describes what God's handiwork first looked like will not satisfy many readers. Nor does it substantially reduce the difficulty of believing that God really did start by creating a chaos to suggest that "Chaos" merely means something *not yet ordered and arranged into* a Cosmos.* Whatever Ovid may have intended by his use of the word "chaos" - and he may merely have meant matter *un*-formed rather than *de*-formed - the fact is that every word in Gen. 1.2 used to describe in detail the condition of the earth at that moment is used elsewhere in Scripture to describe something that has clearly come under God's judgment. Young appeals twice to Isa. 45.18 and proposed that the word תֹהוּ (tohu) is merely a word suggesting something not yet fit to be inhabited. But in most other cases the idea is much more dramatic in meaning, and these other cases must surely weigh against the adoption of what is, after all, only one possible rendering of Isa. 45.18. Young suggests the translation, "God did not create it *to be* a desolation (ie., uninhabitable) but to be inhabited."

Whatever points of disagreement there may be in this particular question, the fact remains that Dr. Young has made out a good case from a linguistic point of view that a break does exist between Gen. 1.1 and 1.2.

Altogether, therefore, we can find strong support from the very earliest times to the present for the view that an interval of unknown duration followed Gen. 1.1 before the work of the six days was initiated

---

* *On the use of the word* χαος *in the Septuagint, see Appendix II.*

either to "*bring order to*", or "*restore order to*" an earth that at that moment was evidently quite unfit for habitation. This view is indeed a long-held one, beginning with the Massoretic and the Jewish Commentators, re-appearing by implication in one of their earliest Aramaic Versions, reflected perhaps by Paul in his letter to the Corinthians, adopted by some of the Church Fathers, held thereafter by early and later Medieval writers who expressly stated and elaborated upon it, preserved in the centuries that followed to influence 18th century translations, seized upon by commentators when modern Geology challenged the Mosaic chronology, and subsequently explored by a few of the best Hebrew scholars right up to our own day. Yet, for some strange reason, it is still identified by many modern writers as a recent invention, without linguistic or exegetical support in Scripture, and never favoured by any scholar with a reputation!

Mirabile dictu!

Chapter 2.

THE LINGUISTIC EVIDENCE.

"But the earth had become a desolation...."

The rendering above departs from that to be observed in almost all the better known English translations in three ways:* the use of a disjunctive (*but* for *and*), the use of the pluperfect in the place of the simple perfect, and the use of *became* in place of the simple *was*.

Of the disjunctive, little need be said. The Hebrew ו (*waw*) stands for both the conjunctive and the disjunctive particles, and the context alone can determine which is the more appropriate. There is, as we have seen, some reason to prefer the disjunctive in view of the indicated pause in the Hebrew text at the end of verse 1. In Appendix XIV will be found a number of illustrations of this use, including some instances in which the correctness of the disjunctive form is borne out not merely by the obvious sense of the passage quoted but by its reappearance as a quotation in the New Testament where the Greek has "but", not "and" (ie., αλλα rather than και

The use of the pluperfect is dealt with in the following chapter, the point being reserved for discussion only after the translation of the verb itself has been carefully considered. The most critical issue is whether הָיְתָה should here be rendered "was" or "became", since

* *See Appendix III.*

the true significance of the verb, and indeed of the second verse as a whole, hinges upon the settlement of this point. Granted that *this* point can be settled, the other two points will probably not be seriously disputed.

Now this discussion does not make easy reading, not only because of the subtleties involved (as will appear) but also because the verb we must examine in its commoner forms happens also to be the very verb we must use in its commoner forms in order to make the examination! One runs into this kind of thing: "In such a case, the word *was* is incorrect....". Or one might put this: "In such a case, the word "was" is incorrect...."; or 'the word WAS is incorrect"; or "the word *was* is incorrect....". At any rate, this points up the nature of the problem! Thus we are forced to employ various devices (underlinings, capitals, italics, and 'quote' marks) in order to make each point clearer.* And this kind of constant typographical switching is most distressing to even a thoroughly dedicated reader. But it seems unavoidable.

In view of the fact that one *can* scarcely construct an English sentence of any complexity without using some form of the verb "to be", it is difficult to realize that there are well-developed languages which make little or no use of it at all in the simple copulative sense. When, in English, we express the straightforward idea, "The man is good", the verb "to be" is used merely to connect together the words *man* and *good.* Many languages, and indeed many children, simply say, "man good", considering the connective verb quite unnecessary. A child will say, "Me good boy": an Indian might say, "Me brave man". Hebrew does the same.

Benjamin Lee Whorf,[60] the 'founder' of that branch of the study of language known as Metalinguistics, observed that a Hopi Indian, for example, has difficulty in understanding why we say, "It is raining". because to his way of thinking the *It* is the *rain.* One might just as well say, "Rain is raining" - which of course is a redundancy. So he wonders why we don't simply say, as he does, "Raining"! Neither

---

* *In the biblical quotations which follow, we have tried to indicate to the reader where the verb "to be" has been supplied in the English though absent in the original by putting the verb in brackets. Thus: Gen. 3.11, "Who told thee that thou (wast) naked?" indicates that (wast) has been supplied to complete the English sentence.*

the *It* nor the *Is* serves any useful purpose in this English sentence and common sense, therefore, would argue the leaving out of both of them. But this would not sound correct to us. Yet, as we have observed, Hebrew shares the un-English view that a verb is not needed here since it really contributes nothing.

Now, in translating, it is quite customary to equate the Hebrew verbal form היה with the English "to be", but it has been recognized by Hebraists for many years that the equation is not strictly valid. In English, *being* is a kind of static concept, things simply "are" this or that. When we say, "The man is tall", we are not speaking of a dynamic *event* but a more or less static situation. "The field is flat" is indeed a static situation. In both these sentences English requires some part of the verb "to be" in order to satisfy our sense of linguistic propriety. Yet in spite of the possession of the verb הָיָה with its supposed sense of "being", Hebrew would not think it necessary here and the verb *is* would therefore not be represented in the Hebrew.

The reader who is limited to English will find that in some editions of the Bible, especially in the Authorized Version, a means is provided, simply by the use of italics, to show where any part of the verb "to be" has been inserted in the English translation to complete the sense though not found in the original Hebrew. For example, if one opens a first edition of the Scofield Bible at (say) page 21, some eleven copulative or connective occurrences of the verb "to be" will be found in italics, appearing in the text as *is, art, be,* and *was:* and on page 395 some 39 examples will be found in the forms *was* and *were* In every instance the word has been supplied by the translators where the Hebrew original did not consider any verb necessary.*

---

* *Any page would, of course, have served to illustrate the point, and any printing of the Authorized Version will show it. Thus, for example, from Jud. 6.10 to 7.14 we have in 6.10* am, *13* be, *15* am *and* is, *22* was *24* is, *25* is, *30* be; *and in 7.1* is, *2* are *and* are, *3* is, *12* were, *13* was, *and 14* is. *All these are copulative and* הָיָה *is omitted in the original. On the other hand, in Judges 6.27 the verb* was *is not in italics since it is found in the Hebrew, and it is clear that the intent of the writer was something beyond the mere copulative force of the verb: as for example*

Continued page 44.

Thus the fundamental idea behind the Hebrew verb הָיָה is not precisely what would be copulative in English but is a far more dynamic concept. This is indicated to some extent by its possible etymology. A number of authorities, including Gesenius and Tregelles, believed that the primary meaning was that of "falling" - comparing the word with the Arabic هوى meaning "to be headlong" or "to fall down". From this came the idea of "befalling" in the sense of "happening", and so "to fall out", and thence "to come to be", ie., "to become". From this idea of having become, we pass easily into the meaning "to be" in the sense *of having existence*, but the copulative sense usually attributed to it seems without logical foundation.

Subsequently, Tregelles came to believe that the concept of "falling" was not really *primary*, and that the notion of "being" came instead from that of "living".[61] From the concept of "living" the idea of "being" is readily derived so that it comes easily to mean "to be": but this kind of being is dynamic being, living being, not the static kind of being which is equative as when one says, "This is (ie., equals) that", but the kind which is implied in such a sentence as "He is alone", or "He is with thee".

Thus while Benjamin Davies[62] gives the basic meaning as "to be" - usually with the sense of "to exist", "to be alive", "to come into being", and so "to become" - Brown, Driver and Briggs list the meanings of הָיָה in the following order: "to fall"; "to come to pass"; "to become"; and "to be".[63] And under the last heading they add subsequently in parenthesis, "often with the subordinate idea of becoming".

The concept of dynamic as opposed to static being is of great importance to an understanding of the Hebrew usage of the word. Boman,[64] in a critical study of the verb, concludes that it is *never* used copulatively at all and that all the usual illustrations of such a use provided in lexicons are not really valid. He does not consider that even Ratschow, who made a quite exhaustive study of Old Testament usage, was really able to give any clear unequivocal instances.

Thus, for example, in Gen.2.25 the sentence, "and they were

"And it came to be that...." In Gen.23.17 the verb 'to be' is set in italics 5 times! We need this insertion of the verb to fill out the sentence, but the Hebrew writer did not see any need for it and so omitted it entirely.

(וַיִּהְיוּ) both naked and were not ashamed", means not so much that at the moment of speaking the writer is observing the simple *fact* of their nakedness but that this was how they lived, daily.[65] They "went about" without clothing and without shame. Subsequently, they suddenly became aware that they were naked and this awareness brought with it a sense of shame not experienced before. This was nakedness in a new way and it occurred quite suddenly - suddenly enough that Adam "discovered" it with a sense of shock. That this was in the nature of a discovery is implied in the Lord's words (in Gen,3.11), "Who told thee that thou (*wast*) naked?". The question would have been pointless otherwise. Thus the real emphasis here is no longer upon the circumstance that Adam and Eve had been living naked in the Garden of Eden but that they had both suddenly discovered a fact which caused them to be ashamed.

Boman argues that the simple "is" or "was" in an English sentence is never expressed in Hebrew and that where it IS expressed it does not mean what the English translation implies.[66] It is used in the sense of eventuality: it is not used for a simple fact or circumstance or situation.

One might wonder how Hebrew would then distinguish between the phrase, "the man is good", and "the good man". In a sense they convey the same basic idea, but there is a subtle difference. In any case Hebrew can make the distinction. The first would appear simply as "the man good" (ha-ish tobh: הָאִישׁ תּוֹב), and the second, as "the man the good one"(ha-ish ha-tobh: הָאִישׁ הַתּוֹב).

One might then ask further, How would the distinction be made between the sentences, "the man *is* good" and "the man *was* good"? In Hebrew, the context is allowed to decide the matter. While it might seem that this would be difficult (as upon occasion it is), the number of such occasions must be remarkably small for there seems to be not the slightest hesitation in omitting the verb, whether the sense of "is" or "was" is intended. Such will be apparent from the footnote with examples on page 43 of this Chapter and from the more elaborate study which will be found in Appendix IV.

Some have felt this to be a real difficulty. Barr, for example, argues that the verb *must* be inserted when the tense is past *and* the situation no longer exists.[67] For example, if a writer meant to say, "The man was good.... but is no longer so", ie., "The man was once good", then he would insert the appropriate form of the verb "to be" to indicate the altered circumstance.

But this rule does not hold. For example, according to this principle, the record of Job's complaint in Chapter 29 should have the verb *was* in the original since the situation has clearly been altered by his diseased condition. Yet, in point of fact, the Hebrew omits it. It is not merely that the situation is no longer true today: the situation was no longer true when the statement was made. Thus Job, in verses 14 and 15 and 20, tells his self-appointed comforters that he was formerly - ie., was once - a father to the blind and feet to the lame: he once enjoyed fame and recognition and his roots once spread beside the waters like a flourishing tree. The meaning of his complaint is unmistakeable. He WAS all those things but is no longer so: yet the Hebrew writer saw no need to express the connective verb "was" in such a situation.

We have another example in the case of Pharaoh's servants in Gen.41. Here the butler recalls (verse 12) how he and a fellow tradesman were in prison and how at that time a Hebrew named Joseph was also with them. Clearly the situation had now changed for the speaker, since he is a free man - and his fellow tradesman is dead. He refers back, therefore, to a situation which from his point of view no longer exists and the English translation in verse 12 properly inserts the verb "was" - but the Hebrew omits it. Some might argue that the situation for *Joseph* had not changed, since he was still in prison! But one must surely consider the circumstances from the point of view of the speaker. The omission of the verb in reporting his speech shows, therefore, that it is not required merely because there is the implication of altered circumstance. He was, as he says, once in the same prison: but he is no longer so, yet the Hebrew writer evidently saw no need for the verb הָיָה in this context.

There are numerous illustrations of this kind of situation in the Old Testament, but many of these require a somewhat elaborate excursus in order to show how we know there has been a change. Some are straightforward enough: as, for example, where Gen. 12.6 records that "the Canaanite (was) then (ie., at that time) in the land". But there are probably far more examples which are in reverse. There are innumerable examples where the situation is quite UN-changed and yet the verb "to be" *is inserted* in the original in the appropriate form. This is a most common occurrence. Thus, for example, throughout the first chapter of Genesis there is the recurrent phrase, "And it was so". Here the Hebrew inserts the verb. According to Barr, this insertion should imply that the situation or circumstance is no longer true. But this is surely not the case. Genesis 1, verses 3, 5, 7, 8, 9, and so forth, would all be properly translated if one were to render the phrase which in English reads, "And it *was* so", as "it *became* so", but it would surely be quite improper to suppose that the author means, "And it was once but is no longer so....".

Thus, the insertion of the verbal form "was" in a Hebrew sentence is not intended to signify that the circumstance is no longer true, for these evenings and these mornings retain their pre-eminence of position in the processes of time. Thus when Barr proposes that the verb is inserted in Gen. 1.2 in order to show that the desolation was a temporary one and no longer exists, he is implying the existence of a rule which certainly cannot be unequivocally demonstrated from biblical usage. And to say at the same time, as Barr does, that on this account "it would be quite perverse to insist on the meaning 'became' here", is clearly going beyond the evidence. Indeed, he would perhaps be forced to admit that to follow out his own proposed rule and render Gen. 1.5, "and the evening and the morning were once a second day but are no longer so", would indeed be absurdly perverse! But, by contrast to this absurd rendering, it would make very *good* sense to render the Hebrew, "and the evening and the morning became the second day", for this is precisely the truth of the matter, and the Hebrew has seen fit to insert the verb in order (as I believe) to make this quite clear. In this eventful period, it did become the second day of the week.

From all of this it would appear that the decisive factor which determines whether the verb will be inserted or omitted is not related to tense. Nor is it related to circumstance, if by this is meant merely that what is reported is no longer the case. Boman seems to come much closer to the truth when he underscores the fact that only where the sense is dynamic does a Hebrew writer introduce the verb הָיָה.[68] He points out that there are three circumstances surrounding its employment which bear out the contention that it is basically a verb of *action* rather than condition.

First of all it can be, and frequently is, used in conjunction with the infinitive or a participle of another verb of action. For example, Nehemiah (2.13) tells how he was in the habit of inspecting the walls of his beloved city Jerusalem while they were still under repair. Thus he says, "And I was (וָאֱהִי) examining (שֹׂבֵר , participle) the walls of Jerusalem". This could easily have been expressed by the appropriate form of the verb שָׂבַר without the associated verb הָיָה. But the object seems to be to underscore the idea of continuous engagement.... A list of examples will be found in Appendix II, and a study of such usages indicates that the idea is best expressed by rendering the verb הָיָה not as "to be" but by some such English word or phrase as "kept---" (Ezek. 44.2), "succeeded in ---" (II Chron.

18.34), "remained ---" (I Ki.22.35), "continually ---" (Gen.1.6), "habitually ---" (I Sam.2.11, Gen.39.22), "was ever ---" (I Ki.5.1), "always ---" (II Ki.4.1, Ezek.44.2), "was daily ---" (Neh. 5.18), etc. All these imply something beyond a static situation, even in Ezek.44.2, for the idea is positive closure of the gate, that is, keeping the gate closed and not merely "leaving it shut". It is a case of maintenance rather than abandonment. In II Chron.18.34 the mortally wounded king obviously did everything in his power to hold himself upright in his chariot so that his supporters would not lose heart. In Gen.1.6 the atmosphere actively divides, ie., maintains, the division between the waters above it and those below: there is nothing static about this process at all. And so it will be found in every instance of usage in connection with either a participle or an infinitive. It is analogous to the English usage in such a sentence as "the water is boiling" or "the man is still angry".

Secondly, it appears in the *niphal* or passive form, as though the sense was "to be be-ed", just as in English an active form (e.g. "fold") is converted to a passive form* ("fold-ed") by the addition of "-ed". It is much more difficult to think of the English verb "to be" in a passive form because to us it tends to be essentially a static concept. In Hebrew, since it is an active verb, the formation of a passive did not seem strange and the verbal form of the active is routinely changed to a passive form without hesitation. Thus in I Ki.1.27 a literal translation would be, "Is it from my lord the King that this thing has been be-ed" (!), which would obviously have to appear in English as "has been done" or "has come about" (in Hebrew אִם מֵאֵת אֲדֹנִי הַמֶּלֶךְ נִהְיָה הַדָּבָר הַזֶּה:). The whole idea here is one of action. Similarly, that often quoted passage from I Ki.12.24 (literally, "For from me this has been done" (כִּי מֵאִתִּי נִהְיָה הַדָּבָר הַזֶּה) is in the Authorized Version, "For this thing is from me". Most lexicographers simply say that in the *niphal* or passive form the verb is best rendered "come to be", ie., "become" or "happen". This is the sense of Deut.27.9 for example: "This day ye have become a people for the Lord your God".

Boman's third point is that the verb הָיָה is often used *in parallel* with other verbs, in sentences which have a clearly active context.[69] For example, in Gen.2.5 it is written, "Every plant before it *was* in the earth and every herb of the field before it *grew*....". And,

* *See Appendix VII for illustrations.*

significantly. this is followed by the words, "And there *(was)* not a man to till the ground". In the first instance the verb is used as a parallel to the verb "grew"; and in the final phrase the verb is omitted because it is a statement of a static situation rather than an activity. Another illustration of this kind of parallelism is to be observed in Gen. 7.17, "And the Flood *was* forty days on the earth", followed by verse 19 which says, "and the waters prevailed exceedingly upon the earth". Clearly the picture is one of the turbulence of an overwhelming flood and not merely of a deep but placid sea of water. Boman suggests quite properly I believe, that throughout the Creation record, the verb הָיָה is used in the sense of "actively coming into being" rather than merely factual existence.[70] God created, or spoke, or made, and "it came to be so", ie., "sprang into being", certainly indicating an active process of realization rather than a static circumstance. Indeed, it is found in parallel with the Hebrew קום which has the meaning of "realization" in such passages as Isa. 7.7 ("It shall not stand, neither shall it come to pass") and Isa. 14.24 ("Surely as I have thought, so shall it come to pass").

Now the verb הָיָה occurs about 3570 times in the Old Testament. It is a very versatile word obviously: and only by associating it with various prepositions (לְ, כִּי, בְּ, מִן, עִם, עַל, etc.) and various verbal forms (infinitives and participles) can its full range of meanings be set forth adequately.* As Boman observed:[71]

> "הָיָה has thus been considered to some extent a general word which can mean everything possible and therefore designates nothing characteristic. Closer examination, however, reveals that this is not the case."

Ratschow[72] examined the occurrences of הָיָה in the Old Testament with a thoroughness hardly to be excelled and concluded that the verb had three essential meanings which are given in the following order: "to become", "to be" in the sense of existing or living, and "to effect". Boman, in discussing Ratschow's findings, states his opinion that these meanings really form a single basic unity with an internal relatedness.

In his discussion he first of all points out something which was elaborated by Benjamin Lee Whorf,[73] namely, that the meanings people

---

* *See Appendix VIII for illustrations.*

attach to the words they use reflect their own views of reality, and that these views are not at all the same as those generally shared by people of another language group. Many non-Indo-European peoples tend to equate things which we would consider quite separate and distinct. For example, to say in English that something IS wood is not to identify the thing itself with the wood that it is made of, but rather to say that it is made "out of" wood. By contrast in many other languages, including Hebrew, the thing and the wood are identified, equated, considered as inseparable. Such a sentence as "the altar and its walls *(were)* wood" (Ezek. 41. 22) means to the Hebrew mind that altar, walls, and wood are a single entity, an equation, one and the same in the particular instance. A verb is not necessary. Similarly, "All the Lord's ways *(are)* grace and truth" would mean to us that there is grace and truth IN all the Lord's ways. But not so to the Hebrew mind. This is not an *aspect* of the Lord's ways, it is a factual commonality. As Boman expresses it, "The predicate inheres in the subject".[74]

Thus he further observes:[75]

> "The most important meanings and uses of *our* verb "to be" (and its equivalents in other Indo-European languages) are (i) to express being or existence, and (ii) to serve as a copula."

But having said this, Boman comments:[76]

> "Hebrew and other Semitic languages do not *need* (my emphasis) a copula because of the noun clause (such a clause as 'the altar is wood'). As a general rule, therefore, it may be said that הָיָה is not used as a copula.... The characteristic mark of הָיָה in distinction from our verb 'to be' is that it is a true verb with full verbal force."

In short, he concludes that whether הָיָה stands alone without any accompanying preposition or is qualified by one, "it signifies *real becoming* (his emphasis), what is an occurrence or a passage from one condition to another...., a becoming in inner reality...., a becoming something new by vocation....".[77] Such is Boman's view, a view supported by many illustrations, some of which will be found later in this text. It is a view arrived at by a most careful study of the whole question in which cognizance has been taken of the previous labours of a large number of recognized European scholars.

It is a view which completely contradicts the rather bombastic statements of some recent writers whom we have already quoted as saying in effect that every Hebrew scholar knows precisely the opposite to be the case! It is a view which strongly supports the argument that chaos was not the initial condition of the created earth.

Other linguists agree with Boman. Non-Indo-European languages do *not* employ the verb "to be" as English does. In an interesting paper entitled, *Language and Philosophy*, Basson and O'Connor examine the relationship between structure of *language* and form of *philosophy*.[78] This examination includes as an important part of their thesis a study of the verb "to be" used in the following ways:

(1) As a logical copula, involving:
- (a) Predication: "the leaf is green".
- (b) Class inclusion: "all men are mortal".
- (c) Class membership: "the tree is an oak".
- (d) Identity: "George VI was king of England".
- (e) Formal implication: "wisdom is valuable".

(2) In an existential sense: "God is".
(3) In any other sense peculiar to the language in question.

> "Some interesting and possibly important information was supplied to us (from a questionnaire sent to a number of philologists and linguists) on this topic. Most interesting was the large number of languages which made a sharp distinction between the *existential* 'is' and the copula.* Semitic languages have in general no copula, but Hebrew and Assyrian both have a special word for 'exists'. Malay (an Austronesian language) is similar to Hebrew in this respect. Tibetan uses 'yin' for the copula and 'yod' for existence, but a sentence like "That hill is high' might use either word according to the sense of the context."

All the lexicons deal with the verb הָיָה at some length. I do not have in my possession, nor is there available to me at the present, a copy of the original work completed by that most famous of Hebrew lexicographers, Friedrich Heinrich Wilhelm Gesenius, in 1812. I do have, however, translations of his original work edited and amended in various ways by some of the scholars who followed him.

---

* *See further Appendix IX*

Christopher Leo's edition of Gesenius,[79] published in 1825, gives a list of the meanings of the verb with illustrative examples from the Old Testament which may be summed up under the following basic headings: "to be" illustrated by reference to Exod. 20.3 (a curious circumstance since it is not copulative!), "to serve as" or "to tend towards", "to become" or "turn into" (with the preposition לְ), "to be with" (ie., associated with, or on the side of), "to happen", "to prosper" or "succeed", and "to have happened".

Tregelles' edition of Gesenius,[80] published in 1889, gives the following meanings: "to be" or "to exist", "to become", "to be done", "to be made" (all without any associated preposition לְ). When followed by modifying prepositions, the verb is given an extended list of meanings which are summarized in Appendix X. Since the main point at issue in this instance is the meaning of the verb הָיָה in Gen. 1.2 where it is accompanied by no preposition of any kind, the other passages will not be examined at this point. In the passive voice, Tregelles gives the meanings as "to become", "to be made", and "to be done".

In 1890 a Student's Lexicon was published by Benjamin Davies,[81] also based on Gesenius (and Furst). He gives the basic meanings as follows: "to be" - whether with the meaning of "to exist" or "to live", or "to be somewhere" - or as the logical copula between subject and predicate. As an illustration of this last, he refers to Gen. 1.2. He then gives a second group of meanings as follows: "to come into being", "to come to pass", "to occur" or "happen"; and in the passive "to be done", "to be made to be".

In each of these Lexicons I have examined every reference in the original Hebrew. In *many* instances the appropriateness of the headings under which they are listed can be very much a matter of opinion as is revealed by the fact that the same reference will be reproduced under different headings be different lexicographers. A list of these references will be found in Appendix XI.

I believe it would not be incorrect to say that as these Lexicons appeared successively through the years, the verb הָיָה was in the course of time viewed somewhat differently. With Gesenius and Leo the principle or basic view seems to have been that the verb meant essentially "to be" in the ordinary English sense, with the concept of "existing" or "living" next, and "becoming" only as a last alternative. By the time we come to Brown, Driver, and Briggs, the modern standard of reference, the position has altered. The basic meanings are now set forth under four headings in *this* order: "to fall out", "to come to pass", "to become", and finally, "to be". And even with respect to this last alternative, at the appropriate place the authors add in parenthesis: "often with the subordinate idea of becoming". Thus the emphasis has shifted: where the copulative sense was originally listed as the primary one, it is now listed as of least importance. Brown, Driver, and Briggs' Lexicon of the Hebrew language is by far the most exhaustive available in English and here we find that far from being a rare or exceptional meaning of הָיָה (as we are so frequently assured these days) the general sense of "coming to be" or "becoming" is one of the most important and most fundamental meanings.

I have examined every reference given in all these Lexicons as well as those provided in some of the more elementary student's dictionaries of Hebrew and I have no hesitation in saying that the evidence tells unmistakeably against the present commonly accepted view among "conservative" biblical scholars who have expressed an opinion on the meaning of Gen. 1.2. Some of these writers will argue that הָיָה may be allowed to mean "became" when, and only when, it is followed by the preposition *lamedh* (לְ). This is *quite* untrue as is easily shown by a study of cases where "became" is manifestly the correct rendering of הָיָה, though the *lamedh* is omitted in the Hebrew. A list of examples where ל is used - and the reasons why - will be found in Appendix XII.

I would not say that the verb is *never* used copulatively (though Ratschow and Boman hold this to be virtually so), but I think it can be shown conclusively that the simple copulative use is the exception and not the rule, and that such exceptions are very rare indeed. In a few cases there appear to be exceptions only because we have failed to observe the real meaning that the Hebrew writer had in mind and our renderings are misleading. As we have seen, the verb can be used to signify an "active existence" in a situation where we would not expect to find "activity". Such a case as Adam's nakedness is an example, for this is how he "went about". In this instance, the English simply says that Adam was naked. But in the Hebrew processes of thinking, this is not a static condition but a living circumstance. The Hebrew mind animated situations far more frequently than we do and it is this animation which gives the Psalms, for example, such tremendous dramatic force. Like many non-Indo-European people, they thought of *things* as having character, not merely characteristics.

Even in Brown, Driver, and Briggs the list of supposedly copulative uses includes numerous instances where the case is very doubtful. For example, they list Deut. 23.15, "The servant which is escaped unto thee....". But surely this is an instance where modern English would require the verb *has* rather than It is not a copulative use of the verb: the verb הָיָה is associated with another verb of dramatic action. One could never properly substitute the word "has" in such a sentence as "The field is flat", and the very fact that one can make the substitution in the former but not in the latter case is sufficient to demonstrate that the difference is a real one. In such a sentence as Gen. 17.1 (also included in the list in Brown, Driver, and Briggs) where the text reads, "And when Abraham was ninety years old....", we are not really saying that Abraham WAS ninety years. Obviously Abraham is not the same "thing" as ninety years. We are actually saying, "When he reached the age of....", ie., "When he became ninety years old....".

Brown, Driver, and Briggs list altogether 45 references to show that הָיָה can mean simply "to be". However, of these 45 references 8 should be excluded, being clearly not examples of a purely copulative use. Furthermore, I believe another 7 at least are equivocal since in every case the translation "became" or "had become" *would be equally, if not more, appropriate.* These are: Gen. 1.2; 17.1; Jud. 11.1; II Ki. 18.2; I Chron. 11.20; II Chron. 21.20 and 27.8. This leaves us with only 30 examples out of a total (included under all headings listed in their lexicon) of 1320 occurrences of הָיָה which have been proposed as illustrations of the possible meanings of the verb. Moreover, of these 30, at least 8 others are ill-chosen because their use is either anomalous (Gen. 8.5) or signifies "came to be" as in Gen. 5.4, 5, 8, 11; 11.32; 23.1; and Exod. 38.24.

As we have already said, it seems possible that some cases of a genuine copulative use of the verb הָיָה which parallels that claimed by most writers for the passage in Gen. 1.2 will be discovered if the Old Testament is searched with sufficient care. But the fact that Ratschow was not willing, after making such an exhaustive study, to admit of a single instance, suggests that such cases will certainly be the exception rather than the rule. By contrast, the number of cases where the copulative sense is indicated by the very *omission* of the verb in the Hebrew is very great indeed. I have not made an actual count for the whole Old Testament but I am sure that it would run into the thousands. There are 600 cases in Genesis alone, for example. A single page in any English printing of the Bible will usually show anywhere from 10 to 20 cases and most Bibles run into a thousand pages or thereabouts for the Old Testament. Simple arithmetic suggests, therefore, that such omissions may run as high as five or ten thousand: five or ten thousand instances, that is to say, in which the Hebrew has omitted the verb entirely because the meaning is simply copulative. On the other hand, the number of cases where the verb can appropriately be rendered by some expression which denotes *becoming* is very, very large indeed.

Whatever else may or may not be said, one certainly would not draw from this the conclusion that the simple copulative use is the *normal* use. While it is highly likely that Brown, Driver, and Briggs could have supplied more examples had they considered it worthwhile, it still remains true that the simple copulative sense is placed last in the list and is then illustrated by a very small sample only, a substantial proportion of even these being a little ambiguous.

By contrast with the actual evidence, one recent writer stated categorically that the sense of "became" is so rare as to be found only six times in the whole of the Pentateuch.[82] As it stands, assuming the writer meant precisely what his words imply, the statement is demonstrably false. For example, the English reader will find the following seventeen instances *in Genesis alone*, viz., Gen. 2.7, 10; 3.22; 9.15; 18.18; 19.26; 20.12; 21.20; 24.67; 32.10 (verse 11 in the Hebrew text); 34.16; 37.20; 47.20 and 26; 48.19 (twice); and 49.15. Other occurrences elsewhere are listed in Appendix XIII: the total exceeds 133.

Furthermore, it must be remembered that these are not by any means all the instances in which הָיָה is translated "became" (or "become", "had become", etc.) but only those observable *in the Authorized Version*. There are many other English translations which supply us with further instances.* And it must be remembered that English translations represent only one group of versions among many. There are Latin, French, German, Greek, and dozens of other versions besides the English ones. In these one may observe many more instances.

For example, the Latin Vulgate has rendered הָיָה as "became" in thirteen instances in Genesis chapter 1 alone! Even more strikingly, the Greek Septuagint translation renders הָיָה as "became" in 22 cases in Genesis 1. Throughout the whole of Genesis this version translated the verb as "became" 146 times: in Genesis and Exodus together the total becomes 201 times: in the Pentateuch as a whole 298 times: and some 1500 times throughout the whole Old Testament including

---

* *See on this, Chapter IV, The Witness of Various Versions.*

the Apocrypha. These totals are, of course, according to my own counting. The count may be slightly out one way or the other, but certainly it is essentially correct and probably errs only by being an understatement if anything. I may have missed a few but I certainly did not invent any! Moreover, the figures do not include cases where הָיָה is rendered by some entirely different word that better expresses by circumlocution its dynamic sense of "becoming".

The sad truth is that the issue can no longer be explored except within the framework of a controversy which has crystallized itself around the "Gap Theory". When the challenge of Geology brought into sharper focus the importance of this particular exegesis, the argument was not unnaturally shifted from the linguistic evidence of the text of Genesis itself to an examination of other passages of the Bible which it was believed contributed light on the matter. So the issue became one of the "interpretation" rather than the precise and careful analysis of Gen. 1.2 which is really the critical issue.

It may be argued with some force that if the case is rested primarily on the linguistic evidence of Gen. 1.2, it can never have compelling weight because by far the great majority of authorities are so strongly against it. But authorities are not always right. For example, from the very earliest times in English translations that I have been able to examine thus far, the fifth verse of the first chapter of the "Song of Solomon" has been rendered, "I am black but comely....". I have so far found only one honourable exception.[93] Yet the truth of the matter is that the Hebrew word translated "but" is more frequently rendered "and" in the English of the Old Testament. There is no question that "but" is perfectly allowable here. Nevertheless, "and" is its more usual meaning, and though there are a number of other alternatives that could have been chosen, such as "yet", "nevertheless", etc., common usage easily confirms the fact that the Hebrew *waw* is much more frequently employed as a con-junctive than a dis-junctive. Normally the context readily determines which it is.* Then why has it been rendered "but" in this passage where, by this simple expedient, the speaker is in effect being made to apologize for the colour of her skin? The answer, of course, is that the choice was made on prejudicial, not linguistic, grounds, though each

---

* *An approximate count shows that the particle is translated in the Old Testament as 'and' some 25,000 times, and as 'but' some 3000 times.*

translator was probably quite unaware of the way in which his bias was expressing itself. The use of "but" has nothing to do with scholarship at all. It has simply been accepted without challenge because the implications of it were not observed.

I am persuaded that we have wrongly reached the same kind of general agreement as to the rendering of Gen. 1. 2, not on scholarly grounds but either because the alternative simply did not occur to the translator or because he desired to dissociate himself from a certain view of the earth's early history which currently, at least, is said to find no support from Geology. The emotional factor is often quite evident from the vehemence with which the alternative rendering is disallowed. Climate of *opinion* is simply against it but not, I believe, the linguistic evidence itself. Some of this evidence is reviewed for several books of the Bible in Appendix IV.

CONCLUSION:

In Appendix IV will be found a rather involved examination of the evidence as found in five representative books of the Old Testament; Genesis, Joshua, Job, two Psalms, and Zechariah. This study has been put in an appendix in order to remove it from the cursive text and to allow the reader to read on through without getting tiresomely bogged down in detail.

The evidence shows that some part of the English verb "to be" occurs in the Authorized Version 832 times in the book of Genesis alone.* Any other English version would, of course, have served the purpose of analysis just as well. However, in the usual printing of the Authorized Version text, italics are used for "supplied" words which simplifies the counting, and of these 832 occurrences, 626 are not represented by any form of the verb הָיָה in the original. In summary, where the copulative use of the English verb "to be" occurs in the Authorized Version, the Hebrew original does not employ the verb הָיָה. On page 58 a breakdown of the tenses involved in these 626 occurrences of the supplied English verb indicates that a substantial number of them (169 in all) are in the past tense.

In this Appendix, a similar breakdown was undertaken of the use of the verb "to be" for the other books of the Bible listed above and a breakdown of the results is tabulated on page 146. From this sample study I think certain things emerge with respect to the use

---

* *See accompanying tabulation, page 58.*

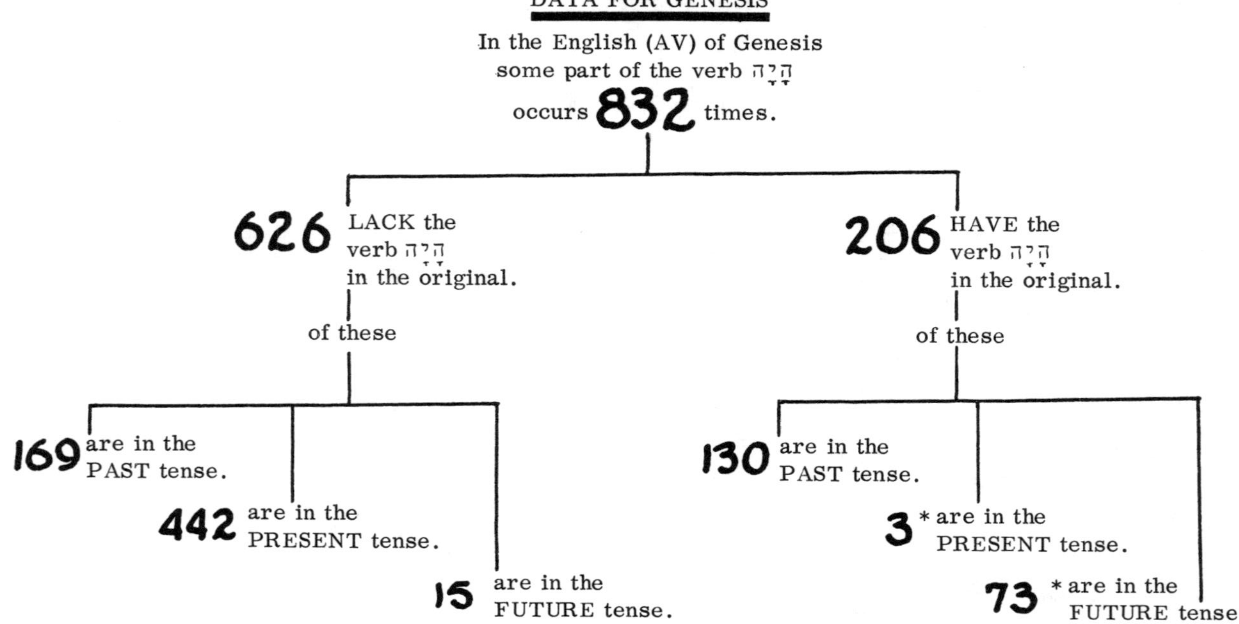
DATA FOR GENESIS
In the English (AV) of Genesis
some part of the verb הָיָה
occurs 832 times.
626 LACK the verb הָיָה in the original.
of these
169 are in the PAST tense.
442 are in the PRESENT tense.
15 are in the FUTURE tense.
206 HAVE the verb הָיָה in the original.
of these
130 are in the PAST tense.
3 * are in the PRESENT tense.
73 * are in the FUTURE tense.

*Of these, 17 are rendered *became*, *will become*, etc., and in other versions many more are so rendered.

in Hebrew of the verb הָיָה.

First of all, it is apparent that the verb הָיָה is not *normally* employed to express the simple copula, whether the tense is past or present. It is more frequently employed, however, when the tense is future.

The second thing emerging from this study is that the Hebrew writers did not find it necessary to employ the verb הָיָה in order to make clear to the reader whether the tense was past or present. In other words, the introduction of the verb (as in Gen. 1.2, for instance) is not simply a literary device to inform the reader that this is how the situation was in the past rather than how it is in the present. In the Book of Genesis, the tabulation shows that in 169 cases the context is allowed to decide for the reader that the events are past and the reader is left to surmise for himself that in 442 cases the tense is present. The context itself, in the absence of any expression of the verb הָיָה in the original, is considered to be sufficiently clear.

The third thing is that the verb הָיָה is employed only when change of a specific kind is involved. This does not mean change in the sense that a past situation is no longer true in the present, but rather that a present situation is changing, has changed from what it was, or will change in the future. The argument that a past situation which has not continued into the present automatically requires the employment of the verb הָיָה does not seem to be valid. The idea of change is very nicely represented in English in a substantial number of cases by some form of the verb "to become" or "to come to be". In a surprisingly large number of cases where הָיָה appears in the original the use of such a form as "become" or "became" as a substitute rendering will be found to clarify the meaning of the text or, at the least, to make very good sense.

In the light of these findings, it can hardly be maintained that to translate Gen. 1.2 as, "but the earth had become a ruin, etc.", contravenes Hebrew usage. If the meaning intended had been simply "the earth was a chaos", even if we understand the word *chaos* in the Greek sense of "waiting to be given form", the verb הָיָה would not normally have been employed in the original.

Chapter 3.

THE PLUPERFECT IN HEBREW.

To my knowledge, there is no work in the English language dealing specifically with the Hebrew verb comparable to that published in 1892 by S. R. Driver[84] entitled, *A Treatise on the Hebrew Tenses.* The expanded title as it appears on the first page is, "A Treatise on the Use of the Tenses in Hebrew and some Other Syntactical Questions". As might be expected from a man with Driver's scholarship, the treatment of tenses is thorough and precise, and massively illustrated with innumerable examples taken from Scripture.

In the present Chapter, our primary concern is with the use of the pluperfect in Hebrew and we shall not here enter into detailed consideration of the other tenses, of such questions as the "*waw* consecutive", the mode of expressing continuing present action, or action in the future. Nor will the philosophy of the Hebrew time-sense be examined in any depth, remarkable as it is, in spite of the fact that much of Driver's treatise deals with this aspect of the subject. All these are of importance for the student of Hebrew, of course, but they are explored here only to the extent that they contribute to an understanding of the Hebrew use of the pluperfect.

Suffice it to say that the formal paradigm of the Hebrew verb presents us with a perfect tense for describing completed action, and an imperfect tense for describing incomplete action: and these two tenses are by various means made to serve all the other tenses, pluperfect, present, and future. For example, the verb *qatal* (קָטַל) "to kill" appears in an appropriate form corresponding to "he is killing": and it appears in an appropriate form "he is killed". The verb also has the passive form, "he is being killed" and "he was killed": and of course there are the usual participles, imperatives, infinitives, etc., both active and passive. Unlike English, the verb has a specific form for the reflexive (which would mean "to kill oneself, ie., to commit suicide), as well as an intensive form "to kill with violence" (ie., to slaughter), and a causative form, "to have someone put to death". Thus in the matter of conjugations the Hebrew verb is well enough supplied but in the matter of tense, that is to say of *time*, it is limited to two forms only.

Clearly a single tense form has therefore to serve a much wider range of meanings than in English. Shades of difference about the timing in the past or the future do not seem to have been considered sufficiently important to justify special forms for either a pluperfect or a future tense. With respect to the latter, it has been suggested that, like other non-Indo-Europeans, they held the view that to speak of something which is to occur in the future is unrealisitc since one cannot really be sure about it. Thus no specific verbal form was ever "invented" to cover it. It can be a promise or an intention, but as far as man is concerned it hardly constitutes a fact! With God, of course, it is quite different. When He says He will do something in the future, it IS a fact, and the certainty that it will be done led the Hebrew writer to use a perfect tense as if it were already a *fait accomplis*. Most divinely originated promises are treated thus, and the verb is written in a form which is referred to by grammarians as the "prophetic perfect".

Brief mention must be made of one odd feature of Hebrew syntax that has puzzled Indo-European readers since it seems an irrational procedure. It is this. When a sentence or a clause begins with the conjunction "and" (*waw*), the verb which immediately follows it and to which it is joined as a prefix, has its tense converted! A perfect is treated as an imperfect and an imperfect as a perfect. Thus the form for the English, "he is killed", if it happens to have the *waw* prefixed to it, is converted as though it were no longer a perfect and completed action but an imperfect and uncompleted action. "He killed" becomes "and he is killing" or "and he kills" or even "and he will kill": ie., any one of the uncompleted modes of expression. This is sometimes referred to by Hebrew scholars as the *waw*-conversive" (ie., *waw* which converts) and sometimes as the *waw*-consecutive" (ie., verb following or consequent to what precedes). We shall not have occasion to revert to this very much in the present study except in quoting Driver to show what it can NOT be made to mean.

Now evidently Hebrew writers did feel it desirable to have some means of distinguishing between the implications of a perfect and a pluperfect tense. If there is only one verbal form to cover both ideas, one necessarily has to adopt some "device" other than changing the verbal form. To convey the idea of a pluperfect as distinct from a perfect, Hebrew writers adopted the practice of deliberately changing the normal word order of the sentence. It is this with which we are primarily concerned in the present chapter.

The normal English sentence, in its simplest form, places the subject first, the verb next, and the object after the verb. In Latin the verb is placed at or near the end of the sentence, after both subject and object. In Hebrew the normal order is verb first, subject next, and object after that. Thus the order is:

In English: "The king appointed his ministers...."

In Latin: "The king his ministers did appoint...."

In Hebrew: "He appointed, did the king, his ministers..."

English, of course, allows changes or departures from the normal in the interests of emphasis, contrast, euphemy, and by poetic licence. Hebrew is remarkably consistent and departs from the norm with rather less frequency than does the English, though it makes similar allowances in poetry and adopts rather similar rules for emphasis or contrast. In the latter case, it is customary to place the subject ahead of the verb in order to emphasize a change. "The king planned this but God determined otherwise" would be a situation in which the Hebrew writer would place the second subject, "God", ahead of its verb, the conjunction being read more appropriately as a disjunction than a conjunction in such a case. However even in this kind of situation the Hebrew would not always change the word order. It really depends upon how great the contrast is felt to be and whether it is desired to draw special attention to it or not. The reason for emphasizing this point is that the change of word order in the sentence, ie., the placing of the subject ahead of the verb instead of the reverse, is a *device which happens also to serve the purpose of converting a perfect into a pluperfect*. Thus when the word order IS changed one has to determine for which cause this has been done, although in some cases it may have been done for both reasons.

The use of a pluperfect in a narrative has a special importance because it frequently indicates a hiatus. When the second sentence is not immediately connected with the one which precedes it, when the narrator is reverting to an event or a circumstance that in point of time is to be placed ahead of and distinct from the events recorded in the subsequent narrative, then it is customary to place the subject ahead of the verb and it is proper to render the verb as a pluperfect. It is not the verb form which is changed but the word order; and since there is disconnection or discontinuity intended by this device, it is usual to preface the sentence with *waw-dis*junctive rather than *waw-con*junctive, which in an English translation would mean replacing the "and" with "but" or "however" or "meanwhile". For example, in such a sentence as, "The king came to the valley but the enemy had fled", the Hebrew would place the subject "enemy" ahead of the verb "fled", thus converting it to a pluperfect "had fled".

In a sentence of this kind, we have a situation in which both contrast *and* discontinuity appear in a single context. There is contrast because, while the king planned one course of action confidently looking for an engagement, the enemy had planned otherwise and had already left in order to avoid one! The situation is such that the departure of the enemy was already completed before the king arrived on the scene - and therefore the context calls for a pluperfect in the translation. The conjunction (*waw*) would properly be rendered a disjunctive "but" or "however" or some such word, and whether we look upon the inverted order as signifying contrast or discontinuity matters little, for both views are equally correct. The context will usually settle the matter in any case. In such a sentence as "The king planned this but the people planned otherwise", the inverted order would be used to signify contrast primarily, but even here a pluperfect might not be inappropriate: "but the people *had* planned otherwise". Thus, in the present issue, the word order of Gen. 1.2 virtually demands a pluperfect if it is once allowed that the verb הָיְתָה cannot be taken as a simple copula. "But the earth had become...." is almost certainly the more appropriate rendering.

Now Driver writes at some length on this point. In discussing the usual idiom chosen by Hebrew writers for the purpose of expressing a pluperfect, he says:[85] "Their custom, when they wish to do this is to interpose the subject between the conjunction and the verb הָיְתָה". He then draws attention to Pusey's comments on the same subject and advises the reader to refer to the well-known *Lectures on Daniel* where Pusey writes at some length on the inverted word order which he says, *"expresses a past time, anterior to what follows but in no way connected in time with what precedes"*.[86]

Driver then gives the following series of illustrations from the Old Testament and comments upon each as indicated. I have not quoted his comments directly because his style is such as to demand that one has read the text which preceded. I have merely summarized his words. But I have done so without in any way changing his intended meaning.

Gen. 24.62: "Now, Isaac *had come* from the way of the well Lahairoi; for he dwelt in the south country. And Isaac went out to meditate in the field at the eventide: and he lifted up his eyes and saw, and, behold, the camels were coming. And Rebekah lifted up her eyes, and when she saw Isaac, she lighted off the camel....". The opening verb is to be read as a pluperfect, for here the writer wishes to combine two streams in his narrative; ie., he has (i) brought Rebekah to the termination of her journey, but (ii) he also desires to account for Isaac's presence at the same spot. In order to prepare the way for their meeting, he is obliged to go back and to detail what had taken place prior to the stage at which his narrative has arrived: he therefore starts afresh with the words וְיִצְחָק בָּא (Now + the subject (Isaac) + the verb, *in this order*). The whole of verse 62 f. bears reference to Isaac and the two streams which are terminated respectively by וַיֵּלֵךְ (verse 61) and וַיַּרְא (verse 62) thus converge in verse 64 which says, "And she lifted up, did Rebekah, her eyes" (וַתִּשָּׂא רִבְקָה אֶת עֵינֶיהָ).

So also in Gen. 31.19: (וְלָבָן הָלַךְ) "Now Laban *had gone away* to shear his sheep, when Rachel stole the images that were her father's". That is to say, the possibility of Rachel stealing the images was a direct consequence of the fact that Laban had gone away.

To a reader who is unfamiliar with Hebrew, these illustrations may be difficult to follow precisely, but Driver chose these examples, among others, simply becuase they do exactly illustrate the point he is making: namely, that the first clause is so constructed in the Hebrew as to convey a pluperfect sense whereas the second clause is not, and this construction is dependent entirely upon the interposition of the subject between the conjunction and the verb.

Driver then clarifies the issue somewhat by providing the reader with a number of biblical illustrations for which he gives the reference and a key word or two. I have set forth these references much more fully because probably not too many readers will take the time actually to look them up - and the force of his observations will thus largely be lost. I have added a note, where appropriate, relative to the Revised Standard Version renderings. Here is his list.

Gen.20.4: But Abimelech had not (actually) come near her. . . . ." The situation here is that Abraham, for fear of being put to death by Abimelech whom he suspected would want to take his beautiful wife Sarah, had posed as her brother instead of her husband. Accordingly, Abimelech had treated the supposed brother with extreme favour, and then taken Sarah off to his palace. . . . *But*, as it happens, he had a dream that came to warn him against his intended action and this dream occurred providentially *before* the King "had come near her". Hence the writer wishes the reader to know, since the narrative is written in retrospect, that Abimelech meanwhile had not yet actually abused Sarah - and so, as things turned out, had done her no harm. It will be noted that both the Authorized Version and the Revised Standard Version have translated the Hebrew as a pluperfect.

I Sam.14.27: "Jonathan had not heard" that his father had given the order forbidding the eating of a certain honeycomb. So Jonathan disobeyed an order of whose existence he was ignorant. It will be noted in this instance that the Authorized Version does *not* observe the tense indicated by the Hebrew word order, whereas the Revised Standard Version has done so. It should be underscored that in all these, as well as in the following cases, the noun precedes the verb.

Num.13.22: "Now Hebron had been built seven years before Zoan in Egypt". The very sense of the narrative here would, one might suppose, guide the translators - even if the Hebrew text did not provide the clue. Nevertheless, for some reason neither the Authorized Version nor the Revised Standard Version translated this passage correctly. This fact should be sufficient indication, as we shall have reason to underscore later, that it is not enough in such matters to appeal to two such standard translations and merely depend upon how *they* dealt with the matter. Driver is right: this is quite clear from the very nature of the context. The Revised Standard Version scholars were not sufficiently careful - and the Authorized Version scholars may not even have been aware of the rule. Both mistranslated the text.

Josh.6.22: "But Joshua *had said* unto the two men. . . ."

Josh.18.1: ". . . . and the land *had* (already) *been* subdued before them". In Josh.6.22 the Authorized Version observed the rule, the Revised Standard Version did not. In Josh.18.1 neither the Authorized Version nor the Revised Standard Version observed it.

I Sam.9.15: "Now, the evening before Samuel came, the Lord *had told* Samuel. . . ." The Authorized Version and the Revised

Standard Version are correct.

I Sam.25.21: "Now David *had said*..." So the Authorized Version and the Revised Standard Version.

I Sam.28.3: "Saul *had put away* all that had familiar spirits". Both the Revised Standard Version and the Authorized Version observed the pluperfect here.

II Sam.18.18: "Now Absalom, in his lifetime, *had taken* and reared up a pillar unto himself...." Both versions agree.

I Ki.14.5: "Now the Lord *had said* unto Abijah...." Here neither the Authorized Version nor the Revised Standard Version (nor the Berkeley translation, I notice) have observed the correct sense.

I Ki.22.31: "But the king of Syria *had commanded* his thirty captains....". The Revised Standard Version agrees, but not the Authorized Version.

II Ki.7.17: "Meanwhile the king *had appointed* the lord, on whose hand he leaned, to have charge of the gate...." This circumstance was fatal to the king, hence it is a piece of information cast in retrospect by way of preparing the reader for what followed. The Revised Standard Version noted the word order, but the Authorized Version did not.

II Ki.9.16: "Meanwhile, Ahaziah, King of Judah, *had come down* to see Joram...." Again, the Revised Standard Version agrees with, but the Authorized Version has not observed, the rule.

It will be noted that in all these instances the sentence is best introduced by the disjunctive particle in order to underscore the fact that there is no immediate connection with what precedes. Driver sometimes has "and" where I have substituted "but" or "now" or "meanwhile". The point needs no defending for the Hebrew *waw* (ו) which stands at the beginning of each of these references has an almost unlimited number of meanings,* so that one may adopt the meaning most suitable to the sense without doing any injustice to the Hebrew original.

After concluding this list of illustrations, Driver adds that in each of these passages, by separating the verb from the conjunction and interposing the subject between the two, "the writer *cuts the connexion* with the immediately preceding narrative, and so suggests a pluperfect" (his emphasis).[87] This is a most significant comment when applied to Gen.1.1 and 1.2.

---

* *See Appendix XIV.*

In *A Resurvey of Hebrew Tenses*, Frank R. Blake[88] gives, as one of the variant meanings of the "perfect" tense form in Hebrew, "a past perfect (ie,, pluperfect)" denoting something more than merely a completed situation and "occurring normally only in multiple sentences". As an example, he refers to Gen. 31.33-34. It will be noted that the pluperfect element of the sentence, "but Rachel had taken....", describes a past act which is pictured as having occurred *before* Laban came to Rachel's tent. By analogy, we should assume, therefore, that the pluperfect is used to describe something which occurred prior to the events which thereafter form the main thread of the story. It describes a circumstance ancillary to the rest of the narrative. Accordingly, it seems likely that Gen. 1.2 is ancillary in the same sense to what follows in Gen. 1.3 ff.

We come now to an example, given by Driver,[89] of a special kind. He points out that in the normal course of events, when Ezekiel has some message from the Lord to declare to his people, he introduces his remarks with a kind of standard formula. This formula does not always involve the same words but it does involve the same sentence structure and word order. Thus in Ezek. 3.22 he says: "And the hand of the Lord (was) upon me...." (וַתְּהִי עָלַי שָׁם יַד־יְהוָה). So also in 8.1 he says, "The hand of the Lord *fell* upon me....", and in 14.2, "And it came to pass that the word of the Lord (was) unto me saying...." So 20.2 - exactly as in 14.2; and so on.

But there is a clear difference when we come to Ezek. 33.22 where the text has וְיַד־יְהוָה הָיְתָה אֵלַי בָּעֶרֶב: ie., "Now the hand of the Lord had been upon me in the evening". Strictly speaking, אֵלַי should perhaps be rendered "unto me" rather than "upon me" but there are textual variations and either would be acceptable. The point is not important in any case, except that one must be as accurate as possible - which the Revised Standard Version has not been, as we shall see. Now Ezekiel's full sentence is: "Now the hand of the Lord had been upon me in the evening.... before he that had escaped came to me: and He had opened my mouth until he came to me in the morning; and my mouth was opened and I was no more dumb".

Thus the sentence opens with a word order which is similar to that of Gen. 1.2, and the context shows clearly that the pluperfect is required in order to make the order of events quite obvious to the reader. And the Revised Standard Version is correct in so far as it renders the verb in the pluperfect, though for some curious reason (I can find no MS variant to justify it) the sentence has been rendered, "Now the WORD (דָּבָר, not יַד) had come upon me the evening before....". The use of the substitute word is not serious, of course, for the meaning is clear enough. Berkeley's version has correctly translated this passage both as to the verbal form and the word "hand".

So Driver underscores the fact that in all these cases the word order is the *only* way in which Hebrew can indicate a pluperfect tense. He denies that they could have expressed it in any other way, for he points out that the normal word order (conjunctive - verb - subject) "which is recognized by all grammarians, cannot easily be reconciled with the idea of a pluperfect: for the construction inherent in the one seems to be just what is excluded by the other. Under these circumstances we shall scarcely be wrong in hesitating to admit it without strong and clear exegetical necessity".[90] By which, in the context of his words, he means that the Hebrew has no way of expressing the pluperfect EXCEPT by an inversion of the word order; for the construction normally used implies a connection with what precedes, whereas the inverted word order is to show precisely the opposite - a disconnection. In all the illustrations provided, the intention of the writer is clearly to express what is properly conveyed only by a pluperfect in English.

If there can be shown to be some other way whereby a Hebrew writer can express the pluperfect, then the case for a pluperfect is weakened somewhat in Gen. 1. 2. For one could always argue that since the mere transposition of word order can, upon occasion, serve rather for emphasis upon a new subject than to express a pluperfect, the writer of Gen. 1. 2, had he really wished to express the pluperfect without any ambiguity whatever, would have chosen the alternative unambiguous method. Is there, therefore, any other way in Hebrew of doing so? The answer according to Driver is, No. With his usual moderation, Driver writes:[91]

> "It is a moot and delicate question how far the imperfect with *waw*-conversive denotes a pluperfect. There is, of course, no doubt that it may express *a continuation of a pluperfect:* for example, Gen. 31. 34 'had taken and had placed them....'. But can the imperfect with *waw*-consecutive *introduce* it? Can it instead of conducting us as usual to a succeeding act, lead us back to one which is chronologically anterior? The imperfect with *waw*-consecutive is.... certainly not the usual idiom chosen by Hebrew writers for the purpose of expressing a pluperfect: their usual habit, when they wish to do so, is to interpose the subject between the conjunction and the verb, which then lapses into the perfect, a

form which we know *allows* scope for a pluperfect signification."

Driver uses the word *allows* rather than *demands* (his emphasis throughout) because, as he has already pointed out, it may be simply a means of giving contrasting emphasis against what preceded.

Now Driver was well aware that quite a few Hebraists were in the habit of translating the simple *waw*-consecutive as though it were a pluperfect, a practice which is to be observed also in a number of cases in the Authorized Version. This he feels is unwarranted.[92] He therefore proceeds to examine with care the supposed examples as set forth by Kalisch (Gen.2.2; 26.18; Exod.11.1), by Ibn Ezra (Gen.4.23), by Keil (Gen.3.19,22), by Hitzig (Isa.8.3; 39.1; Jer. 39.11; Jonah 2.4). He also lists from Keil Gen.2.19; I Ki.7.13 and 9.14, and from Delitzsch Isa.37.5. Following this, certain other passages from Ibn Ezra are cited.

After giving due attention to all the references listed, ie., those above and some others cited by Jewish grammarians, Driver concludes: "Such are the passages from which our conclusion has to be drawn". He sums up the situation by saying:[93]

> "All that a careful scholar like Mr. Wright *(Lectures on the Comparative Grammar of the Semitic Languages*, 1890) can bring himself to admit with reference to the pluperfect sense of any other construction than that of word order inversion, is that while 'no clear instances can be cited in which it is distinctly so used', there are cases in which 'something like an approximation to that signification can be detected'. And it is rejected unreservedly by Bottcher, Quarry, Pusey, and Dillman."

Moreover, he notes that in the Revised Version the wrongly used pluperfect renderings of the Authorized Version have normally been corrected.

It is reasonably certain, therefore, that word order inversion is intended to direct the reader's attention to this chronological disconnection. It will be observed only otherwise in the case of poetry and for contrast. Since Genesis is not written as poetry in our Massoretic text (whatever may be argued out of a desire to label it as some kind of pertic allegory), one is left with no alternative but that either the writer deliberately meant to separate the two verses and to give the sense of a pluperfect or that he meant to effect a clear contrast. And since the latter virtually always is indicated by the introduction of a new subject to the verb, a circumstance not applicable in this instance, we really have no alternative but to render the verb "had become".

Some of those whom Driver quotes to the contrary drew their support from Jewish grammarians. But on this point Driver writes:[94]

> "The authority of the Jewish grammarians, strange as it may seem to say so, must not be pressed; for although they have left works which mark an era in the development of Hebrew grammar, and are of inestimable value for purposes of exegesis, still their syntactical no less than their phonetic principles have always to be adopted with caution, or even to be rejected altogether. Their grammar is not the systematization of a living tradition, it is a reconstruction as much as that of Gesenius or Ewald or Philippi, but often unfortunately without a sound basis in logic or philology. And a question such as that now before us is just one upon which their judgment would be particularly liable to be at fault."

In summary, therefore, Driver's position is that if the usual word order ".... expressive of the smooth and unbroken succession of events one after another is naturally abandoned as being alien to the relation that has now to be represented.... the subject of the circumstantial clause is *placed first*" (emphasis his).[95] Thus, we really have a pretty firm rule, an almost open and shut case.*

Contrary to my own view in this instance, Edward J. Young,[96] in his excellent little book on *Genesis One*. has expressed the opinion that this is an inverted word order because the author really did intend to lay emphasis on the subject "the earth". He believes, in fact, that this is a description of the earth as it came from the hand of the Creator, and that the writer wished to convey to the reader the idea that it was merely a condition pending further creative

---

* *I have been able to find only one possible exception: Gen. 12.1 and 4: "Now the Lord had said unto Abram, Get thee out.... So Abram departed, as the Lord had spoken unto him". In neither instance is the word order inverted. The Revised Standard Version seems, therefore, to have been guided correctly in their rendering of verse 1 as "Now the Lord said to Abram....", but not in verse 4 which they render as the Authorized Version does. Neither Version has observed the rule in verse 4.*

activity and on this account emphasis was used to draw the reader's particular attention to what was to follow. As he puts it, "Verse 2 states the condition of the earth as it was when created and until God began to form from it the present world". Young proposes that the idea of emphasis has been picked up by the Septuagint which has ἡ δε γῆ , ie., "But the earth...." However, of this word δε, Thayer remarks that it is a "participle adversative, distinctive, disjunctive".[97] In a later paragraph he says, "It serves to make a transition to something new, ... the new addition is distinguished from and, as it were, opposed to what goes before". This is how the Septuagint seems to have understood the *waw* of verse 2 which is, unfortunately, in virtually all English Versions rendered improperly as a con-junctive.

If the heavens and the earth were created a Cosmos, and if the earth subsequently became a Chaos, we have just such a situation as demands the construction that appears in the Hebrew of verse 2. But Professor Young feels that God did not begin creation with a Cosmos but with a Chaos ("Chaos", that is, in the classical Greek sense of an "unformed" thing), a view which to my mind contradicts the basic meaning of the Hebrew word בָּרָא (create) in verse 1.

It is possible, of course, to read the pluperfect of the verb "to be" as *had been*. Thus Gen. 1.2 might have been rendered "But the earth had been a desolation.... etc.". However, I think the implications of such a rendering would be of questionable validity. In his book *The Semantics of Biblical Language*, Professor Barr of the University of Edinburgh has stated that the verb הָיְתָה is used in Gen. 1.2 because the intention of the writer is that "the earth was waste and is no longer so".[98] Certainly this could be *a* truth; but one wonders whether it is *the* truth the author had in mind when he penned Gen. 1.2. And I think, personally, that it is equally doubtful whether he meant that "the earth *had been* waste - but was no longer so". Altogether, the least strain is placed upon the original by rendering the verb הָיְתָה simply as "had become", a rendering which accords well with the position it occupies in the sentence and with general usage of the verb elsewhere.

We have mentioned that Driver makes reference to Dr. Pusey in connection with this question. Pusey,[99] in his *Lectures on Daniel*, wrote in several places on the subject. In his Introduction, for example, he says, "The insertion of the verb הָיְתָה has no force at all *unless* it be used to express what was the condition of the earth in the past, *previous to the rest of the narrative, but in no connection at all with what preceded"*. I have already quoted a passage very much like this one, but Pusey's reiteration of the principle involved serves here as an introduction to his much fuller treatment of the circumstances surrounding the use of the pluperfect in Hebrew which occurs somewhat later in his work on Daniel. Thus he says subsequently:[100]

> "There are cases in which words arranged as they are here* (the subject being placed before the verb הָיְתָה and joined with the preceding 'and') form a parenthesis. But then the context makes this quite clear."

He then says: "The idiom chiefly adopted in narrative to detach what follows from what precedes, is that which is here employed, viz: the placing of the subject first and then the past verb".[101]

Then he lists the following references as illustrations: Gen. 3. 1 which introduces what follows but is unconnected with the preceding; Gen. 36. 12; Jud. 11. 1; I Sam. 3. 1; II Ki. 3. 4; II Ki. 5. 1; II Ki. 7,3; Num. 32. 1; Jud. 20. 38; Gen. 41. 56; Ezek. 33. 21; and I Ki. 14. 30. Since these references (with one exception) do not duplicate the series given in illustration of the same point by Driver, it will be worth looking at each one briefly.

Gen. 3. 1: "Now the serpent had become more subtle...."
Gen. 36. 12: "Meanwhile Timna had become concubine to Eliphaz".
Jud. 11. 1: "Meanwhile Jepthah had become a mighty man...."
I Sam. 3. 1: "Now the word of the Lord had become precious in those days...."
II Ki. 3. 4" "Now Mesha, King of Moab, had become a sheep master...."
II Ki. 5. 1: "Now Naaman had become a great man".
II Ki. 7. 3: "Now four lepers had come to be there".
Num. 32. 1: "Now great wealth had come to the children of Reuben".
Jud. 20. 38: "And an appointed sign had been (arranged) by the men of Israel" (a construction very similar to that of Gen. 1. 2).
Gen. 41. 56: "Now the famine had come to be over the face of the whole earth" (repeating a fact, antecedent to the command of Pharaoh).

---

* *He is referring to Gen. 1.2.*

Ezek.33.21: "And it came to pass in the twelfth year of our captivity, in the tenth month, in the fifth day of the month, that one who had escaped out of Jerusalem came to me saying, The City is smitten! Now the hand of the Lord had been upon me in the evening before that he that escaped had come, and had opened my mouth. . . ."

I Ki.14.30: "Now there had been a war between Rehoboam and Jeroboam. . . ." (a construction very similar to that of Gen.1.2).

In all these instances, as with those in Driver's list, the word order bears out the essential point being made - namely, that the verb should be translated as a pluperfect, lending strong support to the view that the best sense of the original Hebrew of Gen.1.2 is that which results from rendering הָיְתָה as "had become" rather than "was".

Thus, in summary, we have three situations involving the verb "to be" in English which are handled by Hebrew in different ways. The verb may be omitted: the verb may be included and placed at the head of the sentence - which is usual: and the verb may be included and placed *after* its subject.

In the first instance, the sense is purely copulative. In the second, the meaning is "to come to pass", "to happen", "to become" and "to be" in the sense of existing or living. In the third, the tense is pluperfect: "had been" or "had happened" or "had become".

The instances illustrating the first or simple copulative use are legion, every page of the English Bible revealing many straightforward examples, such as "Darkness (was) upon the face of the deep" or "And God saw that it (was) good" - in each of which the verb is omitted.

By way of illustrating the second, we may cite: "Cain became a tiller of the soil", "Eve became the mother of all living", "Lot's wife became a pillar of salt", "And it became light", "And it became a custom in Israel", etc., etc.

Of the third usage, we may cite such passages as: "Now the serpent had become more subtle"; "Now Nineveh had become a great city"; "Now Nimrod had become a mighty hunter"; and, in my view of course, "Now the earth had become a ruin and a desolation".

---

* *In Appendix XV will be found further illustrations from the Old Testament which show that the use of an inverted word order to express the pluperfect is by no means a rare circumstance but occurs quite frequently.*

Chapter 4.

THE WITNESS OF OTHER VERSIONS.

The number of English translations of the New Testament increases year by year. We have Moffat's, Weymouth's, Williams', Phillips', and many others. The number of translations of the Old Testament is probably almost as great,and if we include the more ancient versions, they may even exceed those of the New Testament. Moreover, the Bible in whole or in part has been translated into many hundreds of other languages, and the Jewish people themselves have produced quite a few versions in their own vernacular. It is these versions as well as those in various languages other than English - Aramaic, Greek, Latin, and Hebrew (New Testament) - with which this chapter is chiefly concerned.

The best known among the earliest of such other-than-English versions is that commonly referred to as the Septuagint. This Greek translation of the Old Testament was made, supposedly, by some seventy Jewish scholars in the third century B.C. The origin of the word "Septuagint" is to be found in the Epistle of Aristeas who recorded that King Ptolemy Philadelphas (285 - 246 B.C.) at the instigation of Demetrius of Phaleron, had determined to have a Greek rendering of the Holy Scriptures for his library at Alexandria. He accordingly asked the High Priest Eleajar at Jerusalem to send a commission of the most erudite Jewish scholars for the undertaking. With alacrity, Eleajar dispatched 72 elders (six from each tribe) to make this version.

It is considered unlikely that the whole of the Old Testament was translated into Greek at one "sitting", but it is believed that at least the Pentateuch was completed during Ptolemy Philadelphas' time and that the remainder was completed later in Alexandria, probably within 150 years.

Three subsequent Greek versions appeared. One, a literal translation of the Hebrew by Aquila is dated around 128 A.D. A second, by Theodotian is dated about 180 A.D., and a third of unknown date was produced by Symmachus. These three were put into parallel form by Origen along with the original Septuagint and accompanied by a transliteration of the Hebrew text into Greek characters, to form his great critical work, *The Hexapla*, only small fragments of which now remain.

It is with the original Septuagint that we are chiefly concerned here and primarily with its rendering of Genesis Chapter 1. There are numerous copies of this available and these do not differ significantly with respect to the information they supply relevant to the present issue. Remembering that this text originated in Egypt in an atmosphere of broad educational interests where the best of the tradition and folklore and philosophy of the ancient world was being recorded and preserved and where a certain cosmology had already crystallized in a form which saw the first stage of creation as a Chaos rather than a Cosmos, what the Jewish scholars have and have not seen fit to recognize of the precise structure of the Hebrew original will be better understood. It is to be assumed that the translators themselves were scholars in the Hebrew of the Old Testament: but they were also concerned to produce a rendering which would impress their Greek readers with the "soundness" of the Mosaic Cosmology, by which would be meant its essential concordance with the views of the day though entirely free of any polytheistic element, as well as the antiquity of their own history as a people to match that claimed by the Egyptians for themselves.[102,103] These two facts are important: first, because the version makes one odd exception in this first chapter in the handling of the Hebrew verb הָיָה which is otherwise not easily accounted for, an exception which allowed them to present a cosmology that, like other pagan cosmologies, appeared to make creation begin with a Chaos much as the Egyptian and Greek cosmogonies did. Secondly, as is well known, the Septuagint extends the Hebrew chronology considerably, presumably in an attempt to give a comparable antiquity to their own history, like that of the Egyptians.

Here, then, is a picture as it relates to their translation of this verb.

Throughout the whole of Chapter 1, the Hebrew verb הָיָה occurs 27 times. In verse 2 once, in verse 2 twice, in verse 5 twice, in verse 6 twice, in verse 7 once, in verse 8 twice, in verse 9 once, in verse 11 once, in verse 13 twice, in verse 14 twice, in verse 15 twice, in verse 19 twice, in verse 23 twice, in verse 24 once, in verse 29 once, in verse 30 once, and in verse 31 twice. In 22 of these instances the Septuagint has employed some form of the Greek verb γιγνεσθαι ie., "become". Of the remaining 5 occurrences of הָיָה, they have used some part of the Greek verb εἶναι. In four of these 5 cases the verb הָיָה appears as an imperative directed towards the future. Thus in verse 6 where the Hebrew has, "And let it be a divider between, etc....", the Greek has used the future of εἶναι, ie., ἔστω, "it shall be...." This seems quite proper. The sense in all four instances is "to serve as" or "to serve for", and not simply "to become" and although the meaning is similar, it is not precisely the same. We have here not a change in *fact*, only in *function*, a circumstance which is recognized by Lexicographers.[104] In verse 14 the Hebrew has וְהָיוּ לְאֹתֹת (which even by the most adverse of critics of the present thesis would be allowed to mean "become" since the verb הָיָה is followed by the Hebrew *lamedh)*, the Septuagint has ἔστωσαν which falls into the same class of verbal forms as verse 6. The same is precisely true of verse 15 where, as in verse 14, the הָיָה is accompanied by a *lamedh* and should certainly have been rendered "Let them become as lights....", the Septuagint again uses the form of command - ἔστωσαν. In verse 29 there is either a straightforward future sense or a form of command (once again the הָיָה being followed by *lamedh)* and so the Greek employs a simple future of the verb "to be", meaning either "let it be...." or "it shall be...."

Now this, then, accounts for all the occurrences of the verb הָיָה save one, and this exception occurs in verse 2. Here, for reasons which are worth considering, they made an exception. But just to show how really exceptional this case is, it may be well to note in summary that, excluding these occurrences of the Hebrew verb הָיָה which are strictly future or in the imperative mood, ie., verses 6, 14, 15, and 29 (all of which have been rendered in the Authorized Version as "Let it be for", "Let them be for", "It shall be for...."), *the Septuagint scholars uniformly rendered* הָיָה *by the Greek verb* γιγνεσθαι *so showing that they viewed it in this context as meaning "become" and not as a simple copula.* Thus there is only one case out of 23 occurrences of the verb הָיָה in which they have made an exception and treated it as a copula, translating it in verse 2 as ἦν, thereby presenting the reader with the opening words of Gen. 1. 2 as Ἡ δὲ γῆ ἦν: ie., "But the earth was...." a circumstance strongly influencing Jerome as he produced the Latin Vulgate which in turn served as a basic guide in many cases to all the other Western versions from the Authorized to the present day. As a consequence, the Universe appears to have begun as a Chaos.

Now the word *Chaos* had a rather special meaning in Greek thought. It did not necessarily signify what we mean by a situation which has become so badly disrupted that it is a ruin. The Greek concept tended rather to mean only the infinity of space: not an engineered dis-order but an early stage of development before order had been imposed on the Universe. The opposite to Chaos is Cosmos. The first stage in the development of the Cosmos was therefore being presented as a stage of total emptiness - and this total emptiness was termed Chaos. In Appendix II it will be seen that Ovid defined it as, *"Rudis indigestaque moles"*, ie., "A shapeless mass unwrought and unordered". Webster defines Chaos as, "The void and formless infinite; the confused, unorganized state of primordial matter before the creation of distinct or orderly forms". But this interpretation of the word was a later one, held only by Roman authors and not by the Greeks, and when the Septuagint was being written, the word Chaos almost certainly still bore its more ancient meaning, ie., the infinity of empty space. In time it came to be viewed as not so much empty space but as unorganized matter.

Thus it is not really too surprising that the Jews who formed the translation Committee of the Septuagint and who knew too well that the Version they produced was to take its place beside the literature of Greece in the great library at Alexandria, should seek, but without actually distorting the Hebrew text, to make it possible to look upon it as a reflection of the same basic cosmogony as was commonly accepted at that time. Yet they did NOT, be it noted, actually *use* the word Chaos as a translation of the Hebrew *tohu* where it might have seemed the obvious thing to do if this is how they saw the earth's condition in verse 2. I think their use of terms other than the Greek word Chaos is a significant indicator of their view of Gen. 1. 2.

That the words in Gen. 1. 2, however, have a very different meaning from the Greek Chaos or the modern "nebulus", is shown later (in

Appendix XVI) and it seems likely to me that the Jews in Alexandria were quite aware of this. So they left the meaning "open" by a transliteration which was true in part but not the whole truth and could be interpreted by the reader with some freedom to adjust the meaning to his own particular preconceptions. The earth *was* a "chaos", whether initially or as a consequence of some intervening event it is not specifically made clear in the Greek version, even though they did as shown above, use δε instead of και for the particle between verse 1 and verse 2. It may be argued that a Jewish reader would not necessarily see such a significance in the use of δε as many commentators have done since, including Jerome. Yet Onkelos evidently did, for he viewed the situation as a Chaos, not in the Greek sense but in the more modern sense, a destroyed rather than a waiting-to-be-ordered world. In conclusion, therefore, in Genesis chapter 1, wherever הָיָה is clearly indicative of a change or a becoming, the Septuagint has in all but one case (22 out of 23) used the Greek ἐγένετο. And, as Thayer has underscored,[105] it is most important to note that the verb γιγνεσθαι is not to be equated with εἰναι. The Septuagint were, it would appear, consciously departing from their normal practice in verse 2.

Now according to my count the Septuagint rendered הָיָה by ἐγένετο some 146 times in Genesis alone: in Genesis and Exodus together, 201 times; in the Pentateuch, some 298 times; and in the whole of the Old Testament, close to 1500 times. Since the Old Testament uses the verb הָיָה approximately 3570 times, it appears that in nearly half its occurrences the Septuagint considered the correct sense to be "become". A very large number of the cases where הָיָה occurs refer to the future as a changed circumstance where, as we have seen, it is *necessary* to introduce it since it is no longer merely copulative: quite properly this demanded in Greek the simple future of the verb "to be". On a fair number of occasions the Septuagint has taken the Hebrew original and paraphrased it, rendering the verb "to be" followed by some other verbal form as a single verb which comprehends the composite of the Hebrew original. I do not know exactly how often these two situations (future tenses and paraphrastic renderings) occur, but it must account probably for a fair percentage of the balance of appearances of the Hebrew verb הָיָה. When we add those instances in which the Hebrew verb appears as an imperative, and those in which it has the meaning of "existing" (ie., living), we shall not be far wrong if we conclude that in the great majority of cases the Septuagint did not look upon the meaning of the Hebrew verb as mere "being" in the copulative sense but as "becoming" or "coming to be".

In summary, I think it is safe to say that הָיָה is seldom considered by the Septuagint as meaning "is" or "was", and that their rendering of it in Gen. 1.2 as ἦν was probably in order to avoid conflict with the accepted cosmogony held in Alexandria and by the Greeks generally. For such a conflict would have appeared had they translated Gen. 1.2 as "But the earth had *become* unorganized....", since this clearly implies that it had not been so in the beginning.

We have already made reference to the Targum of Onkelos, but in order to make this Chapter more or less complete in itself, a brief review of what this Targum represents may be in order.

The word *Targum*, (from *Ragamu*. "to speak", in certain Semitic languages) is a term for the Aramaic versions or paraphrases of the Old Testament which became necessary when, after or perhaps during the Babylonian exile, Hebrew began to die out as the common language of the people and was supplanted by Aramaic. The first evidence of a Targum as an already existing body of accepted Aramaic paraphrase has been found by some authorities in Neh. 8. 8. According to tradition, Ezra and his coadjutors were the original founders". There grew up a certain accepted rendering into Aramaic of parts of the Old Testament which assumed something of the status that the Authorized Version did in the seventeenth century in England. The Mishnah or official Commentary of the Jews on the Old Testament soon contained a number of injunctions respecting the "Targum", but for many centuries it was preserved orally and not written down.

All that is now extant of these traditional "renderings" are three distinct "Targums" on the Pentateuch, a Targum on the Prophets, Targums on the Hagiographa (Psalms, Job, Proverbs), and the five Magilloth (Song of Solomon, Ruth, Lamentations, Esther, and Ecclesiastes), another Targum on Esther, one on Chronicles, one on Daniel, and one on the Apocrypha.

The most important of the three Pentateuch Targums is named after Onkelos, probably a corruption of Aquila, a proselyte and one of Gamaliel's pupils. Aquila's Greek version became so popular that the Aramaic version current at the time was credited to him. It appears that this Targum originated among the scholars of Rabbi Akiba between 150 - 200 A.D. in Palestine. It was later sent to Babylonia where it was modified and edited and vowelled in the Babylonian manner about 300 A.D. Hence arose the Babylonian Targum.

The *oral* tradition behind it may therefore be traced to about 150 A.D., but it could in fact be considerably earlier. Hence at or about this time we have an Aramaic version of Gen. 1.2 which reads

וְאַרְעָא הֲוָת צַדְיָא meaning as we have already noted, "And (or but) the earth was destroyed", where the Aramaic verb has the meaning "to cut", "to lay waste", or "to destroy", a rendering reflected in the traditional Midrash interpretation quoted from Ginsberg (see page 14 above).

The next version to be examined is the Vulgate. Jerome, or more accurately, Sophronius Eusebius Hieronymous, its author, was born in the city of Stridon on the borders of Dalmatia and Pannonia, some time between 331 and 340 A.D. At about the age of 20, he was sent to a Roman school where he studied the classical authors under Aclius Donatus. He later attended the University at Trier and Aquileia, where he studied theology. After a tour of the East which ended in 373 and after a severe illness, he adopted the ascetic life and spent four years in the desert near Antioch where he studied Hebrew. He was ordained in 379 and three years later visited Rome on official ecclesastical business from Antioch. In Rome he began his work on the translation of the Hebrew and Greek Scriptures into Latin. This great work was completed before he died in 420 A.D. and since that time remained in use throughout the Roman Church.

Of chief concern here is his rendering of the verb הָיָה, especially in the first chapter of Genesis. In his translation he consistently has *factum* (or *facta*) *est* (ie., "became") wherever the Septuagint has ἐγένετο, and in verse 2 he has "*Terra autem erat....*", ie., "The earth, however, *was*....", thus faithfully reflecting the Greek version. Whether he really *was* governed in this by what he found in the Septuagint or was independently convinced that he was correctly translating in each instance, we shall, of course, never know. But this much at least can be said: once he had passed beyond verse 2, he had no hesitation thereafter in equating the meaning of the Hebrew verb הָיָה with the Latin for "became", and he adopted this rendering in 13 occurrences in the first chapter of Genesis alone. His departure from this general principle in verse 2 thus seems odd and looks suspiciously like a Septuagint influence.

Now, if we allow that the term "Version" really means nothing more than "Translation into a different language", we have another non-English "Version" that may be allowed to bear its independent witness - and this is the New Testament *wherever it quotes the Old Testament.* For here the Hebrew original is translated by inspiration (I believe) into Greek.

According to the Oxford Cyclopedic Concordance, there are 277 quotations from the Old Testament in the New, which are more or less exact. There are, of course, many inexact quotations or allusions and many incidents referred to, but these are not sufficiently exact as to wording to allow the drawing of any conclusions about equivalent verbal meanings within the two languages.

Of these 277 quotations, only 29 are of such a form that the verb "to be" is an essential part of the English rendering in the Authorized Version. In one case (No. 5 in the list below) the situation is confused by the fact that the New Testament uses a different sentence structure.

Of the 28 quotations remaining, the Old Testament in 20 cases omits the verb הָיָה entirely, its use being not required since the meaning is copulative. This leaves us with only 9 clearcut examples upon which to attempt the formulation of some kind of guiding principle. The number is far too small to allow of any certainty - yet there seems to be some measure of consistency.

To begin with, here are the 29 quotations.

(1) Matt.23.39 (Mk.11.9): "Blessed *is* He...."
Psa.118.26: identical - *is* is *omitted* in Hebrew.

(2) Mk.10.8: "They shall be into one flesh" (ἔσονται εἰς).
So also LXX.
Gen.2.24:"They shall become....", הָיָה with לְ.

(3) Mk.12.29: "The Lord our God is one Lord...." (ἐστιν).
So also the LXX
Deut.6.4: In Hebrew, *is* is *omitted*.

(4) Lu.4.18: "The Spirit of the Lord *is* upon Me...."
Isa.61.1: In Hebrew, *is* is *omitted*.

(5) Lu.19.46: "My house is the house of prayer...." (ἔσται , "shall be").
Isa.56.7: "My house shall be called...." (different verb used).

(6) Lu.20.17 (Matt.21.42): "The same has become the Head of the corner",ie, οὗτος ἐγενήθη εἰς κεφαλην γωνιας, so also the LXX.
Psa.118.22,23: "Has become, as it were, the head....", הָיְתָה לְרֹאשׁ:

(7) Jn.10.34: "I said ye are gods...." (ἐστε), so also LXX.
Psa.82.6: "I said, gods (*are*) ye....", *no verb* in Hebrew.

(8) Acts 13.33: "Thou art My Son" (εἶ).
Psa.2.7: "Thou, My Son", *no verb* in Hebrew.

(9) Rom.3.10: "There is none that...." (ἐστιν occurs throughout).
Psa.14.1,3: "There, no God.....", Hebrew *omits verb* throughout.

(10) Acts 1.20: "And let his... become.... (γενήθητω); neither shall there be.... (και μη ἐστω).

Psa. 69.25: "Let it *become* that their habitation be a desolated one.... and no one shall become a dweller in their tents...." תְּהִי טִירָתָם נְשַׁמָּה...
בְּאָהֳלֵיהֶם אַל יְהִי יֹשֵׁב.....

(11) Acts 7.32, 33: I *am* the God of your fathers...., ...*is* holy ground...."

Exod. 3.6: verb *omitted* in both clauses.

(12) Acts 7.49, 50: "Heaven *is* my throne...."

Isa. 66.1: verb *omitted* throughout.

(13) Rom. 3.13-16: Verb *is* is omitted throughout.

Psa. 5.9 and 36.1: verb *omitted* throughout.

(14) Rom. 4.7, 8: "Blessed *are* they whose sins are forgiven... covered".

Psa. 32.1, 2: verb omitted in *both* cases.

(15) Rom. 4.18: "So shall thy seed be...."

οὗτως ἔσται το σπερμασον ....

Gen. 15.5: "So shall thy seed become...."

כֹּה יִהְיֶה זַרְעֶךָ....

(16) Rom. 11.9, 10: "Let their table be as a snare.... (γενήθητω εἶς ....)

Psa. 69.22: ".... become before them as a snare...."

יְהִי שֻׁלְחָנָם לִפְנֵיהֶם לְפָח....

(17) I Cor. 6.16: "They shall be (ἐσονται) ..... (εἶs) into (σαρκαμίαν.....)

Gen. 2.24: ...וְהָיוּ לְ "They shall become as it were...."

(18) I Cor. 10.26: "The earth *is* the Lord's...."

Psa. 24.1: Hebrew verb *omitted*.

(19) I Cor. 15.54: "Death *is* swallowed up... where *is* thy victory?"

Isa. 25.8: Verb *omitted* in Hebrew. The quotation reads slightly differently in Hos. 13.14: I will become thy (אֱהִי).... plague, oh death.... I will become (אֱהִי) thy destruction, O grave". This is not an *exact* quote from the Old Testament to the New Testament: where the Greek has ποῦ σου θανατε, τὸ νίκοs.... "Where, oh death, is your victory?"

(20) Gal. 3.13: "Cursed *is* every one that hangeth...."

Deut. 21.23: Verb *omitted* in Hebrew.

(21) Heb. 1.5: "Son of Mine, art Thou..." (υἱόs μου εἶ συ....)

Psa. 2.7: Verb *omitted* in Hebrew ("My Son, Thou....").

(22) II Tim. 2.19: "Those being of Him...." (τοὺς ὄντας αὐτοῦ).
Num. 16.5: Hebrew *omits* verb.

(23) Heb. 1.5: "I will be to him as a Father...."
ἐγω ἔσομαι αὐτῶ εἰς πατερα...
II Sam. 7.14: "I will become to him as a Father...."
אֲנִי אֶהְיֶה־לוֹ לְאָב....

(24) Heb. 1.8: "Thy throne *is* forever...."
Psa. 45.6: Hebrew *omits* the verb.

(25) Heb. 2.6: "What is man that..." (τί εστιν ἄνθρωπος ὅτι..)
Psa. 8.4: verb *omitted*.

(26) Heb. 5.6: "You, a priest..." (συ ιερευς εἰς τόν αἰωνα..)
Psa. 110.4: Hebrew *omits* verb.

(27) Heb. 9.20: "This *is* the blood of the Covenant...."
Exod. 24.8: Hebrew *omits* the verb.

(28) I Pet. 1.16: "Be ye holy...." (ἅγιοι ἐσεσθε - imperative)
Lev. 11.44: "Become ye holy (imperative) for I *am* holy..."
יִהְיִיתֶם קְדֹשִׁים כִּי קָדוֹשׁ אָנִי....
This is an important illustrustration of the principle. The people were to *become* what God *is*. Thus the verb הָיָה is proper in the first but not in the second case.

(29) I Pet. 1.24: "All flesh *is* grass".
Isa. 40.6: Hebrew *omits* the verb.

Of these examples as already observed, nine only [ie., Nos. (2) (6), (10), (15), (16), (17), (19), (23), and (28)] involve the verb הָיָה in the Hebrew of the text of the Old Testament. From this small body of information the following "rules"* seem to appear:

RULE NO. 1. From the five references numbered as (2), (6), (16), (17), and (23) it appears that where in the Hebrew the verb הָיָה is employed followed by לְ, the New Testament writers were led to use either the simple future of the verb "to be" [in (2) ἔσονται, and in (23) ἔσομαι] or the verb "became" [in (6) and (16) - ἐγενηθεν, γενηθητω] followed by the preposition εἰς ("into"). It would seem that the best English *literal* rendering for both the Hebrew and the Greek, where εις appears in the latter and לְ in the former,

---

* *It is virtually certain that these rules will prove to be totally inadequate but at least they make a starting point, and nothing more is claimed for them than just that.*

would be "as it were" or "in effect". Thus:

(2) and (17): "They shall become, as it were, one flesh".
(6): "He shall become, as it were, the head of the corner".
(16): "Their table, let it become, as it were, a snare".
(17): "They shall become, as it were, one body".
(23): "I will become to Him, as it were, a Father".

In each instance the thought expressed is that the end result shall be analogously such-and-such. Thus in (2) and (17) the man and wife do not literally become one body but only analogously. It cannot have reference to the fact that children are to be born who will bodily sum up the parents because many couples are childless and yet are so united as to fulfil the real conditions of "oneness" which is to be the hallmark of a true marriage. In (6) a man shall become in effect a stone, the stone which is the key to the stability and completeness of the rest of the building; meaning surely that the Lord will *analogously* be a corner stone - not in actual fact: and in (16) a table is to become a snare, but only in a manner of speaking. And in (23): "I will become, *as it were*, Father to Him" is a very significant statement for it implies that there is a *special* meaning to this Father-Son relationship, and that this relationship cannot be precisely spelled out in reference to the merely human situation. No human son exists until he is begotten of his father, whereas the Lord's relationship to His Father was something far more than this.

Thus, in each of these cases, there would seem to be an important reason for using the verb הָיָה followed by לְ. In each case, moreover, there is a *change* involved. In many instances in the Old Testament there is a change of state, and in many there is a change of status. Stars are to become time-setters, a woman is to become a man's wife (cf. Gen. 20. 12), a river is to become blood. . . . , and so on. The rule here, then, seems to be that לְ is required when the change is more analogous than real. The stars remained stars, the woman a woman, the river a river: each achieved a new significance.

RULE NO. 2. In three cases, (10), (15), and (19), the Old Testament uses הָיָה without the לְ and one must therefore assume that analogy is not in view, but a real "conversion" into something different. Thus:

in (10), a habitation will literally become a desolation.
in (15), Abram's seed (singular) literally becomes a great host (plural).
in (19), God the Creator will become a Destroyer, of Death.

These passages lend weight to the contention that while הָיָה consistently implies a change of state (or status), the addition of לְ adds a distinct nuance to the sense in which the "becoming" takes place. That is, it takes place only in an analogous sense, whereas without the following לְ the verb may still be properly rendered "become" but it is "becoming" in a more literal sense, a transformation of one thing into another, not "as it were" but absolutely.

We have now accounted for 8 out of the 9 occurrences marked off for consideration. The ninth case (28) is readily disposed of, the clear intent of the text being to indicate a command and the verb in both the Hebrew and the Greek being required to make the Imperative clear.

Thus it seems reasonably certain that whenever the simple copulative use of the verb "to be" is involved, the Hebrew omits הָיָה, though the Greek does not always follow the same rule. However, the Greek *does* show that if הָיָה appears in the Old Testament in any of the passages quoted in the New Testament, some specific method must be adopted to convey a precise meaning which is always more than the mere copula. We may observe that either a future is involved, or a command, or the sense of "becoming", which thus demands the use of the verb γιγνομαι. These conclusions are borne out even in those indirect quotations so far examined. Thus in Rom. 9.29 for example: "(Except the Lord of Sabaoth had left us a seed) we also had become (ἐγενηθημεν και ὡς, etc.) as Sodom...." The original, Isa. 1.9, has: הָיִינוּ לַעֲמֹרָה דָּמִינוּ ie., "We would have become as Gomorrah (as to) our likeness".

In summary, then, on the basis of this admittedly meagre sample, it appears that wherever in the Old Testament no *change* of state or status is intended or implied or commanded or predicted, the verb הָיָה *is entirely absent*. But whenever a change *is* intended or implied or commanded or predicted, the verb is expressed by some form of הָיָה - either with or without *lamedh* following, depending upon whether the transformation is viewed as analogous or real. The New Testament in rendering the Old Testament quotations into Greek seems to have followed this rule. It is also clear that in the 20 cases where the verb הָיָה is omitted, the meaning is purely copulative, a fact borne out by the New Testament Greek which either follows suite and omits any verb or uses the simple present tense of the verb "to be", ie. always εἰναι but never γιγνομαι. When the present tense is not used but some other tense or mood is called for, the future involving a real change from the present, as for example in (2), (15), (17), and (23), or the imperative as in (28), the

Hebrew requires the appropriate form of the verb היה to be expressed. It is, in short, a rule according to the testimony of these 29 quotations that Hebrew does *not* employ the verb הָיָה copulatively: and that whenever it does employ it, it is to convey the future, a command, or the sense of "becoming".

Finally, we may turn to one further form of evidence, namely, the translations which have been made of the New Testament into Hebrew. Of those made by Ginsberg and Delitzsch, Heward observed:

> "It is important to see that the *Kal* or simple conjugation of the verb הָיָה does have the force of 'become'. In the standard Hebrew translations of the New Testament the *Kal* is employed by the Greek γιγνομαι (to become) in more than half the occurrences in Ephesians and Colossians - and no other conjugation."

Such modern versions of the New Testament do not, of course, carry the weight of inspiration, so that the usage in each particular instance has been determined purely by human judgment. Yet it is important to see that here, too, הָיָה has in the majority of cases been taken as a proper verb for the sense of "becoming". To attach this meaning to it most assuredly does not impose a strain upon it. It is its *most* common, not its *least* common, sense. I do not have a Ginsberg or a Delitzsch rendering into Hebrew of the New Testament. The version in my possession was published by the Trinitarian Bible Society (London) with no specific authorship ascribed to it. However, it is most probably based on Ginsberg. Almost all English versions stem ultimately from the Authorized Version which formed their starting point, although the "Modern English" versions owe perhaps least in this regard - and a paraphrase such as Phillips' or The Amplified Version owe even less, of course.

But assuming that the New Testament I have is the work of Hebrew scholars, we may examine it with benefit in order to see to what extent the Greek "became" is rendered back into Hebrew by use of the verb הָיָה. For this purpose, I began with the Student's Concordance to the Revised Version (not the Revised *Standard* Version, note) and from it was led to the following passages, in all of which the Hebrew translation has הָיָה where both the Greek and the English have "become".

Matt. 18.3: "Except ye be converted and *become* as little children....." Of which the Greek is "....καὶ γένησθε ὡς τὰ παιδία...."which is rendered into Hebrew "to *become* as (little) children", ie., לִהְיוֹת כִּילָדִים.

John 1.12: "To them gave He power to *become* the sons of God.....", ".... ἐξουσιαν τέκνα θεου γενέσθαι.....", which in Hebrew is rendered: לִהְיוֹת בָּנִים לֵאלֹהִים , ie., "to *become* sons with respect to God".

John 9.39: ".... the seeing shall become blind, and the blind shall become seeing....", which appears in the Greek as οἱ μὴ βλέποντες βλέπωσιν καὶ οἱ βλέποντες τυφλοὶ γένωντα ", that is to say, "those not seeing, seeing, and those seeing *becoming* blind". The verb γένωντα is perhaps intended to serve both clauses though being introduced but once at the end of the sentence. The Hebrew translation is: הָעִוְרִים יִהְיוּ רֹאִים וְהָרֹאִים יִהְיוּ עִוְרִים , ie., "the blind shall *become* see-ers and the see-ers shall *become* blind". It is quite true that if the present thesis is incorrect, this could just as well have been rendered, "the blind shall *be* see-ers and the see-ers *be* blind", but we have the New Testament as a guide here - indicating that what is intended is "shall *become*", not merely "shall be". And it is therefore to be noted that Hebrew simply has no other way of expressing the sense of "becoming" - nor is it required that the verb הָיָה be followed by לְ in order to convey this meaning, as is so often argued. On the other hand, when a change of *status* IS involved, הָיָה is followed by לְ: as in Acts 1.22 when a believer becomes also an apostle. "One must be ordained to *become* a witness....", is in the Greek, μάρτυρα της αυ ἀναστασεως αὑτου σὺν ἡμῖν γενέσθαι literally, "a witness of the resurrection of Him with us to *become*"). In the Hebrew this has been rendered thus: לָקַח מִמֶּנּוּ אֲשֶׁר אֶחָד מֵהֶם יִהְיֶה עִמָּנוּ לְעֵד...... ie., "He was taken from among us, one who shall *become* with us a witness...." Thus was Matthias ordained and numbered among the twelve.

In the sense of "happening to" someone, the verb הָיָה is used in the Hebrew New Testament in Acts 7.40, "We know not what has become of him....", ie., לֹא יָדַעְנוּ מַה־הָיָה לוֹ , ie., "We do not know what has happened to him".

In Acts 7.52 there is an interesting illustration of the difference between the merely copulative use of the verb "to be" and that use which signifies a changed status. The English reads: "Of whom ye have been now the betrayers and murderers". The Hebrew translation omits the verb before the word "betrayers" but inserts it before "murderers": אֲשֶׁר אַתֶּם הִסְגַּרְתֶּם וַתִּהְיוּ לוֹ לִמְרַצְּחִים ie., "Whom you (are) the betrayers and have become, with respect to Him, as murderers". It may be that the verb is intended to serve for both clauses.... but it may also be that a mere betrayer remains as he was vis-a-vis society, whereas a murderer certainly does not, for his status has definitely changed. At any rate, the associated *lamedh* (לְ) appears *only* before the word "murderers" as though to signify the special sense in which they had become murderers - not by themselves laying hands on Him but by having others perform the deed with their authorization.

In Acts 12.18 we have an excellent example of the pluperfect use, in which the subject precedes the verb. The English reads: "As soon as it was day, then a great stir was there among the soldiers to see what was become of Peter". In Hebrew this passage becomes: הַבֹּקֶר אוֹר וּמְהוּמָה רַבָּה הָיְתָה בֵּין אַנְשֵׁי הַצָּבָא לֵאמֹר מֶה־הָיָה לְפֶטְרוֹס: which, rendered literally, would be: "(Came) the morning light and a great stir *had there come about* among the men of war saying, What has *become* of (ie., happened to) Peter?". The dramatic effect of this sentence is evident enough. Certainly the sense here is "to happen" or "come about", and by paying attention to the word order one observes the use of the pluperfect which adds to the vividness of the whole situation.

In Rom. 2.25 the verb הָיָה appears in the *niphal* or passive voice and has the meaning of "be made into" or "turned into", followed by לְ and the sense is thus: "thy circumcision is made into no circumcision at all", ie., "thy circumcision is converted into un-circumcision in reality". This is a meaning found in the Old Testament also, as in Exod. 38.24, for example.

In I Cor. 9.22 and 23 the Greek has ἐγενόμην τοῖς ἀσθενέσιν ἀσθενής, ...τοῖς πᾶσιν γεγονα πάντα... ἵνα συγκοινωνὸς αὐτοῦ γενωμαι..... : ie., "to the weak I *became* weak.... to all I *became* all things.... in order that I might *became* a partaker of it". In Hebrew, γιγνομαι is here consistently replaced by הָיָה: the verbal forms appearing as הָיִיתִי twice, and יִהְיֶה once.

In I Cor. 13.11, "when I *became* a man", ie., ὅτι γεγονα ἀνήρ, in Hebrew appears as וְכַאֲשֶׁר הָיִיתִי לְאִישׁ, ie., "and when I *became* as a man" and thus achieved the status of manhood, הָיָה again being followed by לְ signifying this change of status.

In II Cor. 5.21, speaking of "achieving" the righteousness of God in Christ Jesus, the Hebrew is לְמַעַן נִהְיֶה אֲנַחְנוּ בוֹ לְצִדְקַת אֱלֹהִים, meaning "In order that we might *become* in Him as the righteousness of God". The *lamedh* signifies a change of status once again. The Hebrew נִהְיֶה is for the Greek γενωμεθα.

In Gal. 3.13: "(Christ) hath redeemed us from the curse of the law) *becoming* on our behalf a curse...." appears in the Greek as γενόμενος ὑπερ ἡμῶν κατάρα. In the Hebrew translation this is written as בַּאֲשֶׁר הָיָה לְקְלָלָה תַּחְתֵּינוּ, ie., "in which he *became* on our behalf a cursed thing". *Lamedh* follows הָיָה since this was indeed a change of status for the Holy One of God.

In Rev.11.15 appear the words, ".... saying, The kingdoms of this world have *become* (the kingdoms) of our Lord". Here the Greek reads: λέγοντες ἐγένετο ἡ βασιλεία τοῦ κόσμου τοῦ κυριου ἡμῶν, and the Hebrew has: לֵאמֹר הָיְתָה מַמְלֶכֶת הָאָרֶץ לַאֲדֹנֵינוּ or literally, "saying, The kingdoms of the earth have *become* our Lord's".

Now in the light of Thayer's conclusion that γιγνομαι is never to be confused with ειναι in Greek since its proper meaning is "becoming", not "being", it is a little surprising to discover that in the Authorized Version (as indexed by Young's Concordance) the Greek verb γιγνομαι is translated "to be" some 250 times and "to become" only 42 times. However, an examination of those instances where the sense "to be" has been given to this verb in the Authorized Version will soon reveal that the rendering "become" would be equally valid, if not to be preferred, in the great majority of cases. Indeed at the heading of this list, Young himself gives the *true* meaning of the Greek verb as "to become"! A few random cases will reveal the validity of the above observation.

Matt.5.45 (Young's first entry) is given as "That ye may be the children of your Father", which is clearly more correctly to be read as, "That ye may *become* the children of your Father....", a statement exactly in accord with Jno.1.12. In Mark 6.26, "the king was exceedingly sorry", means in point of fact that he *became* exceedingly sorry", for this is what we really mean in such a context since it was a consequence of what preceded.

Luke 2.13, "Suddenly there was with the angel...." is clearly a change, more expressively, "suddenly there *came to be* with the angel...." John 4.14, ".... shall be in him a well of water...." is clearly, ".... shall *always* be in him a well of water...." And so forth. I do not say that it must *always* be so rendered, for sometimes the sense involves an imperative, for example. But in the majority of cases it should be. In a number of instances the range of meanings of the Hebrew verb הָיָה is found here in this Greek verb γιγνομαι by much the same processes of idea-extension. It may mean "to happen", "to come about", "to live" or "exist" (as in I Cor.2.3 for example), and so forth. It has occasionally the meaning of "counting for" or "amounting to". *But* it is very, very seldom indeed that γιγνομαι is employed as a mere copulative. I think it possible that it is so employed more frequently than the Hebrew הָיָה is since the latter almost certainly *never* is, but its *normal* meaning is "to become" just as by contrast the *normal* meaning of ειναι is "to be".

This is quite clearly borne out by the lexicographers. Thus Thayer gives its meanings as:[106] (1) "to become", "to come into existence", "to begin to be", "to receive being"; (2) "to become", ie., "to come to pass", "to happen"; (3) "to arise" in the sense of "appearing in History"; (4) "to be made", "to be done", "to be finished"; and (5) "to become" or "to be made" in situations where a new rank, or character, etc., is involved. This last is analogous to the force of הָיָה where a change of status is in view, as when a woman becomes a wife.

It will be observed that Thayer does not list in his five classes of meanings the simple copulative idea - *is, was, shall be,* etc. On the other hand, he expressly states that this is the prime significance of the Greek verb ειναι ."to be". It would seem, therefore, that the scholars who translated the New Testament of the Authorized Version either were not aware of the true distinction between ειναι and γινομαι OR did not themselves distinguish between "being" and "becoming" in English. If one examines Young's list of occurrences under the word "to be" as an English translation of the verb γινομαι (the 3rd column of page 73 in my edition of that Concordance) one finds that *almost always* the verb γινομαι is rendered in the *Hebrew* version of the New Testament by הָיָה and the sense is strictly "became". There are occasional exceptions. In Matt. 9.29 an entirely different Hebrew verb is used (קום) which means "let it be established for you....", which is surely most appropriate. Another exception is in Matt. 16.2 where the translator of the Hebrew version must have considered the word *is* in this verse ("when it *is* evening") as purely copulative, for he has decided to omit the verb entirely. This could possibly be a case where γιγνομαι is used copulatively. But certainly such occasions do not seem very frequent. Indeed, even in Greek, the simple copulative verb is apt to be omitted where one might expect to find it according to English modes of expression. When it is omitted, the Hebrew version follows suite - as in Matt. 24.32 for example, "Ye know that summer *is* nigh....", or in Matt. 24.37, "But as the days of Noah *were*...." In Matt. 26.5 and 27.45 the Hebrew translator took the sense as simply copulative and omitted the verb הָיָה , though γινομαι appears in the Greek.

One must clearly bear in mind that the Hebrew version of the New Testament is *not* an inspired one. It constantly involved human judgment. And although perhaps the translator worked prayerfully at his task, we cannot expect of it the same inerrancy that we may expect to find in the original Scriptures. I think we must either assume that in such seemingly copulative uses in the New Testament Greek we have in reality something *more* than appears to the casual reader (in which case the Hebrew version is not accurately interpreting the text) or we have some cases where the normal verb "to become" is for some reason being used exceptionally. It is *possible* of course, that our Greek New Testament is itself a version, a translation of an original Aramaic, at least where the Gospels are concerned, as Lamsda would argue.[107]

From such examples* it would appear that whereas in moving from Greek to Hebrew the Greek *may* be viewed as copulative and will not be represented by any corresponding verb, in moving from Hebrew to any other language it is safe to interpret the absence of the verb הָיָה as *prima facie* evidence that the sense of the original *is* copulative. In short, in so far as arguments have validity when based on a study of an uninspired Hebrew version of the Greek New Testament, there is evidence enough that the verb הָיָה is virtually always employed in Hebrew when the meaning is something other than the simple one of "being". Thus הָיָה is not the normal word for "*being*" even in the minds of modern translators, but it is the normal word for "*becoming*" and there is, in fact, no other way in which a Hebrew writer can express the idea of *becoming* except by its use.

Thus, in considering the meaning of Gen. 1.2, we have two factors to take note of. If the verb is merely copulative, the writer could have made this quite clear by omitting it entirely. Then there would have been no doubt about it. But he did NOT omit the verb. On the contrary, there was no other way in which he could have expressed the idea of "becoming" and the presence of the verb should therefore be taken as having this significance. It is no longer sufficient to appeal to the old cliché that הָיָה means "become" only when followed by *lamedh*. The many versions in English do not support this argument at all. A quite cursory examination of the Authorized Version shows 30 or more passages in which הָיָה *without* the *lamedh* is rendered "became" or "become". Indeed, in more than one third of the occurrences of הָיָה in the original text, this is the case. A similar examination of the Revised Standard Version shows about the same number of occasions, actually about 25% of all occurrences of הָיָה

---

* *Further examples will be found in Appendix XVII.*

in the original. And the even more recent Berkeley Version reveals ten cases in Genesis alone.* Such lists do not include the numerous occasions where הָיָה is followed, not by *lamedh*, but by some other preposition, such as כְּ , etc.,# where it is still rendered as 'became' in the English versions. Nor do these lists include numerous occasions where the meaning is *clearly* "became" in spite of the fact that no English version currently available has indicated the fact: such passages, for example, as Exod. 23.29, "Lest the land *become* desolate......", or Ezek. 26.5, "It shall *become* a place for the spreading of nets...."

Thus, no special pleading is required to establish the fact that the verb in Gen. 1.2 is most unlikely to be a mere copula. Those who decline to adopt this principle of rendering הָיָה as *became* rather than *was* are surely far more in danger of attempting to "explain away" the original text than are those of us who do accept it, for we are being guided by what certainly seems from the evidence to be the rule rather than the exception.

---

* *See Appendix XVIII for lists of references to these Versions.*

\# *See Appendix X for references.*

Chapter 5.

MODERN OBJECTIONS.

One of the remarkable things about this whole controversy has been the extraordinary vehemence of those who oppose the concept of a hiatus between verse 1 and 2 and it may be taken, I think, as an index of the amount of precise knowledge generally available. In order to give added force to their words, critics sometimes gather together all the peripheral ideas which happen to have become attached to the central thesis which they oppose and present this hodgepodge of miscellaneous opinions as if it were a quite essential part of it. They then proceed to demolish this artificial construct with the ease that one might expect. But adherents of the theory frequently do not subscribe to these more venturesome reconstructs at all. In this volume we have tried as far as possible to avoid any but the basic issues.

One particularly recurrent phrase in the New Testament which is often held to give strong support to our view of the significance of Gen. 1.2 is dealt with in Appendix XIX. This is the reference to "the foundation of the world" which may possibly be better rendered "the disruption of the world". But I cannot underscore too strongly that such an argument is *not* the basis of this thesis. Interpreting this recurrent phrase in one particular way may strengthen one's conviction that this is indeed the true significance of Gen. 1.2, but it does not, in my view, constitute an unequivocal proof. Yet, in spite of this disclaimer, it seems rather likely that some critic will set out to demolish the contents of this Appendix, thereby supposing that he has once for all disposed of the argument! But in the meantime, I should like to deal briefly with the comments and conclusions of some of those who have written against the position taken in this volume.

In 1946, as already mentioned, two Papers were published in The Transactions of the Victoria Institute (London), one by a Mr. P. W. Heward and the other by Professor F. F. Bruce.[108] Heward wrote in favour of the thesis presented here and Bruce against it. To my mind, both did an excellent job, neither being unfair to the other, nor exaggerating their own claims. In the discussion afterwards, several points were raised on both sides and answered fairly and well. Naturally, I read Heward's Paper with greater sympathy than that by Bruce, but I believe it is objectively true to say that there was no exaggeration and no mis-statement in Heward's review of the evidence. Of Bruce's Paper, which was courteous and just at all times, I believe there are, nevertheless, two criticisms of a minor nature that are valid. Bruce refers to Dillman's Commentary as essentially supporting his own position. However, as we have already noted previously, Dillman apparently changed his mind regarding the correct translation of הָיְתָה in Gen. 1.2. I am sure that Professor Bruce was unaware of this or did not feel it really altered Dillman's basic position, for in spite of his later admission I do not think he wholeheartedly acceeded to the idea of a gap between verse 1 and 2.[109] This fact makes Dillman's admission as to the meaning of הָיְתָה in verse 2 all the more significant and in a very real sense nullifies the basis of Bruce's appeal to Dillman for support - at least, in so far as verse 2 is concerned.

The other point is in connection with his treatment of Jonah 3.3b, a sentence which in its structure precisely parallels Gen. 1.2. Bruce concludes that if Gen. 1.2 is to be rendered "the earth became a ruin" after God had created it otherwise, then we must say that Nineveh became a metropolis after Jonah entered it. But I do not believe this is what the author intended - and neither does Professor Bruce. However, there are (as we have shown*) numerous instances where,

---

* *See Chapter III.*

in narrating a series of events, the Hebrew writer reverts back to a prior circumstance that bears on what is to follow. Such sentences are best handled by translating the opening conjunction (*waw*) as "Now, etc. etc.". Thus Jonah 3 3b would be rendered, "Now Nineveh had become..." That is to say, the writer never intended the reader to suppose that Nineveh became great just because Jonah entered it, but rather that it had already grown into a very large city by the time he arrived there. It should be mentioned in passing that Driver admits here the propriety of "become" in this passage. This rendering would, of course, be quite acceptable for Gen. 1.2 also - although "But the earth had become...." would be perhaps more appropriate than "*Now* the earth, etc.". I do not think Bruce's argument is logical in this case, but these are not very serious criticisms and certainly they are not criticisms of the style or tone of either Paper.

It is with some surprise, therefore, that one finds a reference to these two Papers in a work by F. A. Filby entitled *Creation Revealed*,[110] where a footnote tells us that while Bruce's Paper is a scholarly piece of work and conclusively against our view, the Paper by Heward "contains a number of statements which are only partly true, interspersed with much padding and special pleading". I wonder which were the "partly true" statements? And I cannot find any evidence of "special pleading": but I suppose this depends upon one's initial bias.

In his book, Filby opens his summary review of the 'gap' theory with a general statement to the effect that it is to be attributed to "the Scottish Preacher, Dr. Chalmers", a statement which is far from the truth, as we have seen. He then sets forth the theory as he understands it and concludes that it is without foundation:[111]

> "The contention that the verb in verse 2 means 'to become' waste and void rather than it 'was' so has been examined by scholars, and the judgment of the best Hebraists is that the text is most naturally translated 'was'."

So the subject is summarily dismissed with the observation:[112]

> "The gap-theory is then unscriptural, unscientific, and unreasonable, and - rejecting it completely - we can return to the simple (*sic*) study of verse 2."

Recently, I had occasion to see a small Paper by a Christian writer, well known and of some stature, entitled, *The Length of the Creative Days*, in which the issue is again given cursory notice and equally summarily dismissed. The author, referring to it as a "theory which we reject", says:"[13]

> "Our objections to this theory are (1) that it rests upon not one single grain of evidence, and (2) that it was invented in order to harmonize geology with Scripture and not simply to interpret Scripture as it stands."

Subsequently, he adds:

> "It is true that the verb 'to be' in Hebrew is sometimes used to mean 'became' if the context demands it, but the verb as it stands is 'was' as anyone (*sic*) who has studied Hebrew will testify. There is not the slightest hint in the context that the *unusual* (my emphasis) meaning 'became' should be read. In fact, we should either find the preposition 'to' (לְ) before the descriptive adjective or noun if the word is to read 'become' (see Gen. 2. 7) or else we should find from the context that 'was' has some such meaning as 'was potentially'. Neither of these is the case."

In the light of what has been shown of the facts in this volume, it seems hardly necessary to make any comment on these observations.

Another very unfortunate effort at criticism of this view appeared in the Annual Volume of *The Creation Research Society* for 1965. Since this is a Journal which I have consistently found to be most valuable and which is always carefully documented, the article seems to me to have been even more out of character. Here the theory has very short shrift at the hands of one author who informs the reader that:"[14]

> "It is true that there are six instances in the Pentateuch where the verb is translated 'became' (Gen. 3. 22; 19. 26; 21. 20; Exod. 7. 19; 8. 17 and 9. 10). In each of these cases, however, the context clearly shows that a change of state has occurred.... Because Gen. 1. 2 lacks contextual support for translating this verb 'became' no English version of Genesis has ever translated it this way."

One continually runs into this appeal to the absence of "contextual" support. But what *is* the context of such a passage as this if not the bias of the reader? It is, after all, only the second verse of the Bible. Can one establish a "context" in such a situation?

As for the statement that there are only six instances in the Pentateuch where the verb הָיָה is rendered "became", one can only hope that this was a printer's error. There are at least seventeen cases where הָיָה is rendered "became" *in Genesis alone* according to the Authorized Version (for a list of these, see page 55). Other English Versions, such as the Revised Standard Version, etc., increase this total. So it is difficult to know how this list of six occurrences was arrived at. In any event, it is apparent that even this miscount is based on only a single translation, and an English one at that. What of other translations whether in English or any other lanugage? What of the Vulgate with its thirteen occurrences in Genesis Chapter One alone: and what of the Septuagint with its twenty-two occurrences in Genesis One, and with some 1500 in the Old Testament as a whole? It is sincerely to be hoped that the real facts of the case will in time become more common knowledge so that statements like this will not pass unchallenged, even by a Christian editor not trained as a Hebraist.

The same writer proposes that "became" is only proper for the Hebrew הָיָה when it involves a "change of state".[115] Who is to say with any certainty that verse 2 does not indicate a change? This is really the whole point at issue. I believe there *was* a change, a breakdown in the originally created order. The writer's argument has no force whatever, for it simply begs the issue....

One of the earliest critics of this view was Professor M. M. Kalisch who had no sympathy with the ideas held by such scholars as Delitzsch, or Kurtz, or any other continental scholar of like mind. In his *Historical and Critical Commentary of the Old Testament*, published in 1858, he says:[116] "It is inadmissible to translate Gen.1.2 'But afterwards the earth had become...' " Presumably he had Dathe in mind, for this was Dathe's rendering. But he states his opinion of those who shared Dathe's views as to the implications of Gen.1.2 in no uncertain terms. He says:[117]

> "Now most of the modern followers of this opinion believe that an indefinite interval of time elapsed between the creation of matter recorded in the first verse and the formation of the world in its present admirable order, a period sufficiently extensive to account for the various and repeated changes both in the condition of the earth and the sidereal systems.

> So that the first chapter does not, in fact, fix the antiquity of the globe at all. But the supposition is absolutely untenable for the following reason: verse 2 evidently stands in very close connection with verse 1 which it qualifies and defines*. The connecting particle 'and' (*waw*) expresses here necessarily immediate sequence....; It is utterly impossible to separate the first two verses and to suppose between them an immense period of time."

His "proof text" is Exod.20.11. He assumes that this passage records the whole creative process as being completed in six days. He thus holds that since the sun was not "created" till the fourth day, the world as a scene of living things could not have existed before then.

He is, however, overlooking the fact that Exod.20.11 does not say that God *created* the world in this period of six days, but only that He *appointed* it (עָשָׂה, *'asah*) in a period of six days.

The verb used here is rendered "make" on numerous occasions of course, but it often has the sense of "appointing", just as the word is so used in the Greek of Heb.6.20, "made a High Priest"; or the English phrase "made a judge", for example. The work of the six days need not have involved the *creation* of the sun and stars at all. They were probably already in existence. See further on Exod.20.11 in Appendix XX.

He is also ignoring the fact that "and" (ו) often opens a sentence

---

* *With this pronouncement one may contrast Driver's conclusion in his* Hebrew Tenses *(p.84); where after giving a number of instances in which the usual Hebrew word order is departed from (as it is in Gen.1.2) in order to express a pluperfect, he says: "And each of these passages, by avoiding* waw *consecutive (the usual way to express continuing action,ACC) the writer* cuts the connection *(Driver's emphasis) with the immediately preceding narrative, and so suggests a pluperfect". Obviously Driver and Kalisch can hardly both be right. And in view of the fact that Driver's statement not only occurs in a scholarly but classic work on the Hebrew verb but is in this case based on a series of illustrative examples, I am inclined to accept Driver's word against the rather dogmatic statements of Kalisch.*

or paragraph or even a chapter or a whole book with no connection whatever with what went before. Ezekiel opens with it, for example! With what does it here have a "necessary" connection? A new section, in I Chron.11.1, is begun after a seven year interval, and in Ezra 7.1 after an interval of 58 years.... Further illustrations will be found in Appendix XII. That the word is often *dis*-junctive must have been known well enough to Kalisch, so that one wonders how he can say that it must necessarily be interpreted *con*junctively.

Kalisch is fully persuaded that the ideas of people like Delitzsch and Kurtz, who sought to supply the details of the events in the interval from other parts of Scripture, are quite worthless in themselves and unbecoming to scholars. He is quite ungracious in his references to them. On the other hand, Delitzsch was a man of very different temperament, gracious in his reference to those who disagreed with him and unhesitatingly giving credit to their soundness of scholarship (where this was due) even in his detractors. Delitzsch, as we have seen, held very firm and quite elaborate views respecting the circumstances surrounding the condition described in Gen.1.2 - but he did not base his views on the linguistic evidence, never actually agreeing that 'became' would be a more correct translation. This latter opinion of his is not infrequently quoted as proof of the unscholarliness of the "gap" theory (as it has been by Dr, Henry Morris[118]) but those who refer thus to Delitzsch's opinion are often not aware that he actually supported the view strongly, even though he did not base it on Gen.1.2.

Driver was much impressed by Delitzsch, both as a scholar and as a commentator,* and while in his Lexicon and in his *Hebrew Tenses*, Driver rendered Gen.1.2 as "and the earth was..." whenever he referred to it, he nevertheless frankly acknowledged that the view supported by Delitzsch and Pusey and others, though in his opinion improbably, was "exegetically admissible".* Like Kalisch, Driver felt that since the sun had not been "created" until the fourth

---

* *Of Delitzsch, Driver wrote* (Hebrew Tenses, *p.xi, xii) "And by sobriety, fullness of information, and scholarship combined, Delitzsch has succeeded in making his commentary indispensible to every student of the Old Testament."*

\# *Driver does not always follow his own "rules". Thus although he wrote at length on both the use of* הָיָה *as meaning "became" and the changed word order as signifying a*

day, it was "scientifically incredible" that a world could have supported the higher forms of life in a world without sunlight.[119] This objection is based on a misunderstanding which again results from confusing the two verbs *bara* and *'asah*, "to create" and "to appoint".

Driver's liberal views were shared by John Skinner who, while holding that the Bible was a remarkable enough document of antiquity, felt no qualms in challenging its accuracy. Skinner contributed the volume on Genesis in *The International Critical Commentary* of which Driver was one of the editors. In this volume, Skinner dismisses our interpretation with aplomb! Thus he writes:[120] "This view that verse 1 describes an earlier creation of heaven and earth which was reduced to chaos and then re-fashioned, needs no refutation". As F. F. Bruce rightly remarked when referring to this observation in his Paper in The Transactions of the Victoria Institute, this is "an excessively cavalier dismissal of a view which has been supported by men of the calibre of Pusey, Liddon, etc.".[121] It is indeed.

The curious thing is that Skinner virtually concedes the point he is dismissing here when, later on, he comes to deal with the words *tohu wa bohu* in his comments on Gen. 1.2. He refers to Jer. 4.23 f. where the words recur, but he is at pains to assure the reader that there is no real parallelism here. In a way, I agree. Jer. 4.23 does *not* read in the Hebrew, "the earth *became tohu wa bohu* but "the earth was.....", for the verb הָיְתָה is omitted. Unlike the situation in Gen. 1.2, its use is not required since evidently we have a copulative sentence here. Apparently Skinner did not observe this fact. However, having said that no light is thrown upon the words *tohu wa bohu* as they appear in Gen. 1.2 by their use in Jer-

---

pluperfect, he did not always commend his own views by adopting them himself to translate his own biblical illustrations. It seems that more often than not he gave the reference which was appropriate but merely reproduced the Authorized Version rendering as being most familar (or accessible) to his readers. Thus in dealing with the pluperfect, he chides Kalisch for rendering Gen. 2.2 as a pluperfect (p. 23), arguing that it is not an example, but then giving it elsewhere in the same work he renders it as one (p. 22)! It appears that he has merely reproduced the Authorized Version in such cases. His rendering of Gen. 1.2 as "was" may really be nothing more than another example of the Authorized Version being quoted for simplicity.

emiah, he then adds, with a strange lack of consistency:[122]

> "Our safest guide is perhaps Jeremiah's vision of *chaos-come-again* which is simply that of a darkened and devastated earth, *from which life and order have fled*" (my emphasis throughout).

One wonders how more precisely he could have supported our view of the implications of Gen. 1.2. Yet apparently he did not see the significance of his own words.

In his *Hebrew Thought Compared with Greek*, Thorlief Boman writes at length and, to my mind, most convincingly to the effect that the Hebrew verb הָיָה seldom, if ever, appears as copula. Yet he still holds that it *is* copulative in Gen. 1.2, though in a special way. Thus he says that the verse should not be rendered "the earth became" but "the earth was...."[123]

Now his argument is a little difficult to summarize briefly but in essence it is thus. In such a sentence as, "the altar is wood", the verb *is* is quite redundant because the altar and the wood are equated. "The one *inheres* in the other", as he puts it.[124] Similarly, in the sentence, "God is graciousness", the verb is not needed because graciousness inheres in God. And so on. Yet I am not sure that he is really right. Not all altars are wood, and certainly there is plenty of wood that is not in the form of an altar. Perhaps graciousness and God do inhere, yet sometimes graciousness is found in man too - where it certainly does not *inhere*. The trouble is that the principle can be applied specifically, but cannot be stated as a generalization. He concludes that the verb הָיָה is omitted where *inherence* is involved, but it must be introduced where it is *not*. Hence he argues that in Gen. 1.2 the verb is required because otherwise the earth and chaos are inherent in one another, ie., the earth *is* chaos. But then he says that earth is the scene of human civilization, which to the Greek mind was the definition of Cosmos. And since Chaos and Cosmos cannot co-exist, the earth cannot inherently be identified with Chaos - for it is identified with Cosmos. Of course, in the New Testament the word for *Cosmos* is rendered "world" for this reason, because the earth is the habitation of man. Thus he says, because Chaos cannot inhere in the word "earth", we *must* introduce the appropriate form of the verb הָיָה. As he puts it:[125]

> "Here *tohu va bohu* (chaos) does not inhere in 'the earth' for the latter is always the region of civilization and humanity,

> which excludes the possibility on conceptual grounds. The predicate could not be equated in this sentence directly with the subject for that would result in the impossible meaning that chaos and cosmos are identical concepts."

But there is no need to say that the earth *was* both Chaos and Cosmos at once. It is quite sufficient to take the text to mean that what was created a Cosmos had now *become* a Chaos. It is hard to see why Boman objected to this so strongly. The text is then "satisfied" both conceptually and linguistically. Indeed, how else than by adopting the wording that exists could the Hebrew writer have expressed such a thought? By Boman's own reasoning, had the writer wished to say simply that the earth was a Chaos, he would have omitted the verb.

Indeed, this is precisely what Jer.4.23 does. Jeremiah's vision was a vision of a moment. He saw the earth as a Chaos. More than this, he saw a *Cosmos* as a Chaos, for he actually says that the evidence of civilization lay in ruins...., men and cities had been overwhelmed. He was not concerned in reverting to the past in order to say that this scene of devastation had come about over a period of time by such-and-such a process. He merely says that when he saw it, it presented to his mind's eye a scene of devastation. It is almost as though the Author of Scripture had given us this passage in order to assist us in our understanding of Gen.1.2 which so nearly parallels it while at the same time differing from it in such an important detail - the introduction of הָיְתָה. At any rate, Jer.4.23 demonstrates clearly that Chaos can be equated with a scene which was once a Cosmos. And Boman's case, therefore, fails to stand.

I think Boman's work is most valuable, and my criticisms of his reasoning here does not make his study any less valuable. Yet it suggests that for some odd reason whenever the subject of Gen.1.2 comes up for study, normal vision becomes distorted. Somehow Gen.1.2 *must* be made to mean that when God created the world He began the process with a Chaos!

Those who happen to disagree are apt to have even their intellectual integrity challenged! Thus Professor J. Barr, in his *Semantics of Biblical Language*, says:[126]

> "It would be quite *perverse* (my enphasis) to insist on the meaning 'become' (in Gen.1.2)."

His argument is that the verb הָיְתָה must be accounted for in this sentence by assuming that the author meant "the earth was a waste but is no longer so". Thus it is proper to use the verb only when a situation being described was a *temporary* situation which has since been changed. Since the verb *is* used here, this must be the author's only reason for employing the verb הָיְתָה in this case.

But I think it very questionable that this *is* the author's meaning. Yet, as we have already seen in Chapter II, there are numerous occasions upon which a clear intention to this effect does *not* employ the verb. It will be recalled, for instance, that Job tells his "friends" that he *was* (once) a father to the fatherless, sight to the blind, and so forth.... He is clearly not one of these things now, at the time of speaking. If there was a straightforward rule such as Barr implies, this would assuredly be the place to apply it, and the verb הָיָה should be inserted. But it isn't. By contrast, it is often found where in the nature of the case there can be no "change" intended. Thus very frequently we find the phrase, "so-and-so was 150 years old and he died". The author does not mean that he was *once* of such an age, surely? But the verb is inserted. The simplest and surely the most satisfactory explanation is to assume that the man in question had become so many years old, ie., had reached this age when he died. If Professor Barr is serious in making this suggestion, he should have given a few unambiguous illustrations. But he has not done so. His use of the word "perverse" is unfortunate.

We meet with the same odd insistence in Raymond F. Surburg's contribution to the volume, *Darwin, Evolution, and Creation.* As he puts it: [127]

> "Although held by many Christians today, this theory cannot be substantiated from the Bible.... The Hebrew text does not say the earth *became*, but the earth *was* waste and void. Even if it were possible to render *Hayetha* as 'became', the words 'waste and void' indicate an unformed state and not one resulting from destruction. In his *Survey of Old Testament Teaching*, J. Walsh Watts asserts 'In Gen. 1.2a the verb is a perfect. It indicates a fixed and completed state. In other words, original matter was in a state of chaos when created: it came into being that way'."

To say that 'waste and void' means unformed in the sense of the Greek concept of Chaos might be reasonable if the Old Testament was a reflection of Greek mythology. In this case, the Septuagint translators would surely have adopted the Greek word χαος to translate *Tohu*. But they chose not to do so. It is, however, fairly clear that wherever the words "waste" and "void" occur elsewhere in Scripture they do NOT indicate an unformed state, they indicate something more positively undesirable. In many cases, especially when they occur together as in Jer.4.23, they mean a situation "resulting from destruction" and brought about by divine judgment. Would it not have been more accurate to state frankly that elsewhere the normal sense of the word here interpreted to mean "unformed" would be better rendered *de*-formed" or "desolated"? In blanket statements like this, most readers are at the mercy of the writer unless they are very familiar with the Old Testament and are aware of how these descriptive terms are employed in other passages.

Bernard Ramm is also rather cavalier in his treatment of the subject. He describes efforts to harmonize Geology and the Bible by this method as "abortive". He then says:[128]

> "The effort to make *was* mean *became* is just as abortive. The Hebrew did not have a word for *became* but the verb *be* did service for *to be* and *become*."

In point of fact, the reverse is much more nearly so. They did not *need* a word for "to be" in the simple sense, so made their word for *become* serve for *to be* and *become*. The modern lexicons bear this out by giving the meanings of הָיָה as "to become" (in various paraphrastic ways), and then also - and finally - as "to be". "To be" is not its primary meaning. Ramm continues:[129]

> "The form of the verb *was* in Gen.1.2 is *qal*, perfect, third person singular, feminine. A Hebrew concordance will give all the occurrences of that form of the verb. A check in the concordance in reference to the usage of this form of the verb in Genesis reveals that in almost every case the meaning of the verb is simply *was*.

Again, after what has been set forth of the evidence thus far, comment is hardly necessary. It may be helpful, however, to recall that in a great number of cases, 1500 out of 3000 or more, the Septuagint substitutes the Greek "became" (in the appropriate tenses, of course), and that in another 25% of the cases the verb is used in the sense of living or existing, and is not copulative at all - and finally, that for every case where the verb is inserted in the original and rendered as *was* (whether correctly or otherwise), one can find ten cases where the copulative "was" is omitted *entirely* in the Hebrew. As we have seen, this is sufficient indication in itself that the Hebrew did NOT use הָיָה for "was" in the simple English sense. They actually felt no need for such a verb at all. Only when the sense was something other than the simple "was" did they insert a verbal form. Ramm's treatment of the subject is, therefore, in the final analysis, unworthy of a man of his scholarship.

His *emotional* involvement here is revealed by his next comment:[130]

> "Granted in *a* (my emphasis) case or two (!) *was* means *became*, but if in the preponderance of instances the word is translated *was*, any effort to make one instance mean *became* especially if that instance is highly debatable, is very insecure exegesis."

Allowing his premises, what he argues is perhaps not unreasonable. But his basic premise is surely in error. One does not need to "make one instance mean *became*"; one actually has to do the very reverse if the evidence presented in this thesis is sound. And I do not know how else one could approach the problem, nor how one could arrive at any other conclusion in the light of the facts than that the truth is really quite the reverse.

The Septuagint normally translated הָיָה (with or without the לְ) by the Greek γιγνομαι and not by the Greek ειναι. And it is therefore important to note, as Thayer has done,[131] that γιγνομαι *cannot* be equated with ειναι. Since, therefore, הָיָה obviously cannot be equated with both γιγνομαι *and* ειναι, then הָיָה must be equated with γιγνομαι and must have the primary sense of *becoming*.

Again, Ramm observes:[132]

> "This whole matter was debated in the Journal of *The Victoria Institute* (London). P. W. Heward defended the Pember-Scofield-Rimmer interpretation of Gen. 1.2 and F. F. Bruce defended the traditional interpretation. To the author, Bruce is *easily* (my emphasis) the winner of the debate."

Easily - in what sense I wonder? Ramm quoted E. K. Gedney who wrote to twenty Hebrew scholars in the United States asking them if there were any exegetical evidences justifying the interpretation of Gen. 1.2 as having reference to a ruined earth.[133] They replied unaminously in the negative. But J. R. Howitt did much the same with respect to the meaning of the word "day" in Genesis Chapter One. Unaminously the answer was "a period of 24 hours".[134] Would Ramm accept *this* as final, I wonder? So what really is proved by this kind of "appeal to opinion"? Can one be sure that *any* of these men who were questioned were aware of the background information that is now available on the matter? They would, however, (as United States residents) presumably be reasonably well acquainted with the Fundamentalist position on the matter. And on this account, human nature being what it is, they may have simply dismissed the subject as quite unworthy of serious study. And in the matter of the meaning of the word "day", Ramm himself says, "The case for the literal day cannot be conclusive...."[135] So whether "weight of authority" is "conclusive" or not depends on one's own particular bias. Subsequently, Ramm observes:[136]

> "We reject the literal interpretation (involving days of 24 hours) because by no means can the history of the earth be dated at 4004 B.C...."

Thus in the final analysis the issue is really being decided for Ramm, not by exegetical methods at all, but by Geology, the Geology of "majority opinion".

I have been for years reading on both sides of the issue. I have accumulated a substantial (and very valuable) research library in order to give some "edge" to this reading. I have yet to see a really *sound* counter-argument to the view presented in this volume, but I have read innumerable attacks upon it, and the arguments presented in these attacks are atrociously repetitious. Few, if any, of its critics have really taken the trouble to study the evidence adequately. It is an unfortunate situation. When Surburg says that the Hebrew text does not say "the earth became...." but "the earth was....", he is speaking imprecisely.[137] The *Hebrew* says וְהָאָרֶץ הָיְתָה. The Hebrew is *Hebrew*, not English! To say that it says "was" is simply begging the question: he is merely *making* it say "was". The reasoning is circular. If I render it "became", I could as easily prove I was right by pointing to my own translation! This kind of argument contributes nothing to our real understanding of the Word of God unless one says *why* one is rendering it in this way as opposed to either of the alternatives "became" or "had become".

Altogether, I do not find that *any* of the objections raised carries weight. They can all be answered either from the statements of other objectors or from Scripture itself. Certainly the basic objection on linguistic grounds that the verb הָיָה only rarely means "became" is patently incorrect. But once it has become fashionable to dismiss a piece of evidence, it usually happens that the dismissal becomes more and more dogmatic as the writer has less and less factual knowledge of the evidence. Knowledge usually leads to caution - the hallmark of scholarship. It is ignorance that encourages dogmatism and it is usually in direct proportion to it. Let us hope that a spirit of open mindedness will yet prevail to permit a more dispassionate reconsideration of the matter.

Chapter 6.

THE RULE APPLIED WITH ILLUSTRATIONS.

Robert Young, the author of that most valuable research tool, *An Analytical Concordance of the Old and New Testament*, also produced a *Literal Translation of the Bible*.[138] In his Introduction he sets forth very carefully with support from various authorities certain views regarding the use of tenses in Hebrew. He then applies these rules rigidly. The resulting narrative, while perhaps more precisely correct from the view of Hebrew syntax and grammar (assuming his "rules" are valid), is difficult indeed to read cursively with profit. The English is stilted and does not "flow". The sentences are staccato and just occasionally hardly seem to make sense at all. The lesson one learns from this is that translation demands a certain amount of freedom. In order to make literature live, a translator is justified in taking some liberties not on linguistic grounds but for dramatic reasons, though the dangers of doing this are very considerable.

Now, my reason for using this example is simply to emphasize the need for caution in insisting on obedience upon all occasions to some rule that has, after all, only been established by reference to general usage. In language, this is the only way that rules *can* be established. But when a translation is made for reading (as well as for study), then some departure from the rules sometimes has to be allowed. Thus I would not argue that הָיָה must always and on all occasions be rendered "become" or "became" or even "come to be" (ie., "happen") whenever it is found in the present or past tense. The fact is that there are sentences even in English where the word "be" really *means* "become" and yet we commonly accept the word "be". For example, "I refuse to be a party to it" really means "I refuse to *become* a part to it". So one should not *always* translate according to the letter of the law.

In the opening words of his Preface, Driver, after noting that Hebrew is particularly careful in distinguishing between the sense of "being" and "becoming" and after pointing out how little attention we are apt to pay to this difference, remarks:[139]

> "So cumbrous is the mechanism which has to be set in motion in order to express the difference, so palpable is the strain to which our language is subjected in the process, that we feel irresistibly tempted to discard and forget it."

And again:[140]

> "On the agreement of a verb with its subject in number, a point to which in certain cases the ancient Hebrews attached no importance whatever, we ourselves are sensitive and precise: on the other hand, the difference between *being* and *becoming*, *seyn* and *werden*, ειναι and γιγνομαι has never been fully appropriated or naturalized in English...."

The only time one ought to be particularly careful is when there is a possibility of a real misunderstanding as to the sense, when there is an ambiguity that it is important to avoid. It *is* an important issue with respect to Gen. 1.2 whether one renders the Hebrew as "But the earth became...." or merely "But the earth was...." In such a case, to my mind, the true sense must be clearly established by reference to the rules of the language and rendered into English in such a way as to make that sense unambiguous.

In a few cases it will not matter at all: in others it may be critical. In a large number of cases which fall between these extremes, there may be considerable gain in rendering it correctly and unambiguously. Let me give a few illustrations, in none of which is הָיָה followed by לְ, yet all of which are by one translator or another rendered "became" or "had become", etc.

In Gen. 3.1, the Hebrew should be rendered, "Now the serpent had become more subtle than any beast of the field".* I believe this indicates that some circumstance had *changed* its character rather than that God had created it so from the beginning.

In Gen. 3.20, it would be more proper to render the passage as Driver does, "Eve became the mother of all living". It is virtually certain that at that time Eve was not yet a mother. The development which subsequently establishes her as the mother of the human race is here recorded in retrospect and it seems likely that Adam's *first* name for Eve was simply *Ishah*, or Woman. This kind of retrospect observation surely applies to Gen. 2.23 also, for *Adam* could not possibly have said that a man should leave his mother and father and cleave to his wife, since such a thought would at that time be quite foreign to his experience. I do not mean by this that the saying is not divinely inspired. Adam may very well have renamed his wife Eve *after* she began to beget sons and daughters and they in turn begat children.

In Gen. 21.20, there is a nice instance of precision in the use of the verb הָיָה. Speaking of Ishmael, the original tells us "And it came to pass (וַיְהִי) that God (was) with the lad (אֶת־הַנַּעַר) and he grew and dwelt in the wilderness and *became* a drawer of the bow". The Vulgate has *factusque est* , ie., "and he became...." And the Septuagint has εγενετο. The passage is quite similar to that of Gen. 4.2 (except for the inverted word order found there) which according to Driver (perhaps guided in part by the LXX) is rendered "And Abel *became* a shepherd of the flock, while Cain *had become* a tiller of the ground".

A particularly delightful passage is to be found in Gen. 29.17 which I would render more exactly from the Hebrew (and yet quite literally too!), "Now Rachael had become sparkling eyed and beautiful, but Leah always was weepy eyed". I realize that this sounds far-fetched at first sight, yet the fact is that the actual use of the verb הָיָה (and the word order) in the first instance justifies the use of "had become" in the pluperfect: and its absence in the second case implies a static situation - which I have expressed somewhat paraphrastically but not unreasonably by the words "always was". And whereas the original

---

* *Pusey so renders this passage.*

does suggest "sparks" when speaking of Rachael's eyes, it also suggests "wateriness" when referring to Leah! The Authorized Version is perhaps gentler with Leah than the Hebrew original. It is quite true that the change in word order could merely be to contrast with what precedes. But this contrast is not really specific in the text, and I think it is quite reasonable to say that Rachael as she grew to womanhood had become a strikingly beautiful woman, whereas Leah may have been watery-eyed from childhood.

An excellent illustration of how some translators heeded and other did not heed the sense of "becoming" in the verb הָיָה is in connection with Joseph's dream and the fate that intervened before it was fulfilled. In Gen. 37.20, I would render the Hebrew "Let us see what will *become* of his dreams". Both Driver and the Revised Standard Version have adopted this rendering. But the Septuagint have understood the meaning of Gen. 37.20 rather differently for they rendered it τί ἔσται τὰ ἐνύπτα αὐτοῦ, ie., "What his dreams *will be*... The Septuagint translators evidently took the text to mean that the brothers wanted to cast Joseph into the pit and leave him there - to dream dreams of a somewhat less promising kind! This *could* be the meaning since the tense is *future* and therefore הָיָה would be required in the appropriate form since the circumstances are viewed as being changed - or at least the nature of his dreams! Yet I think the real significance of their remarks is that they wished to thwart the "promise" of the dream he had already told them about.

In Gen. 2.18 ff., we have another striking case where precision in translation is revealing. First, it is stated that it was not a good thing that Adam should be alone. He needed company of some kind. So, as I interpret the occasion, the Lord brought to the man various animals whose nature and habits (and size, presumably) might suggest to Adam that in these he would find the answer to his loneliness. It would not be so exceptional if he had done so, for many both young and old people today find greater pleasure in the company of some pet animal than they do in the society of their fellow man.

Adam's response to each creature, thus presented for his consideration as a companion, was at once reflected in the "name" he gave to it. In this process of naming, I do not think there was anything arbitrary at all. He was not merely providing a dictionary label for each creature so that it could be referred to thereafter without ambiguity. He was *identifying its nature*. The text says: "Whatsoever he called (each animal) that (*was*) the name thereof". Now in the original the verb הָיָה is absent. Had it been included, the sense of the text would then have been "that became its name" - and superficially this is exactly what we might have expected the text to say. The usual interpretation of the passage is that he gave each animal a label and that the label "stuck": ie., *that* became its name thereafter. But from the way the Hebrew has actually stated the matter, I think the meaning is much more profound. This was a case of precise "identification". Adam identified each creature as to its nature - and that really was in fact its nature: in short, he was absolutely right in his assessment. *This*, in fact, is why not one of them appeared to him to be a sufficient companion. In his unfallen state, his judgment did not deceive him. What he said of each animal was true: he marked each one for what it was, a creature far below himself whose nature was quite unlike his own. His own name was *Ish*, a word in some way describing his very nature. The woman he correctly identified as *Ishah* for he recognized her as his own counterpart: but not so, any of the other creatures. Thus what appears as a naive fairy tale turns out to be a record of a profound exercise in human judgment, an exercise which may indeed have exhausted him and prepared him for the very deep sleep which followed.

By thus observing the rule with greater care, one may discern in this simple record an event of far greater significance than a mere invitation to engage in a game of attaching labels to animals. The story as so understood tells us some very important things about Adam's mental capacity at that time as well as about his relationship to the animals that shared his paradise. As we are told in the New Testament (I Tim.2.14), Adam was not deceived in anything he undertook - even in eating the forbidden fruit. Thereafter his judgment undoubtedly began to suffer the noetic effects of sin and it seems unlikely that after the Fall he could any longer have identified with such perfect precision the kind of creature that each was by nature nor recognize his own true nature except by revelation. Our own judgment easily misleads us now into imagining that man is not fundamentally different from certain forms of animal life which, assuming that they existed, would almost certainly have been among those brought for his assessment.

One of the better known passages often appealed to by those who share the view presented here is Jer.4.23-26 which reads, "I beheld the earth and lo, it *(was)* without form and void; and the heavens, they had no light.... and, lo, there *(was)* no man.... and the fruitful place was a wilderness.... etc." The passage is an important one in the present context for several reasons, both for what it does say and what it does *not* say.

The overall picture reveals some striking similarities with the situation in Gen. 1.2, the ruin and devastation, the darkness, and the absence of man. That Jeremiah is referring not to the first stages of God's creative activity but to a historical situation which faced him at the time of his vision is clear. But this does not lessen the force of his words nor the significance of the fact that his terms are precisely those employed in Gen. 1.2. Skinner freely admits that we must see here a picure of a scene "from which life and order have fled.... a darkened and devastated earth".[141] Yet, like many others, he maintains that the very same terms when used in Gen. 1.2 must mean something quite different! There *is* a difference, an interesting one, between Gen. 1.2 and Jer. 4.23, and that is in the omission of the verb הָיְתָה in Jeremiah. Evidently Jeremiah's vision is not a vision of the *occurrence* of the event in which he sees first a beautiful, inhabited, and fruitful land suddenly becoming a devastation. What his vision encompasses is the after effect, the *fait accomplis*; in short, simply a scene of total destruction. Hence the verb הָיְתָה is unnecessary.

But since the terms תֹּהוּ and בֹּהוּ (*tohu wa bohu*) which describe the earth in Gen. 1.2 are here applied to a scene of devastation, it is difficult to avoid the conclusion that this *is* the correct meaning of those two terms when juxtaposed in this alliterative way. Possibly, when used independently, the meanings may be slightly less dramatic, having merely the sense of "vanity" (at least in the case of *Tohu*): but when employed together, the meaning of each seems to be strongly reinforced in the destructive sense, not merely negatively "in vain" but positively destroyed.

For a better assessment of the meaning of *Tohu*, the reader will find a full list of references in Appendix XII. While *Tohu* will not always be found to signify "destruction" but rather that which is not approved or is to no good purpose, it does not appear to equate very well with the classical Greek concept of Chaos which has the sense of something not so much mal-formed, as un-formed. Thus, while Jer. 4.23 is not (by reason of its omission of the verb הָיְתָה) an exact parallel to Gen. 1.2, the terms it uses are certainly stamped with a meaning that conveys the sense of devastation and ruin in JUDGMENT rather than mere incompleteness.

This naturally leads to another critical passage in the Old Testament in which the word *Tohu* occurs twice, namely, in Isa. 45.18 and 19. Verse 18 is often quoted by those who support the view I hold because it seems so clearly to determine the correct sense of the same word in Gen. 1.2. Now Isa. 45.17-18 reads as follows:

> "But Israel shall be saved in the Lord with an everlasting salvation: ye shall not be ashamed nor confounded world without end. For thus saith the Lord that created the heavens; God Himself that formed the earth and made it; He hath established it, He created it not in vain *(Tohu)*, He formed it to be inhabited: I am the Lord; and there is none else."

It is customary to point out that in this passage it is expressly stated that the Lord did *not* create the earth a *Tohu*. It is therefore argued, reasonably enough, that Gen. 1.2 cannot be a direct continuation of Gen.1.1, since this would imply that God *did* create the earth a *Tohu*. I believe the argument is a strong one and ought to be given due weight. But it is not compulsive, much as one might wish it were, because the word *Tohu* may legitimately be rendered "in vain" by treating it as an adverbial accusative. The propriety of adopting the Authorized Version rendering must be admitted in the light of verse 19 which reads "I have not spoken in secret, in a dark place of the earth: I said not unto the seed of Jacob, Seek ye Me in vain (*Tohu*)".

Certainly in verse 19 the translation is much more reasonable than it would have been had *Tohu* been rendered "a ruin", for then the sentence would have read, "Seek ye Me, a ruin" - which is nonsense.* If one must render *Tohu* "in vain" in *this* passage, it cannot be altogether unreasonable to so render it in verse 18 where such a rendering does, after all, make very good sense.

There are, however, two points worthy of note here. First, that the sentence structure in verse 19 *forces* one to render the noun adverbially and thus to read it as "in vain". To do anything else makes nonsense of the sentence. By contrast, this is not true in verse 18. *Either* rendering is equally sensible. Thus some other consideration must settle the issue or at least tip the scales in favour of one rendering as against the other. And here I think there IS something to be said in favour of rendering the noun *as a noun*. The burden of the passage is that Israel has suffered a serious setback as a nation. Yet, says the prophet, all is not lost. Israel shall yet be saved, and next time it will be for ever. For the Lord once created a world which He beautifully appointed as a habitation for

---

* *However, the RSV has "a chaos" in both verses, verse 19 reading, "seek me in chaos", which is allowable enough, but an odd sentence.*

man, which He established with that end in view. And it is true, Isaiah seems to be saying, that the earth fell into ruin and was utterly devastated in judgment, but that is not the *way in which* it was created: nor was it the *end for which* God had formed it. He intended it as a habitation for man; and God intended Israel as a people for Himself. Both goals will yet be achieved, even as the first goal has already been.

Seen in this light, the passage might well justify the two different renderings of *Tohu*, the first as "a ruin", the second as "in vain", each sentence being structured differently to convey the difference in meaning. There is nothing forced or strange about this kind of literary device. Yet - for all this - there is no absolute certainty, and each reader must decide the issue for himself, pending further light.

As we have said previously, a good case is not made stronger by an appeal to a passage, the sense of which is not unequivocably clear, and to my mind, Isa.45.18 is a strong witness only to those who already accept the alternative rendering of Gen.1.2. Some have argued that the command to Adam to "re-plenish" the earth tells in our favour also, but unfortunately the Hebrew word מָלֵא (translated both here and in Gen.9.1 as "re-fill") does not necessarily bear this meaning: it is the normal verb for the simple idea of "filling", though it was also used on occasion to mean "refill".

Many passages in the Bible have been interpreted as having reference to the circumstances surrounding the devastation of Gen.1.2, but the case for an alternative rendering cannot be rested upon them. Granted that there was such an event, then such passages may well shed light on the matter, but the basic point at issue must be settled on other grounds first.

In conclusion, then, it is my conviction that the issue is still an open one, that all the objections raised against it thus far are not really valid, that the rules of Hebrew syntax and grammar not only *allow* this alternative rendering but positively favour it. The sense of "becoming" is not foreign to the verb הָיָה, nor is it merely a less common meaning that is to be allowed under certain rather limited circumstances: it is *the* basic meaning of the verb, the simple copulative sense being exceedingly rare, and the existential sense (though not rare) a special sense which really arises from the more basic meaning of *living*. Added to this is the word order inversion which can only be accounted for in one of two ways, while one of these (a change of subject) certainly cannot be argued very forcibly in view of the fact that the last word of verse 1 is the first word of verse 2.

There is no requirement for the following *lamedh* where the "conversion" of one thing to another is a real conversion and not merely an analogous one; and therefore there is no need for it here. And the descriptive terms in the sentence are none of them such as one would expect to find applied to something that has just come from the creative Hand of God. Nor is it easy, in the light of its use elsewhere in Scripture, to equate *Tohu* with the un-formed Chaos of Greek mythology.

By and large, therefore, I suggest that the rendering, "But the earth *had become* a ruin and a desolation", is a rendering which does *more* justice to the original and deserves more serious consideration as an alternative than it has been customary to afford it in recent years.

It is, after all, quite conceivable that some catastrophe *did* occur prior to the appearance of Man for which we do not yet have the kind of geological evidence we would like. Only twenty years ago uniformitarianism reigned supreme - but recently the Theory of Continental Drift has shaken this long established doctrine to its foundations. There could be other surprises yet in store for us. For myself, in the meantime, the most important thing of all is to know as precisely as it can be known, exactly what the Word of God really says.... even if for the time being it does conflict with current geological theory. All we can hope to do is to contribute light to minds of greater precision who may thus be enabled to hit upon the exact truth.

* * *

APPENDIX I

(Reference: p.37)

Excerpts from Some Supporting Authors.

This Appendix contains extracts from the works of authors not listed in Chapter 1, chiefly because they merely affirm what others have said and, with two exceptions, did not publish their views until the issue between the Bible and modern Geology had already become a serious one. Most of them can only be quoted as being among those who adopted the alternative rendering because they were impressed by the geological evidence as then interpreted. Many of them were recognized Hebrew scholars. Included among these extracts are also a few cases where admissions are made in favour of my thesis by scholars who nevertheless do not support it - for example, a note from Snaith.

The names are listed chronologically according to the original author of the quotation rather than the secondary author who happens to have supplied us with it - for example, Gleig's statement is listed under his own name although my sole source of reference was from Hoare and not from the author himself.

At the end we have included three lists of scholars who wrote in favour of this alternative, of whom I have very little information but thought it worthwhile to list with my source of reference, for the sake of those who may be in a position to examine their works at first hand.

Episcopius, Simon (1583 - 1643) of Holland, according to the *New*

Schaff-Herzog Encyclopedia of Religious Knowledge (in Vol.III, page 302, article by O. Zockler, "Creation and Preservation") is said to have been the first to render verse 2, "And the earth became waste and void".

Rosenmuller, J. G., a German Lutheran, 1736 - 1815, in his *Antiquissima Telluris Historia*, published in Ulm in 1776, wrote the first serious scientific defence of this view, according to the *New Schaff-Herzog Encyclopedia of Religious Knowledge*, Vol. III, p. 302.

Chalmers, Thomas, in his original Lecture in Edinburgh in 1814: "The detailed history of creation in the first chapter of Genesis begins at the middle of the second verse; and what precedes might be understood as an introductory sentence, by which we are most appositely told, both that God created all things at the first, and that, afterwards, by what interval of time it is not specified, the earth lapsed into a chaos, from the darkness and disorder of which the present system or economy of things was made to arise. Between the initial act and the details of Genesis, the world, for aught we know, might have been the theatre of many revolutions, the traces of which geology may still investigate". Quoted by Edward Hitchcock, *The Religion of Geology*, Collins, Glasgow, 1851, p.52.

Eadie, Dr. John, Professor of Theological and Biblical Literature in Divinity Hall of the United Presbyterian Church, Glasgow, (quoted by Dr. T. Fitzgerald in the *Transactions of the Victoria Inst.*, Vol. LXX, 1938, p. 86): Dr. Eadie, writing in the early part of the last century, observed: "The length of time that may have elapsed between the events recorded in the first verse (of the first chapter of Genesis) and the condition of the globe, as described in the second verse, is absolutely indefinite. How long it was we know not; and ample space is therefore given to all the requisitions of geology. The second verse describes the condition of our globe when God began to fit it up for the abode of man. The first day's work does not begin until the third verse.... This is no new theory. It was held by Justin Martyr, Origen, Theodoret, and Augustine - men who came to such a conclusion without any bias, and who certainly were not driven to it by an geological difficulties".

Bush, George, Professor of Hebrew in New York City University, in his *Notes, Critical and Practical on the Book of Genesis*, published by Ward, London, 1838, (p.25 f.), treated the subject at some length. On page 27 he wrote: "As there is no distinction of past, perfect, and pluperfect tenses in Hebrew, we are to be governed solely by the exigency of the place in rendering any particular word in one of these tenses or the other. 'Was', therefore, in this instance, we hold to be more correctly translated by 'had been' or, perhaps, 'had become' - ie., in consequence of changes to which it had been subject in the lapse of ages long prior to the period now alluded to....

"It has, indeed, been generally supposed that it describes the rude and chaotic state which ensued immediately upon the creating command; but this we think is contrary to the express declaration of Jehovah himself, Isa.45.18: 'For thus saith the Lord that created the heavens; God himself, that formed the earth and made it; he hath established it, he created it not desolate (TOHU)' - ie., the action described by the word 'created', did not result in the state denoted by the word TOHU but the reverse - he formed it to be inhabited".

Smith, J. Pye, *Lectures on the Bearing of Geological Science upon Certain Parts of the Scriptural Narrative*, London, 1839.

"A philological survey of the initial sections of the Bible, (Gen. i,1, to ii,3) brings out the result:

1. "That the first sentence is a simple, independent, all-comprehending axiom, to this effect: that *matter*, elementary or combined, aggregated only or organized, and *dependent, sentient, and intellectual beings* have not existed from eternity, either in self-continuity or succession, but had a beginning; that their beginning took place by the all-powerful will of one Being, the self-existent, independent, and infinite in all perfection; and that the date of that beginning is not made known.

2. "That at a certain epoch, our planet was brought into a state of disorganization, detritus, or ruin, (perhaps we have no perfectly appropriate term) from a former condition.

3. "That it pleased the Almighty, wise and benevolent Supreme, out of that state of ruin to adjust the surface of the earth to its now existing condition, the whole extending through the period of six natural days.

"I am forming no hypothesis in geology; I only plead that the *ground is clear*, and that the dictates of the Scripture *interpose no bar* to observation and reasoning upon the mineralogical constitution of the earth, and the remains of organized creatures which its strata disclose. If those investigations should lead us to attribute to the earth and to other planets and astral spheres an antiquity which millions or ten thousand millions of years might fail to represent, the divine records forbid not their deduction". From his *Lectures on Scripture and Geology*, London, 4th ed., p.502, as quoted by Edward Hitchcock in his *The Religion of Geology*, Collins, in Glasgow, 1851.

Harris, John, *The PreAdamite Earth: Contributions to Theological Science*, Ward and Co., London, no date, p.354: "On the whole, then, my firm persuasion is, that the first verse of Genesis was designed, by the Divine Spirit, to announce the absolute origination of the material universe by the Almighty Creator; and that it is so understood in other parts of Holy Writ: that, passing by an indefinite interval, the second verse describes the state of our planet immediately prior to the Adamic creation; and that the third verse begins the account of the six days' work.

"If I am reminded that I am in danger of being biassed in favour of these conclusions by the hope of harmonizing Scripture with Geology, I might venture to suggest, in reply, that the danger is not all on one side. Instances of adherence to traditional interpretations chiefly because they are traditional and popular, though in the face of all evidence of their faultiness, are by no means so rare as to render warning unnecessary. The danger of confounding the infallibility of our own interpretation with the infallibility of sacred text, is not peculiar to a party.

"If, again, I am reminded, in a tone of animadversion, that I am making science, in this instance, the interpreter of Scripture, my reply is that I am simply making the works of God illustrate his word, in a department in which they speak with a distinct and authoritative voice, that 'it is all the same whether our geological or theological investigations have been prior'; and that it might be deserving consideration, whether or not the conduct of those is not open to just animadversion, who first undertake to pronounce on the meaning of a passage of Scripture irrespective of all the appropriate evidence, and who then, when that evidence is explored and produced, insist on their *a priori* interpretation as the only true one.

"But in making these remarks I have been conceding too much. The views which I have exhibited are *not* of yesterday. It is important and interesting to observe how the early fathers of the Christian church should seem to have entertained precisely similar views: for St. Gregory Nazianzen, after St. Justin Martyr, supposes an *indefinite* period between the creation and the first ordering of all things. St. Basil, St. Caesarius, and Origen, are much more explicit. To these might be added Augustine, Theodoert, Episcopius, and others, whose remarks imply the existence of a considerable interval 'between the creation related in the first verse of Genesis, and that of which an account is given in the third and following verses'. In modern times, but long before geology became a science, the independent character of the opening sentence of Genesis was affirmed by such judicious and learned men as Calvin, Bishop Patrick, and Dr. David Jennings. And 'in some old editions of the English Bible, where there is no division into verses, and in Luther's Bible (Wittenburg, 1557), you have in addition the figure 1 placed against the third verse, as being the beginning of the account of the creation of the first day'. Now these views were formed independently of all geological considerations. In the entire absence of evidence from this quarter - probably even in opposition to it, as some would think - these conclusions were arrived at on biblical grounds alone. Geology only illustrates and confirms them. The works of God prove to be one with this preconceived meaning of his word. And there is no ground to expect that this early interpretation will gradually come to be universally accepted as the only correct one."

A footnote gives the references for the quotes in the above as being from Dr. S. Davidson's *Sacred Hermeneutics;* Principal Wiseman's *Lectures on the Connexion Between Science and Revealed Religion;* and Dr. J. Pye Smith's *Scripture and Geology.*

Gray, Rev. James, in his book, *The Earth's Antiquity in Harmony With the Mosaic Record of Creation* (referred to by William Hoare in a footnote on p.145 of his book *Veracity of the Book of Genesis),* takes the view (Chapter IV, p.211, 2nd. edition) "that the first verse in Genesis is not to be understood according to the currently entertained notion, as merely giving a summary account of the after-recorded work of the six days, but is an independent proposition enunciating THE CREATION, primordial as to time, - the reference being retrospective rather than prospective". In a subsequent footnote on p.151, Gray is again quoted (p.120 and 144 of *his* work) on Gen.1.2 as follows: "Such a disturbed condition of terrestrial things is here narrated, as we should naturally conclude would be found after the violent action of one or another of those grand disturbing agents, either of fire, by earthquakes, or of water by deluges, which we know to be Nature's ordinary mighty destroyers and rennovators on the earth..... a state following upon the last catastrophe anterior to the period of its divinely recorded re-organization as the abode of man".

Hoare, Willam H., *Veracity of the Book of Genesis*, (Longman, Green, Longman, &Roberts, London, 1860), has this statement in a footnote on p.143: "Episcopius and others thought that the creation and fall of the bad angels took place in the interval he has spoken of: and misplaced as such speculations are, still they seem to show that it is natural to suppose that a considerable interval may have taken place between the creation related in the first verse of Genesis and that of which an account is given in the third and following verses".

Gleig, the Rt. Rev. George, Bishop of Brechin and Primus of the Scots Episcopal Church (quoted by W. H. Hoare, *Veracity of the Book of Genesis*, etc. p.179): "Moses records the history of the earth only in its present state. He affirms indeed, that it was created, and that it was without form and void when the Spirit of God began to move on the face of the fluid mass; but he does not say how long that mass had been in a state of chaos, or whether it was or was not the wreck of some former system which had been inhabited by living creatures of a different kind from those that occupy the present.

"We read in various places of Scripture of *a new heavens* and *a new earth* to succeed the present earth and visible heavens, after they shall again be reduced to chaos by a general conflagration, and there is nothing in the books of Moses positively affirming that there was not an *old earth* and *old heavens*, or, in other words a former creation....

"There is nothing in the sacred narrative forbidding us to suppose that they are ruins of a former earth deposited in the chaotic mass of which Moses informs us that God formed the present system. How long it continued in such a chaotic state it is in vain to enquire...."

Jameison, R., *Commentary: Critical and Expository: Genesis - Deuteronomy*, (Nisbet, London, 1871, p.3): the author notes that in many Hebrew manuscripts a mark indicating a pause occurs after Gen.1.1. "This break between Gen.1.1 and 1.2 is observed even where no verse division exists".

Browne, the Rt. Rev. E. Harold, Lord Bishop of Ely, *Genesis: Or the First Book of Moses* (Scribner, New York, 1873, p.32), writes, under comment on Gen.1.5: "Literally, 'and it was (or became) evening, and it was (or became) morning, day one'", thereby bearing out the more precise translation of the verb *hayah*. Under verse 2 he merely acknowledges that this may be a picture of either primeval emptiness or "desolation and disorder succeeding to a former state of life and harmony...." He feels the issue cannot be settled conclusively but he does say that the two words *tohu* and *bohu* "express devastation or desolation", listing several passages in which the meaning of *tohu* is clearly this: viz., Job 12.24; 26.7; Isa.24.10; 34.11; and Jer.4.23.

Garland, G. V., *Genesis With Notes* (Rivingtons, London, 1878, p.3): With reference to Gen.1.1 and 2: "The first of these verses declares that the universe, and particularly that portion of it 'the earth', of which the second verse specially treats, as being the future habitation of man, was originally created by God. The second verse then proceeds to describe the condition of the earth at the period when God made (עָשָׂה , Gen.2.), or framed, or readjusted it (καταρτιζω Heb.11.3), out of the then existing materials for the use of man".

Reusch, Dr. Fr. H., *Nature and the Bible: Lectures on the Mosaic History of Creation In Its Relation to Natural Science*, (translated from the 4th edition by Kathleen Lyttelton, T. & T. Clark, Edinburgh, Vol. 1, 1886, p.120). He says: "Those who hold this theory - with its many individual modifications - are men of no little authority, they are, among men of science and philosophers, Jacob Bohme, Friedrich Schlegel, Julius Hamberger, Heinrich von Schubert, Karl von Raumer, Andreas Wagner; among theologians, Kurtz, Baumgarten, Dreschler, Delitzsch and others among Protestants; Leopold Schmid, Mayrhofer, and Westermayer among the Roman Catholics". In a footnote he adds this information: "Kurtz, *Bible and Astronomy*, Delitzsch, *Genesis*; Dreschler on *Delitzsch*; and Keerl, *Schopfungsgesch*; Raumer, *Kreuzzuge*; Hamberger in the *Jabrh. fur Deutsche Theol*; Wolf, *Die Bedeutung der Weltschopfung* Mayrhofer, *Das dreieine Leben*; Westermayer, *Das Alte Test*".

Exell, J.S., *Pulpit Commentary on Genesis*, (Kegan Paul, Trench, Trubner, London, 1897, p.4). Exell in commenting on verse 2 mentions Delitzsch's view of this verse as signifying "the ruin of a previous cosmos" and adds that he attributed the ruin to the fall of angels basing his view on Job 38.2 - 7). He gives as reference *Biblical Psychology*, Section 1, p.76, in Clark's *Foreign Theological Library*.

Edersheim, Alfred, *The World Before the Flood and the His-*

tory of the Patriarchs (Religious Tract Society, London, no date, p.18,19): "Some have imagined that the six days of creation represent as many periods, rather than literal days, chiefly on the ground of the supposed high antiquity of our globe, and the various great epochs or periods, each terminating in a grand revolution, through which our earth seems to have passed before coming to its present state, when it became a fit habitation for man. There is, however, no need to resort to any such theory.

"The first verse in the Book of Genesis simply states the general fact that 'in the beginning (whenever that may have been) God created the heaven and the earth'. Then, in the second verse, we find the earth described as it was at the close of the last great revolution preceding the present state of things: 'and the earth was without form and void; and darkness was upon the face of the deep'.

"An almost indefinite space of time and many changes may therefore have intervened between the creation of heaven and earth as mentioned in verse 1, and the chaotic state of our earth as described in verse 2."

Pember, G. H., *Earth's Earliest Ages*, which title is extended to read as: *and Their Connection with Modern Spiritualism and Theosophy* (Hodder and Stoughton, 1901, 9th ed., 494 pp.). The author's thesis is that Gen. 1.2 pictures a world brought into ruin as a result of the judgment of God against the rebellion of the Angels who under Satan had been responsible for the government of the Old World while it was being prepared for man, but had thought to become independent of Him. Satan was cast out of heaven along with the Angels who had followed him, and they have since tried in various ways to bring God's reconstituted world order, including man, into a like state of chaos. He believes these Angels to be, to a large extent, still free to intrude into human affairs and to act upon man's will - always with a view to making him disobedient to God.

Their increasing activity in the present age Pember believed to be a sign of the nearness of the second great judgment to be brought on the World, of which the Flood of Noah's time was the first.

Pember does not present his thesis as a Hebrew scholar, but rather as a student of ancient and present day forms of spiritism and demon worship.

Anstey, Martin, *The Romance of Bible Chronology*; (Marshall Brothers, London, 1913, p.62 and 63 - with his emphases): "The opening verse of Genesis speaks of the Creation of the heavens and the earth, in the undefined beginning. From this point we may date the origin of the world but not the origin of man. For the second verse tells of a catastrophe - the earth *became* a ruin and a desolation. The Hebrew verb *hayah* ('to be') here translated 'was'), signifies not only 'to be' but also 'to become', 'to take place', 'to come to pass'. When a Hebrew writer makes a simple affirmation, or merely predicates the existence of anything, the verb *hayah* is *never expressed*. Where it is expressed it must always be translated by our verb 'to become', and never by the verb 'to be', if we desire to convey the exact shade of meaning of the original.

"The words תֹהוּ וָבֹהוּ (*tohu wa bohu*) translated in the Authorized Version 'without form and void' and in the Revised Version 'waste and void' should be rendered 'a ruin and a desolation'. They do not represent the state of the heaven and the earth as they were created by God. They represent only the state of the *earth* as it afterwards became - a ruin and a desolation.... or better still 'had become', the separation of the *waw* from the verb being the Hebrew method of indicating the pluperfect tense....

"Gen. 1.2 does not describe a stage in the process of creation, but a disaster which befell the created earth: the original creation of the heaven and the earth is chronicled in Gen. 1.1. The next verse, Gen. 1.2, is a statement of the disorder, the ruin, and the state of desolation into which the earth subsequently fell. What follows in Gen. 1.3-31 is the story of the restoration of a lost order by the creative word of God".

Fitzgerald, Dr. Thomas (in *The Transactions of the Victoria Institute*, London, Vol. LXX, 1938) lists the names "of several scholars of high repute who can be cited in support of the translation which Dr. Hart-Davies finds it impossible to accept. The whole question has been very thoroughly argued in the works of John Harris, D.D., *The Pre-Adamite Earth* and *Primeval Man*: *The Principles of Geology*, by Rev. David King, LL.D. (2nd. edition, - enlarged and revised): *The Bible and Modern Thought*, by Rev. T. R. Birks, M.A.: *Neology Not True*, by Rev. Charles Herbert, M.A. (2nd edition): *Daniel the Prophet*, Rev. E. B. Pusey, D. D., Regius Professor of Hebrew, Oxford: and Jameison, Fausset and Brown's *Commentary - Genesis*. There is also a valuable paper on the subject by Rev. A. I. McCaul, M.A., Lecturer in Hebrew at King's College, London, published in *The Transactions of the Victoria Institute*, London, Vol. IX. On p. 150 of that volume, the Rev. A. I. McCaul states his belief that the Septuagint intended by its rendering that the earth was "invisible" because in darkness, and "unfurnished" because its life had been destroyed.

Smith, Professor T. Jollie, in a Paper in *The Transactions of the Victoria Institute*, Vol. LXXVIII, 1946, p. 29, wrote: "I think that verse 1 and verse 2 in Genesis 1 may be legitimately separated .... *Hayah* does generally mean 'became' or 'came to pass'.... Its use as a mere copula *is* most extraordinary".

Snaith, Norman H., *Notes on the Hebrew Text of Gen. I- VIII* (Epworth Press, London, 1947, p. 8 and 9), has the following against Gen. 1.2 and 3: "verse 2. הָיְתָה, 3 f. s. pl. qal. of הָיָה (verb 'to be', though more often it means 'to become').
"Verse 3: יְהִי, 3 m s. jussive qal shortened from 3 m s. imperfect qal (יִהְיֶה) of הָיָה (let there *come to be*, ie., *become*).
וַיְהִי - Pronounce wa-ye-hi (with -e very short for shema). "And there *came to be* (ie., there *became*). Thus he indicates the admissability of rendering הָיָה as "became" or some equivalent in English.

Sauer, Erich, *Dawn of World Redemption* (Revell, New York, 1953) on p. 35 says: "About 1000 A.D. Edgar of England espoused (the interpretation). In the 17th century it was especially emphasized by Jacob Boehme, the mystic....

"Many German upholders of this teaching.... as for instance the Professor of Geology Freiherr von Heune (Tubingen);.... from the Catholic point of view there are Cardinal Wiseman and the philosopher Freiderich von Schlegel".

Ramm, Bernard, in his *Christian View of Science and Scripture* (Eerdman's, Grand Rapids, 1954, p. 196) has a footnote in which he gives the following information: "Dr. Anton Pearson sets forth the history of the gap interpretation as follows: 'It was first broached in modern times by Episcopius (1583-1643), and received its first scientific treatment by J. G. Rosenmuller (1736-1815) in his *Antiquissima Telluris Historica* (1776). It was also used by theosophic writers in connection with notions suggested by Bohme, e.g. F. von Meyer and Baumgarten. It was picked up by such theologians as Buckland, Chalmers, J. P. Smith and Murphy. (*An Exegetical Study of Gen. 1.1-3*, Bethel Seminary Quarterly, 11.14 - 33, November, 1953).

"This theory was also defended by J. H. Kurtz, *Bible and Astron-*

omy, (3rd. German edition, 1857) and in the footnote of p.236 it is traced from Edgar, King of England in the tenth century, to modern scholars as Reichel, Stier, G. H. von Schubert, Knieival, Dreschler, Rudleback, Guericke, Baumgarten and Wagner".

Other men listed include Adam Sedgewick, *Discourses on the Studies of the Universe*, Cambridge, President of the Geological Society (England); and Pratt, *Scripture and Science Not at Variance*.

* * *

APPENDIX II

(Reference: p.39)

The Classical Concept of Chaos.

According to the Greek poet Hesiod, in his *Theogony* (Bk. 116, chap. 123) written somewhere around 775 BC., there was at the very beginning only a yawning unfathomable abyss, an infinitude of empty space which was the womb out of which the Universe came into existence. This empty space was referred to as "The Chaos". Chaos existed before all else, before the gods came into being, before the material Universe was created, and therefore before the earth itself was formed.

The conception of Chaos as the confused mass out of which in the very beginning the separate forms of material things arose, is not in view. This concept belongs to a much later period.

In his *Metamorphoses* (I: 7), the Roman poet and historian Ovid equates Chaos with the crude, shapeless mass into which the Architect of the World introduced order and harmony, thereby creating the Cosmos. But the original Greek concept had placed Chaos before even the gods themselves, and it had at that time no material substance in it to be organized. Ovid completed his *Metamorphoses* somewhere around 10 AD., or nearly eight centuries later. If it is remembered that the Septuagint Version of the Book of Genesis was written about 120 BC., it will be seen that the concept of Chaos was probably being re-interpreted, meaning either the first empty space which preceded all things OR the first state of unorganized matter. As far as I know, there is no way of being certain which it was.

However, the Septuagint was undoubtedly written with Greek readers in mind, and probably to most Greeks the concept of Chaos was still the traditional one, a vast emptiness with matter not merely yet unformed but not even in existence as a material substance at all. To the Hebrew scholars in Alexandria who prepared the Septuagint Version, such could hardly be taken as the meaning of Gen. 1.2 since the heaven *and* the earth were already in existence created by God, as Gen. 1.1 clearly states. Moreover, the very idea involved in the Hebrew word *bara* makes it very unlikely that they had in mind "an infinitude of empty space" such as the Greek concept of Chaos signifies, because this Hebrew word basically means "to smooth off" or "to polish", a meaning which implies already existing material. Young, in his *Analytical Concordance*, suggests the meaning of the word on the basis of biblical usage as being "to cut" or "carve", both of which terms can only be applied to something which already exists in substantial form. "Creation", to the Hebrew mind, implies something more substantial than an empty space.

It is popularly said that the word means "to create out of nothing". This concept is not actually inherent in the Hebrew word *bara*, or perhaps one should say rather, that it is not *necessarily* inherent. The proof of this is found first in the fact that Adam was created out of the dust of the ground, and not out of nothing: and the word itself is employed elsewhere in Scripture of human activity. See, for example: Josh. 17.15 and 18 where it is used of "cutting down" trees, in Ezek. 23.47, of "dispatching" people, ie., by slaughtering them; in Ezek. 21.19, of "cutting out" in the sense of choosing, much as the ranch hand "cuts out" from the herd certain cattle for a special purpose. In I Sam. 2.29 it is used in the sense of "carving out" for oneself the choicest cuts of meat from the sacrifices being offered to God, a nice illustration of how the true sense of the word illustrates a text which even the Jerusalem Bible feels is obscure. It is only obscure so long as one attributes to the Hebrew word *bara* the meaning of creating as its fundamental meaning. But clearly this is not its fundamental meaning.

And while we are on this subject, it may be worth observing that, contrary to a statement which has been mis-applied to the biblical use of this word times without number to the effect that the word is only used of divine activity, it is quite evident that this is not the case. It *is*, however, only found applied to divine activity in the *light* or *qal* form, a form which signifies the most effortless kind of activity. That Creation was of such a nature to God is nicely brought out in three Psalms, where we are told that creation was the work of God's fingers (Psa. 8.3), punishment the work of His hands (Psa. 39.10), and salvation the work of His arm (Psa. 77.15) - each involving, as it were, a larger part of His total energies.

* * *

APPENDIX III

(Reference: p.41)

Gen. 1.2 According to Various Versions.

In the beginning God created the heaven and the earth.

And the earth was without form and void; and darkness was upon the face of the deep. And the Spirit of God moved upon the face of the waters.

King James Version.

In the beginning God created the heavens and the earth. But the earth was empty and void, and darkness was over the face of the abyss.

Martin Luther.

When God in the beginning formed the heaven and the earth, (then) the earth was waste and void, etc.

Peter von Bohlem.

In the beginning God created the heaven and the earth. But (then) the earth became waste, etc.

August Dillman.

In the beginning God created the heavens and the earth. And the earth was waste and void and darkness was upon the face of the deep.

Revised Version.

In the beginning God created the heavens and the earth. The earth was without form and void and darkness was upon the face of the deep.

Revised Standard Version.

In the beginning of God's preparing the heavens and the earth, the earth hath existed waste and void, and darkness is on the face of the deep and the Spirit of God fluttering on the face of the waters.

Robert Young.

When God began to create the heavens and the earth, the earth was a desolate waste with darkness covering the abyss and a tempestuous wind raging over the surface of the waters.

J.M.P. Smith and E.J. Goodspeed.

In the beginning God created the heavens and the earth. The earth was unformed and chaotic, and darkness lay upon the face of the deep.

Berkeley.

In the beginning God created the heavens and the earth. And now, as far as the earth was concerned, it was waste and void, and darkness was upon the face of the deep.

H. C. Leupold.

When God set about to create heaven and earth, the world being then a formless waste, with darkness over the seas and only an awesome wind sweeping over the water....

E. A. Speiser.

In the beginning God created the heavens and the earth. Now the earth was a formless void, there was darkness over the deep and God's spirit hovered over the water.

Jerusalem Bible.

At the beginning of the creation of the heavens and the earth, the earth it was without form or life, and darkness was upon the face of the deep.

U. Cassuto.

In the beginning of creation, when God made heaven and earth, the earth was without form and void, and darkness was over the face of the abyss and a mighty wind swept over the surface of the waters.

New English Bible.

Au commencement Dieu crea le ciel et la terre. La terre etait informe et vide; les tenebres couvraient l'abime.....

Crampon.

At the beginning God created the heaven and the earth. The earth was unformed and empty; clouds covered the abyss....

In principio erat inanis et vacua, et tenebrae erant super faciem abssi....

Latin Vulgate.

In the beginning, God created the heaven and the earth. But the earth was unsightly and unfurnished, and darkness was over the deep....

Septuagint, (Bagster Edition).

These renderings point up several problems. There is a question as to the precise meaning of the first word (B'reshith, בְּרֵשִׁית) which is not actually "in *the* beginning.... "but "In (the) beginning....", the definite article being absent in the original. Various attempts have been made to render this without the definite article by circumlocution, as will be noted.

A second problem is the exact relationship between the first and second verses. This has been circumvented by various means as the translations show, in some cases using a disjunctive, or a connective "then", or ignoring the connective entirely.

* * *

APPENDIX IV
(Reference: p.45)

The Use of *Hayah* in Genesis, Joshua, Job, two Psalms, and Zechariah.

In order to examine the evidence *in situ* as it were, a study was made of the context of all occurrences of the verb "to be" which are to be found in the English of the Authorized Version of the Old Testament in the following books: Genesis, Joshua, Job, two Psalms, and Zechariah. Genesis was chosen for obvious reasons; Joshua, because it represented a historical book of a later period; the book of Job, because of its rather unique dramatic form; Zechariah, a minor prophet, because it provided a sample of prophetic literature towards the end of Old Testament times; and two Psalms because they were representative of Hebrew poetry.

The information thus derived is set forth in a more or less tabular form for each book as a separate entity, and is then summarized as a whole. What emerges is that a great deal of what has been commonly assumed regarding the use and the meanings of the Hebrew verb הָיָה has been somewhat imprecise - even when discussed by the very best authorities, such as S. R. Driver. This, in turn, has been repeated by secondary authorities ("quoters" and "quoters of quotes") with even less precision! The end result is that the original authorities have been credited at times with views on the subject which, though in a sense they could be considered as logical extensions of their stated views, are now sufficiently inaccurate that even the originators would probably not have approved of them. It is hoped that although the kind of information presented in this Appendix is dry and uninspiring, it will nevertheless contribute something towards a re-statement of the whole matter so that those who are concerned with the issue may be better guided by at least a knowledge of what is clearly *not* true.

In this study, all occurrences of the verb "to be" in any of its various forms in English (*be, am, are, was, will be*, etc.) were examined, whether represented in the original Hebrew by some form of the verb (and therefore set in bold type in the Authorized Version), or merely inserted by the translators to complete the English sentence structure (and therefore set in italics). Thus bold face type as well as italics are included in the total count, each sub-total being properly identified as to its category.

The following is what was observed. In the whole of Genesis, the verb "to be" appears 832 times according to my count. Of these, it is inserted by the translators, where so required in English though not represented in the original Hebrew, a total of 626 cases. It is found set in bold type, indicating the presence of הָיָה in the original, in 206 cases. From this one may see that the simple copulative sense of *am, is, were, shall be*, etc., is not in the majority of cases represented in the Hebrew whether the tense is past, present, or future. The verb הָיָה was felt to be necessary in only 25% of the contexts (206 out of a total of 832) where English seems to demand it. This might be presumptive evidence that the verb is *as a rule* employed in a Hebrew sentence only when the meaning is something more than merely copulative.

Most authorities today admit this but assert at the same time that the general rule applies only in cases where the tense is present. When the tense is past or future, it is usually held that the verb is required even where the usage is copulative. For this reason, it is agreed that in Gen. 1.2 the verb הָיְתָה had to be employed because the tense was past, and that the correct rendering is therefore the simple "was".

The basis of this argument seems logical enough. Unless the verb is expressed in Hebrew one cannot distinguish between such statements as "the man was good", "the man is good", and "the man will be good", since all three would appear in Hebrew without distinction simply as "the man - good" (הָאִשׁ תוֹב) with no further guidance to the reader as to whether the situation was past, present, or future.

But in point of fact, Hebrew writers do not seem to have felt any such need to be more explicit since of the total number of cases where the verb is unexpressed, 626 in all, some 184 cases or 30% clearly apply to a past or future situation. Of this number, only 15 are future.

Consider, then, these 15 future cases in which the verb is unexpressed. The number is surprisingly small when compared with the number of references to past situations, but this is really to be expected. Future events are much more likely to be looked forward to as involving a change from present circumstance and since Hebrew writers seem to have consistently employed the verb הָיָה whenever a change of circumstance or of status is involved, it would be a much less common thing to run across a future that did NOT require the verb to be expressed. It is obvious that in such as sentence as, "We are poor but we shall be rich", a change is indicated which would require that the verb normally be expressed: but if the sentence happened to read, "We are poor and always will be poor", signifying no change in the present situation, the verb would not normally be expressed. Such a situation as this would then perhaps best be translated by the compound phrase, "We shall *continue to be* poor". Life being as it is, most future circumstances are hopefully viewed as a change from the present rather than a continuance of it; and indeed most future references *are* to a change. This fact is reflected in Genesis where, out of a total of 88 references to the future in the English of the Authorized Version, the original expresses the verb (to indicate such a change) in 73 or three-quarters of them. And of the other quarter, the fifteen already referred to, the majority also indicate a change, in spite of the omission of the verb. This appears to be a contradiction of the general rule, but an examination of them shows that there is another qualifying factor in the application of the rule which is important and logical. These 15 occurrences are as follows: Gen. 3.16; 4.7; 6.15; 16.12; 17.15; 29.15; 43.23; 41.31; 46.6; and 49.8, 10, 12, 13 (twice) and 20.

The passage in Gen. 46.6 is clearly one involving no change - past, present, and future all being bleakly uniform: "For these two years the failure *has been* in the land: and yet *there are* five years in which there *shall be* neither ploughing nor harvest". All the others involve a prospective change in one form or another in spite of the absence of the verb. But the reason for the absence of הָיָה where it would otherwise be expected is really clear enough. Each situation is self-explanatory because of an associated sentence or clause which enables one to see unequivocally what the writer has in mind. The structure of the closely linked sentences is such that one cannot read the text at all without being made positively aware that a change is in view. This awareness stems from the existence of either contrast or repetition in sentence structure. Contrast is self-evident in Gen. 17.15 where Abraham is told, "Thou shalt not call her name Sarai but Sarah *shall be* her name". Repetition is evident in such a passage as Gen. 16.12 where the record reads, "He will become a wild man and his hand *shall be* against every man". So unnecessary is the verb in the second clause that the meaning would (even in English) be perfectly obvious if it were omitted and read merely as, "He will become a wild man with his hand against every one". A change of circumstance or metaphor is involved in most of these 15 passages, but the change is made abundantly clear by the very structure of the sentence and no special device is needed to insure the reader's understanding.

An excellent example of the presence and absence of the verb הָיָה as appropriate to the requirement of the writer's meaning may be found in Gen. 34.15: "If ye will become as we *are*....", which in the original is: אִם תִּהְיוּ כָמֹנוּ . The first verb proposes a change and must therefore be expressed: the second is a static situation (ie., strictly copulative) and is therefore unexpressed in Hebrew.

The reason for labouring the point is that we so continuously and so unconsciously employ similar sentence structures with subtle yet important distinctive meanings that we are not in the habit of analyzing them. Only by insisting on attention to them can one gain a hearing at all! And as soon as one has convinced the reader that there is a real distinction, one at once has to account for apparent exceptions! After all, the employment or the omission of the verb הָיָה is merely a literary device to help the *reader* - not an austere law threatening the writer with some penalty (other than being misunderstood!) if he fails to obey it. If the meaning which is served by the literary device has been made quite clear in some other way or by something already said, there is obviously no need to adopt the device and slavishly insist on expressing the verb. It is in order to bring out this point that I have entered into this uninspiring but rather necessary excursus. I am keenly aware that a critic may otherwise accuse me of being superficial by the very simple expedient of pointing to exceptions without telling his readers how they might be more exceptional in appearance than in fact. So I am anxious to avoid being superficial - even if my conclusions should ultimately turn out to be quite wrong. The prime object is to elucidate the issue, an issue that is complex and has been confused by inadequate appraisal of the evidence.

Let me therefore recapitulate by stating the case thus, as I see the evidence: When there is no change in view the verb is never required - whether in the past tense, the present tense, or the future. Where a change is involved, it is required unless the fact of the altered circumstance has already been made abundantly self-evident by some other means. Thus: no change no verb. Some change - some form of the verb expressed, or the change is clearly indicated to the reader by some other means. Where the verb is expressed in the past or future tense, a change is almost certainly in view. The absence of the verb may or may not in itself tell the whole story but the presence of the verb (unless it has one of its rather special meanings) always indicates that a change has occurred, or is occurring, or will occur in the situation in the future. The verb הָיָה is, in such a case, best rendered into

English by some such word as *became* or *had become* (for the past), *becomes* or *is becoming* (for the present), and *will become* (for the future). The word "become" is not always the best English word to use but the meaning of it seems most closely to represent the original. Such a phrase as, "it came to be" (which is, after all, merely an alternative of "it be-came"), is familiar and acceptable; as is, "it shall come to pass" (which, again, is merely an alternative for "it shall come to be" or, more simply, "it shall be-come"). I believe that the vast majority of occurrences of the verb הָיָה when employed in its more basic meaning can sensibly be rendered by some equivalent of the English word "become". In the future tense this fact can readily be verified by reference to its 73 occurrences, many of which are listed in Appendix V. In the present tense, there are but 3 occurrences in Genesis, according to my count, namely, Gen. 32.10, amd 42.31, 36. In the first, "became" is quite appropriate: "Now I am become two bands". In the second, the meaning is less precise: the Authorized Version reads, "We are no spies", a statement which may mean, "We have not come as spies", since - were it merely copulative - it would (by almost universal agreement) not require the expression of the verb, least of all since it is in the present tense. The third case (verse 36) is clear enough since the speaker is complaining of a change in his fortunes because, suddenly, "all things have come to be" against him. The omission of the verb would have conveyed the meaning that things had *always* been against him.

In Genesis, the verb appears 60 times in the past or future tense in the well known English rendering, "It came to pass" or "it shall come to pass", both of which clearly describe a new situation or - to use a modern term, a "happening". Since both phrases could be equally well served by substituting the word "be" for "pass", they would quite appropriately be read as, "it came to be that...." or "it shall come to be that....", and the word "be-came" or "be-come" therefore once more appears as a proper rendering of the verb הָיָה. As already noted, in 17 passages in the Authorized Version of Genesis the verb is in fact translated "become" or "became".

Besides these, there are some 63 passages in Genesis in which the verb is expressed, appearing in the Authorized Version in the form "was" or "were". These occurrences can all be rendered, and indeed should be rendered (to be more precise), by some English verbal phrase which is more than a mere copulative. In many cases it is best rendered "became" or "had become" and such a rendering does more justice to the sense of the original. But there are a number of interesting and rather special meanings of the verb הָיָה which are curious in that they are strangely encompassed by some English phrase employing the word "come". This strikes me as a noteworthy circumstance. The following passages include some chosen quite randomly from Joshua, a book which - as I have stated previously - was also analyzed for the purposes of this chapter.

In Josh. 15.4,7,11; 16.3,8; and 18.12 (twice), 14, and 19, the allotted territories of the various tribes are being defined. The verb הָיָה is used when the boundaries are stated. The English renderings are varied but all mean "reached to" or "terminated at". The verb could have been rendered "came to", just as we may say "my property comes to here", indicating with a marker where the line actually falls. In Genesis the phrase, "and it *came* to pass", belongs in this class, of course. It is found throughout Genesis 1 in verses 7, 9, 11, 15, 24, and 30, in all of which the meaning is clearly "and it became so". A beautiful illustration of this is to be found in Psa.33.9 where the Hebrew reads: כִּי הוּא אָמַר וַיֶּהִי which in the Authorized Version is rendered, "For He spake and it was *done*", but actually should read, " "For He spake and it *became*", ie., "came to be". The word "done" is quite properly printed in italics in the English translation since it is not represented in the Hebrew, but it was felt necessary to complete the sense. Such would be the case if one renders וַיְהִי as "and it *was*". But the word "done" proves unnecessary when the sentence is correctly rendered, a circumstance which confirms the non-copulative meaning of the verb הָיָה. Evidently the Septuagint translators did not make the mistake that the English translators did, for they rendered it thus: ὅτι αὐτος εἰπε και ἐγενήθησαν ie., "For He spoke, and it became".

When Lot's wife *became* a pillar of salt, we have a third class. A fourth class includes statements of simple arithmetic, as in Josh. 21.40, "So all the cities.... of the Levites were (ie., came to).... 12 cities".

Thus we have "came to", ie., reached; "came to pass", ie., transpired; "be-came", ie., turned into; "came to", ie., added up to; and "came", ie., arrived (Job 1.13 and 2.1). I am not by these remarks seeking to prove any point in particular but merely trying to show how the English word "came" *can* be played upon so as to mean some surprisingly different things! And the fact is that the Hebrew word הָיָה is remarkably similar in many respects to the extension of the English word "come", as shown in Appendix VI.

In summary, a future situation in which no change is in view, a future which is merely a guarantee of the continuance of the present, does not require the verb הָיָה to be expressed: nor does the simple English copulative "to be" in any of its present tense forms require the verb to be expressed either. Similarly, a past which is viewed as a static situation, a past which "always was" or "was at the time", a past which is merely referred to by the writer as a point of reference or as a starting point for his narrative, a past which though it no longer holds true did not at the time involve some altered situation, such a past is expressed without the use of any part of the verb הָיָה. A man whose name (*was*) so-and-so (Gen.10.25, etc.), a divinely appointed situation which (*was*) good (Gen.1.10, 21, etc.), one city which (*was*) greater than another (Josh.10.2), a place that (*was*) wicked, a man who (*was*) such-and-such an age,.... all these involve no implied change in circumstance leading up to the situation described. They are simple statements of fact at the time. The verb הָיָה is uniformly omitted.

But if the man *became* of such-and-such an age before God dealt with him in some special way, then the situation is viewed quite differently and the verb הָיָה must normally be expressed unless the eventuality can be otherwise indicated to the reader. Thus, for example, the verb is required in such a sentence as, "And when Abram became 90 years old", then the Lord appeared to him and told him that his name was now to be changed because he was to become a father of many nations (Gen.17.1-4). Or, as another example, "(Jabal) became the father of such as dwell in tents... and his brother's name (*was*) Jubal" (Gen.4.20, 21). The first part of the sentence involves a change for he was not a father at all until he reached maturity, so the verb הָיָה being expressed in the original is more precisely rendered into English as "became"; but the second part of the sentence does not involve any change, being merely an observation of a fact - and the verb הָיָה is accordingly unexpressed in the original.

Undoubtedly, it will be possible to find real or apparent exceptions here and there, but certainly the normal practice is *not* to express the verb הָיָה at all where the meaning is simply copulative, whether in the past, present, or future tense. And, equally, the introduction of the verb הָיָה means either that a change has taken place leading to the then situation, or is taking place, or will take place, or that the verb is being used by the writer (usually in conjunction with some qualifying preposition such as *in*, *at*, *with*, *within*, etc.) to give a special sense. In no such case is it merely copulative. When expressed, it has such meanings as "became" (Gen.19.26); "accompanied" (Josh. 1.5); "added up to (totalled)" (Josh. 21.40); "existed" (Josh. 17.1,2, etc.); "happened" (for a beautiful illustration, see Gen. 41.13, "And it came to pass as he interpreted to us, so it happened": וַיְהִי.....כֵּן הָיָה); "reached to" or "from" (Josh. 18.12 has both usages); "went about daily" (ie., actively, not statically - as in Gen. 2.25); "belong to" (Josh. 14.9; 17.18; and Job 42.12); or even "lay within" (as in Josh. 19.1). In Gen. 39.2 three of these meanings appear in one verse! Thus the text reads, "It came to pass..... he became a prosperous man.... he lived daily in his master's house". Other special meanings seem often to involve the English word "fall", as in the phrase, "It befell" or "It fell out that". This, too, is striking, for in French also there is some evidence of the same kind of association of ideas where, for example, the word *devenir* may mean both "to befall" or "happen" as well as "to become", the *venir* in the word, of course, being the English "come". As already noted, some scholars believe that the Hebrew הָיָה is related to a more primitive root meaning "to fall".

As a corollary of the statement made earlier to the effect that the verb הָיָה implies really an active situation rather than a static one, it is also to be observed that the word "became" should not be substituted for the English "was" where the verb הָיָה is unexpressed in the original. To make this substitution conveys a meaning to the text which is either clearly not the writer's intention; or it simply makes nonsense. Thus where Genesis 1 has the recurrent phrase, "and it *was* good", one cannot sensibly substitute *became* for *was* and read it as "and it became good". What God creates or what He instantly commands into being does not as a process "become" good. It *is* good. It may, of course, *become* something, viewed as an event in such a recurrent phrase as, "and it was so". But here the verb is always expressed in the original - and with perfect propriety. But once in being, the "goodness" of the thing so created is inherent: it is thereafter copulatively "good". The difference in the original of these two often repeated phrases in Genesis 1 is brought out by the Authorized Version practice of using bold face or italics as the original demands. And as I have already observed, for this very reason this Version has much to commend it to the English reader over other versions. Only upon one or two occasions does the Authorized Version seem to make a mistake in its use of type. One such instance is Gen. 40.16 which should have read, "The interpretation (was) good", rather than, "was good", since the original omits the verb. It is reasonable to conclude, therefore, from these facts, first of all, that the idea of "becoming" *must* be expressed - unlike the mere copula which will not be: and secondly, that there is no other way in which it *can* be expressed in Hebrew.

Let us consider briefly the evidence on these points to be derived from a study of the text of Joshua, Job, Psa. 22 and 68, and Zechariah.

Joshua.

A comparison of Joshua with Genesis presents essentially the same kind of picture in the matter of proportional usage and specialized meanings. Genesis is, of course, longer than Joshua (1445 verses as against 658) and thus the grand totals differ accordingly, but the frequency is of the same order.

In the English of the Authorized Version, the verb "to be" occurs 269 times in all. Of these, 182 are not represented by any verb in the original. In 87 cases, the verb הָיָה appears in the Hebrew, these being of course set in bold type in the English. Of these, 38 have been or should (in the interests of consistency) have been rendered, "it came to pass" or "it shall come to pass" (both of which involve a process of becoming), and 13 might very properly have been rendered "come to be", "become", "became", "had become", or "will become" [namely, Josh. 3.4 (come to be); 4.6,7; 9.5 (pluperfect); 14.4,9 (future); 15.1; 17.8 (future); 20.3; 23.13; 23.27 (twice); and 24.32]. The balance have specialized meanings, such as "being with" in the sense of accompanying (Josh. 1.17; 3.7; etc.), or "added up to" (as in Josh. 21.40), or "were situated in" (as in Josh. 8.22; 18.14; 19.1,14; etc.), or "reached from" (as in Josh. 13.16) or "reached to" (Josh. 13.23). None of these are copulative usages. Nor are the several remaining examples copulative, for in these a future event is described which differs from the then present circumstance; as for example in Josh. 20.6: "until he stand before the congregation for judgment, and until the death of the high priest that shall be in those days". To my knowledge, only one possible exception is observable in which the verb הָיָה has the appearance of having been used unnecessarily in a sense, and this is Josh. 10.14 which reads, "And there was no day like that, before it or after it". Perhaps even this is not really exceptional since, in a sense, the use is existential.

Certainly, whatever else may be said for the text of Joshua, it does not lend support to the idea that the verb הָיָה has normally a copulative sense of "to be".

Job.

The Book of Job is slightly different in an interesting way that I think must be related to the dramatic form of the narrative. It is interesting because the historic present is more frequently used and because in certain circumstances when the verb הָיָה would normally have been employed, it has actually been omitted. The object, by shortening the sentence, is perhaps to heighten the sense of urgency.

In the Book of Job according to the Authorized Version, a total of 270 occurrences of some part of the verb "to be" will be found, with only 26 (or 10% of them) set in bold type indicating the verb הָיָה in the original. The omissions which therefore number 244 are represented in the English text by such words as *are, was, will be*, etc. The overwhelming majority of these are simply copulative. There are, as already stated, a few special cases where the omission is probably for dramatic effect. These are to be found occurring in such verbal phrases as "(*were*) eating" (Job 1.13, 18), "(*was*) yet speaking (Job 1.16, 17, 18). This is a not uncommon device in Hebrew literature, the participle of the verb (here "eating" and "speaking") being used sometimes with הָיָה * and sometimes without it, instead of the simple imperfect normal to an English sentence. It is also apparent that the writer has avoided to a large extent the use of the past tense, for of all the italicized verbal forms of "to be" which occur in the Authorized Version text of Job, only 8% are past compared with 27% in the text of Genesis. It seems as though, in the mind of the translators at least if not in the mind of the original writer, the use of the "historic present" was felt to be more appropriate to the narrative form employed.

The very first verse is a good illustration of three different meanings attached to the sense of "being". The text reads, "There was a man.... whose name (*was*) Job.... and it happens that that man was perfect...." The first "was" clearly means "lived", the verb being used in its existential sense; the second is the simple copulative and is therefore omitted in Hebrew; and the third is used in the historic sense, "and it *came* to pass...." Here, then, we find a strictly copulative sentence set forth in a way which by the omission of the verb הָיָה makes clear that the writer's meaning is quite distinct from that of the two other occurrences of the verb in the same passage.

The existential use of הָיָה is to be observed in such a passage as Job 16.12: "I lived at ease", which has been rendered in the Author-

* *For example, see: Gen. 4.17; 37.2; Jud. 16.21; I Sam. 2.11; and many others. And see further, Appendix II.*

ized Version as, "I was at ease". The sense of "becoming" is to be observed in such a passage as Job 17.6 which in the Scofield edition of the Authorized Version reads: "He hath made me also a by-word of the people; and I was (אֶהְיֶה) as one before whom men spit". It seems to me that the speaker is trying to indicate that a drastic change in his situation has now taken place with respect to his previous status in the community. And therefore, in the interest of greater precision, I suggest that the verb should be rendered "I am *become* as one who.....", though admittedly by making this change I am robbing my opponents of an example (if they should choose to use it) of a supposed copulative occurrence of the verb הָיָה. However, since the writer of Job has not once in the other 240 or so instances of a purely copulative situation employed any part of the verb הָיָה, we have good reason to suppose that he employed it here because he intended the meaning to be something other than a mere copula.

The dramatic style of the writer is revealed by the not infrequent omission of the verb הָיָה in connection with various prepositions (בְּ , etc.) where normally one would expect it. Such a case is Job 29.5 where the verb is omitted, though in the English it is followed by "with": "When the Almighty (was) yet with me". This may be contrasted with the more normal (ie., prosaic) construction indicated for the same phrase in Josh. 1.5, 17 (twice); 2.19; 3.7 (twice); 6.27; and 7.12. Here, too, we seem to have the shortened sentence structure.

Besides Job 17.6 already referred to, there are a number of other occurrences where the text might better have been rendered using the verbal form "became", "become", etc., though the Authorized Version has not done so. In all of these, needless to say, the verb הָיָה appears in the original. I have in mind such passages as the following, all of which indicate a real change in the situation:

10.19:	"I should have become as though I had not been" (ie., never existed).
11.17:	"Thou shalt become as the morning".
12.4:	"I am become as one mocked by his neighbour".
16.8:	"Wrinkles - which become a witness against me".
24.14:	"and in the night becomes a thief".
30.9:	"And now I have become their song, yea, I have become their by-word".
30.29:	"I have become a brother to jackals".

Essentially the same picture emerges from Job as from Joshua and Genesis in the matter of grammar and syntax except for the already noted much less frequent use of the past tense of the verb הָיָה which is replaced by a historic present for effect. In Genesis the verb appears 130 times in the past tense, in Job only 17 times: in Genesis all occurrences of הָיָה (regardless of tense) total 206 as compared with only 26 in Job. Thus the style of Job would certainly seem to have been deliberately compressed - almost staccato at times.

Psalms.

Two Psalms were chosen, 22 and 68, solely on account of their convenient length, and for statistical analysis they have been treated as one. Perhaps in the very nature of the case, the language of the Psalms seems to be written very much in the present tense and references to the past are comparatively few. In fact, the Hebrew verb is not used once in a past or a future reference at all in either of these Psalms. In the *English* there are 27 occurrences where some part of the verb "to be" is supplied by the translators, of which 22 are in the present tense. Since these are undoubtedly correctly supplied as to tense, and since the data for all the Psalms combined indicates the same general pattern (31 in italics in past tense, 524 in present tense, and 34 in future tense), there is no doubt that this is a feature of Hebrew psalmody. Which is to say, that the verb הָיָה is not felt to be necessary in the vast majority of cases, actually appearing only as one simple case in these two Psalms, and in this one instance (Psa. 22.19) with what is probably the existential meaning. Since there are in all some 31 references to the past and 34 to the future which have not demanded the introduction of the verb הָיָה in the original, the Psalms as a whole would appear to confirm the general rule that הָיָה is not required when it functions as a simple copula, regardless of the tense.

Zechariah.

In Zechariah, there is a significant difference from the Psalms, for the whole bent of the text is towards the future and out of a total of 42 occurences of the verb הָיָה , 37 or 88% are references to the future, 4 are references to the past and only 1 is a reference to the present. It seems likely that this general pattern is true of most of the *prophetic* books or passages of Scripture,in view of the fact that the words look forward to a situation yet to come which will be different from things as they now are. This kind of change in

Hebrew literature, where the verb "to be" is involved, appears regularly to require the use of the verb הָיָה , and in a very large number of cases the English has rendered the sentence, "and it shall come to pass...." As already indicated, this could quite as properly be written, "It shall come to be....", ie., "It shall be-come..."*

The Table on page 146 is included merely to summarize the data reported upon in this Section. It should be underscored that these numbers represent my own counting, a count usually undertaken during evenings after a full day's work and therefore not pretending to be infallible though certainly not grossly in error. Where the totals do not tally (as in the case of Job's Italics total, for example), the reason is that there were a few occurrences of the verb "to be" in English which could not be classified among the others, being part of some verbal clause such as "were eating", etc. The percentage figures given represent the proportion of the appropriate total which each category of entries has within each book. The figures for Psalm 22 and 68 have been combined.

Percentages are calculated to the nearest whole percent.

In Genesis, Joshua, and Zechariah, the verb is omitted from twice to three times as frequently as it is employed (206/626: 87/182: and 42/74). In Job the verb is omitted approximately ten times as often as it is employed, and in the Psalms, twenty-seven times as often. It is clear that the copulative use in its simple form is exceedingly rare compared with what the English sentence demands.

---

* *It is hard to say to what extent the Authorized Version has been responsible for determining the sense which we continue to attach to some words, but it may be worth noting that according to the Oxford English Dictionary (Vol. 1, p.715 b, published in 12 volumes by the Clarendon Press, 1933) under the article on the word BE: "(This verb) was in Old English a distinct verb.... meaning 'become', 'come to be', and thus serving as a future tense to* am *and* was, *By the beginning of the 13th c. the Infinitive and Participle, Imperative and Present Subjunctive of* am *and* was, *became successively obsolete, the corresponding parts of BE taking their place so that the whole verb* am *and* was *and* be *is now commonly called from its infinitive the verb 'to be'." In other words, even the verb "to be" once really meant "to become".*

Tabulation of the data from the Study of the Five Books noted.

Book	Italics				Bold face				Grand totals
	Past	Pres.	Fut.	Total	Past	Pres.	Fut.	Total	
Gen.	169=27%	442=70%	15=3%	626	130=63%	3=2%	73=35%	206	832
Josh.	72-40%	7=4%	7=4%	182	57=66%	5=5%	25=29%	87	269
Job	20=8%	15=85%	15=7%	244	17=65%	7=27%	2=8%	26	270
Psa. 22,68	3=1%	2=17%	2=17%	27	0	1=100%	0	1	28
Zech.	9=12%	15=21%	15=21%	74	4=10%	1=2%	37=88%	42	116

APPENDIX V

(Reference: p. 137)

Some Occurrences of the Use of Hayah in the Future Tense.

Gen. 1.29
2.24
3.5
4.12
4.14 (2x)
6.3
6.19
9.2
9.3
9.11
9.13
9.14
9.15
9.16
9.25
9.26
9.27
12.12
15.4
15.5
15.13
16.12 (2x)
17.5
17.8
17.13
17.16 (2x)
18.18
21.10
24.43
26.3

Gen. 27.39
27.40
28.14
28.20
28.21
28.22
30.32
31.8 (2x)
34.10
34.15
34.16
35.10
37.20 (2x)
41.27
41.36 (2x)
41.40 (2x)
44.9
44.10 (2x)
44.17
44.31
46.33
47.24
47.25
48.5
48.6
48.19 (4x)
48.21
49.17
49.26

* * *

APPENDIX VI

(Reference: p. 138)

The Idea of "Coming" in the Verb Hayah.

A propos of the observation that the verb הָיָה seems to be remarkably like the English word *come*, since it can be nicely rendered by phrases such as "came to pass", "came to be", and, of course, "be-came", the following passages will be of interest.

Gen. 15.1:	"after these things the word of the Lord *came* to Abraham in a vision".
I Sam. 15.10:	"The word of the Lord *came* to Samuel".
II Sam. 7.4:	"In the same night the word of the Lord *came* to Nathan while he was carrying out the command of the Lord".
I Ki. 18.1:	"the word of the Lord *came* to Elijah".
II Ki. 20.4:	"the word of the Lord *came* to (Isaiah)".
Isa. 38.4:	"then the word of the Lord *came* to Isaiah".
Jer. 36.1:	"this word *came* to Jeremiah".

It is interesting to observe that in French the word for *become* is de-venir. Moreover, in the same language, the English word *becoming* in the sense of being "suitable" or "well be-fitting" is con-venir.

* * *

APPENDIX VII

(Reference: p. 48)

The Use of Hayah in the Passive Voice.

The verb הָיָה which to our way of thinking is an active verb, in Hebrew appears in the *Niphal* or Passive voice also. The following references illustrate how this usage is found, in every case the verb being in the *Niphal*.

Deut.4.32:	"whether there *has been* (done) such a great thing..."
Jud.19.30:	"There *was* no such thing (done) nor seen..."
Jud.20.3:	"How *was* there (done) this wickedness?"
I Sam.25.6:	"Peace *be* upon..."
I Ki.1.27:	"*Has* this thing *been done* by my lord the king?"
I Ki.12.24:	"This thing from me *has been*", ie., has been done.
Neh.6.8:	"*There are* no such things (done) as thou sayest".
Prov.13.19:	"The desire that *has been* (satisfied) is sweet to my soul".
Isa.5.5:	"It *shall be* (given over) to being consumed".
Jer.48.19:	"Ask him that fleeth and her that escapeth, and say, What *is* (done)?"
Ezek.21.12:	"Cry and howl, son of man, for it *shall be* (done) upon my people".
Ezek.39.8:	"Behold.... it *is* (done), saith the Lord."
Micah 2.4:	"A doleful lament *has been* (made)".

* * *

APPENDIX VIII

(Reference: p. 49)

The Expression of "Continuation" of State or Action by a Compounded Use of Hayah.

This construction is used to indicate "continuous habit", "incipient action", or "the *continuation* of a state". It points up very clearly the sense in which the verb הָיָה is a verb of action - not merely of state, since even when it is used of a state it is given the rather special meaning of a deliberate continuation in that state.

In order to make the original verbal forms identifiable, the verb הָיָה is written in capitals and the following participle of the associated verb in italics. For example, when followed by a participle:

Gen. 4.17:	"Cain WAS (occupied) in *building*...."
Exod. 3.1:	"Moses WAS *shepherding* the flocks...."
Josh. 10.26:	"They WERE *hanging* upon the trees till evening".
I Sam. 2.11:	"The child WAS *ministering* unto the Lord".
I Sam. 18.9:	"Saul WAS *eyeing* David from that day forward".
I Ki. 5.1:	"For Hiram WAS always *loving* towards David".
I Ki. 13.24:	"His carcass WAS *lying* cast in the way".
I Ki. 22.35:	"The king WAS *propping himself up* in his chariot".
Ezra 4.4:	"The people of the land WERE *weakening*...."
Neh. 1.4:	"And I WAS *fasting*...."
Neh. 13.26:	"And he WAS indeed *being loved* of his God".

As we have noted in connection with the use of הָיָה in the Book of Job, the same basic construction is understood, but for dramatic effect the verb הָיָה is deliberately omitted. Thus in Job 1.16-18 the verb is missing at three places: (were) *speaking*, and (were) yet *speaking* (twice). See also:

Job 14.17: "(is) being sealed up"
Job 18.10: "(is) being laid"
Job 20.26: "(shall be) being hidden"
Job 36.8: "If they (are) being bound"

And followed by an infinitive:

Gen. 15.12: "and the sun WAS *about to go down*".
Josh. 2.5: "and the gate WAS *about to be shut*".
II Chron. 26.5: "And he WAS *about to be seeking* (ie., began to seek) God...."
Isa. 5.5: "It SHALL BE (ie., come to be) *eaten up*".

* * *

APPENDIX IX

(Reference: p. 51)

The Existential Sense of the Verb Hayah.

The existential sense might be argued here as an explanation for the introduction of the verb, making the sense to read, "And the earth existed chaotically". But the existential use requires not a simple predicate but a clause such as would be introduced by the preposition "in" or "as", as when Joseph lived (Authorized Version: "was") *in* his master's house (Gen. 39.2) or when we are told "that there lived (Authorized Version "was") a man *in* the land of Uz whose name (was) Job" (Job 1.1). In the purest existential sense the verb will have no predicate at all nor any other clause following. The paramount example is to be found in the title of the Almighty, the great "I am", the One Who always exists.

It might also be argued that Gen. 2.25 is a parallel of the use of the verb הָיָה in its existential sense ("They lived, naked....") and that here we do have a predicate in the presence of the word "naked". But this word is an *adjective*, not a noun like *tohu* (תֹהוּ) in Gen. 1.2. The sentence reads "They lived naked" not "were a nakedness".

It is true that a noun can upon occasion be used adverbially so that the translation of Isa. 45.18 has been rendered, "He created it not in vain", the words "in vain" being for the Hebrew *tohu* (תֹהוּ) which is therefore treated as an adverb just as it seems to be also in Isa. 45.19. The latter reads (correctly, I feel sure), "I said not unto the seed of Jacob, Seek ye Me IN VAIN...." Since *tohu* is here rendered as an adverb, why should it not also be read as an adverb in Gen. 1.2? Thus verse 2 is taken to read, "And the earth existed formlessly or chaotically". In which case the rendering might justly account for the introduction of הָיָה into the sentence on the grounds that this is a parallel to Gen. 2.25 which could then be rendered, "And they both existed (lived) nakedly and were not ashamed, etc.". In this case a noun (in verse 2) and an adjective (in verse 25) are similarly treated as adverbs and the verb הָיָה is allowed its existential meaning. By this method one might justify the traditional translation of Gen. 1.2.

That an adjective can be treated as an adverb is a well established fact in Hebrew, *though normally only in poetry*. Yet it is still to be noted that while *tohu* does appear elsewhere in probably at least one passage and possibly in two as an adverb, this cannot actually be said of the second descriptive term in Gen. 1.2, namely, *bohu* (בֹּהוּ) rendered "void". It is further to be admitted that the copulative sense of the verb "to be" might allow one to interpolate it before *bohu* so that the sentence would then read, "And the earth existed chaotically and (*was*) a void". This, however, requires some rather special manoeuvering. Yet such an alternative must be allowed as a possibility pending further investigation and we shall not progress towards the truth unless we test out *all* possibilities. It is not yet time to assert or deny either alternative dogmatically.

Although such a possibility must therefore be admitted, it must be underscored that the alternative can only be justified by a process of "special pleading" which is far less substantiated from Hebrew literature than the alternative we are proposing. And indeed, in the present state of my knowledge, it cannot actually be substantiated at all. Thus if it is once agreed, on the basis of the information brought to light in this volume, that the verb הָיָה is not used copulatively and that therefore the rendering *was* in Gen. 1.2 is not strictly correct so that it should be revised to read "became", the alternative requires no special pleading, for there is plenty of substantiating support from the rest of the Old Testament.

It has been customary to say that those who argue for the translation, "And the earth became a chaos", can only press their point by appealing to exceptional Hebrew usage. The fact is really quite otherwise as the evidence shows. And the case becomes even stronger when the unusual word order involved here is given due recognition.

* * *

APPENDIX X
(Reference: p. 52)

The Meaning of Hayah with Various Particles Following.

1. הָיָה followed by כְּ meaning "to become like " someone:

Gen. 3.5: "Ye shall become like God...."
Gen. 18.25: "that the righteous should become as the wicked".
I Sam. 17.36: "the Philistine shall become as one of them".
Isa. 24.2: "The people shall become like the priest, the servant shall become like his master, the maid shall become like her mistress, the buyer shall become like the seller, the lender shall become like the borrower, the taker of usury shall become like the giver of usury to him."
Hos. 4.9: "The people shall become like the priest".

2. הָיָה followed by עִם meaning "to go with" or "accompany", "support", "to be in fellowship with":

Gen. 26.3: "Stay in the land and I will be with thee...."
Gen. 48.21: "Behold I die but God will be with you...."
Josh. 1.5: "As I was with Moses, so I will be with you...."
Jud. 1.19: "And the Lord was with Judah".
I Sam. 18.12: "Saul was afraid of David, because the Lord was with him".
I Ki. 1.37: "As the Lord hath been with my lord, even so be he with Solomon".
II Chron. 17.3: "And the Lord was with Jehosophat".

3. הָיָה followed by לְ, meaning "to belong to":

Isa. 5.1: "A vineyard belonged to my beloved".
Gen. 30.30: For it was little which belonged to thee before I came".
Jud. 18.27: "and they took the priest which belonged to him".
I Sam. 9.2: "And he had a son whose name was Saul".
Deut. 5.7: "Thou shalt have no other gods before Me".

4. הָיָה followed by בְּ, meaning "to be among" or "classed with":

I Ki. 2.7: "Let them be (numbered) among those eating".
Prov. 22.26: "Be thou not (classed) as one of them".
Prov. 23.20: "Be not (numbered) among drunkards".
Amos 1.1: "Who was one of (numbered among) the herdsmen".

* * *

APPENDIX XI
(Reference: p. 52)

The Meanings of Hayah according to Various Lexicographers.

(1) Leo's Translation of Gesenius' Hebrew Lexicon:

in Kal form means:

1. "to be"
2. "to serve for"
3. "to be with", "party to", "consent to"
4. "to turn into"
5. "to happen", "to come to be"
6. "to succeed"

in Niphal form means:

1. "to cause to be done", "to be done"
2. "to become" in the sense of "to have been done"
3. "to have happened"
4. "to be undone" or "done in"

(2) Tregelles' Translation of Gesenius' Hebrew Lexicon:

in Kal form means:

1. "to be", ie., "to exist"
2. "to belong to"
3. "to be something", ie., "to serve as"
4. "to be about to", "to be going to"
5. "to be with" or "on the side of", "party to"
6. "to become" or "be made"
7. "to come to pass"
8. "to be turned into"
9. "to happen to"
10. "to become like" or "be made like"

in Niphal form means:

1. "to become", "be made into"
2. "to be done", "done with" (ie., past)

(3) Benjamin Davies' *Student's Hebrew Lexicon*:

in Kal form means:

1. "to be", whether meaning "to exist" or "to live", "be somewhere"
2. "to belong to"
3. "to be for something", "to serve as", or "turn out to be"
4. "to belong with", or "be of the party of"
5. "to be over" for protection
6. "to be appointed to"
7. "must needs be"
8. "to be about to"
9. "come into being", or "become"
10. "to behave like"
11. "to belong to"
12. "to come to pass", or "happen"

in Niphal form means:

1. "to be done" or "made"
2. "to become"
3. "to happen"

(4) Brown, Driver, and Briggs: *Hebrew and English Lexicon:*

Basic meaning: "to fall out", "come to pass", "become", etc.

in Kal form means:

1. "fall out", "happen"
2. "occur" , "take place", "come about", "come to pass"
3. "arise", "appear", "come"
4. "come upon" (of events)
5. "come upon" (of power)
6. "come upon" (ie., originate)
7. "turn out to be"
8. "become like"
9. "be constituted as"
10. "turn into"
11. "take the place of" (ie., "be for")
12. "come to belong to"
13. "exist", "be in existence"
14. "abide", "be with", "remain", "continue"
15. "be at" (ie., situated), "stand", "lie"

16. "amount to", "be equal to"
17. "accompany"
18. "to be in the company of"
19. with a participle = continuing state
20. "be about to" (ie., sun about to go down)
21. "to be"

in Niphal form means:

1. "to become"
2. "to be done"
3. "to be realized","finished", "gone"
4. "to be done" (ie., exhausted)

* * *

APPENDIX XII

(Reference: p. 53)

Meanings of Hayah Followed by Lamedh.

While it is *not* true that the verb הָיָה must be followed by לְ in order to establish the meaning "become", "became", etc., it *is* true that when the preposition לְ does accompany the verb it cannot mean anything else. But in the latter circumstance it has the sense of becoming in a rather special way.

If there is a general principle, it would seem to be this. When something *becomes* something else, there may be two kinds of conversion involved. (1) A thing may be so completely changed and become something so entirely different that it is no longer what it was before, a situation which would not normally require the *lamedh*. (2) A thing can be merely viewed as having become something different only in a manner of speaking as (a) when one individual becomes a multitude, (b) when there is a change in status, or (c) when a thing becomes something else *analogously*.

We have already dealt at some length with (1): namely, the use of *hayah* without *lamedh* following. On the other hand, in (2) the situation is rather different because the change, though real enough, *in a sense* involves no change at all. Thus one individual becomes many individuals, a woman becomes a wife, and a man becomes a stone of stumbling. In these examples each object remains fundamentally what it was before and yet each is changed. The individual remains even while he multiplies, the woman achieves a new status, and the man takes on a new significance. It is my contention that, although there are some exceptions undoubtedly, these last three kinds of *becoming* require that the preposition לְ follow the verb הָיָה . In a very great number of cases the sense is brought out rather nicely by rendering the *lamedh* by the words "as it were", though the English does not demand these words, the reader being left to surmise what is intended. For example, Abraham becomes a nation; or in the matter of a change of status, one of the commonest illustrations is in connection with marriage, a woman becomes a wife wherein although she is the same woman,her status has been changed. Or again, when a man becomes a stone which the builders reject, he does not strictly become a stone at all - but only analogously, as it were, a stone which the builders cannot, or will not, use.

As illustrations of (2) (a), we have:

Gen. 18.18	Abraham becoming a great nation.
Gen. 32.10	Jacob becoming two bands.
Isa. 60.22	A little one shall become a thousand.

As illustration of (2) (b), we have:

Gen. 20.12 Gen. 24.67 Ruth 2.13 I Sam. 25.42 II Sam. 11.27	most have reference to becoming a wife.
Deut. 27.9	a people who are not the Lord's becoming the Lord's people.
II Sam. 7.24	thc Lord to become Israel's God.

As illustration of (2) (c), we have:

Gen. 2.10	a single watershed out of Eden becomes four heads.
Gen. 2.24	a man and a woman are to become one flesh.
Deut. 28.37	a people becomes an astonishment.
II Ki. 21.14	a people becomes a prey and a spoil.
II Ki. 22.19	the inhabitants of a place become a desolation.
Psa. 69.22	a table becomes a snare.
Isa. 8.14	he shall become a stone of stumbling and a rock of offense.
Jer. 5.13	prophets shall become wind.
Jer. 50.37	men shall become as women.

..... all of which involve the sense of "as it were".

In the Hebrew Version of the New Testament, Jonah *becomes* a sign and accordingly here, too, הָיָה is followed by לְ (Lu. 11.30).

It will be understood that in *all* the above references הָיָה is followed by לְ. As already stated, there appear to be a few exceptions, but by and large the "rule" is a useful one and the majority of passages in which לְ is employed can be subsumed under one of these headings. In a few cases the rule seems to involve implications which might require some careful re-thinking. The rod becoming a serpent (Exod. 7.10), and the water becoming blood (Exod. 7.19), are cases in point, for according to my "rule" since the *lamedh* appears in the original the rod didn't *really* become a serpent, but the water really *did* become blood! Regarding the water, there is a wide consensus of agreement today that it became infested with micro-organisms which give it a thick red soupy appearance, making it *look* very much like blood. This still happens occasionally in different parts of the world with the consequent destruction of fishes in it. It can hardly be better described in a popular way than as "blood". If this is what actually happened, then we ought to find the appropriate לְ following. But such is not the case in Exod. 7.19 (twice) and 21, which would therefore be an exception challenging the proposed rule.

As to the rod becoming a serpent, it will be difficult for many people to surrender the conviction that it really did become a serpent, and not merely an appearance only: yet the magicians were able to do the same thing - perhaps by some process of suggestion. Nevertheless, Exod. 7.12 goes on to say that Aaron's "rod" ate up the "rods" of the Egyptians. This seems almost certainly to indicate that in both cases we are dealing with real serpents because if one assumes that Aaron's rod became a real serpent - with an appetite - it seems unlikely that he would be fool enough to eat up a bunch of rods which merely looked like serpents. One must therefore assume here that the rods did become real and not merely as-it-were serpents. In which case, we have another clear exception to the rule.

Nevertheless, in such matters, rules are established by general usage rather than by particular usage, and the great majority of cases fit nicely into the framework suggested. As already observed, Hebraists, like Driver, have underscored the great importance of not confusing the sense of *becoming* with the sense of *being*. Yet it is so easy to substitute the one for the other in English that we have difficulty in being persuaded that such a distinction can really exist or that it has any fundamental importance even if it does.

The translators of the Revised Standard Version of the Old Testament appear to have followed a rule that when הָיָה is accompanied by לְ the verb is to be rendered "became", etc. According to the Concordance of that Version, there are approximately 450 listed occurrences of the English word "become" or "became" in the Old Testament. Examination of these shows that about 80% of them include the associated לְ . To some, this will perhaps be powerful evidence that לְ is required in order to give the meaning of "become" to the verb הָיָה . Yet from all that has been said, it is clear that this is not the case, nor is the Revised Standard Version consistent, as such verses as Gen. 37.20; 39.2; Deut. 33.5; Josh. 9.21; I Sam. 14.15; 16.21; etc. etc., show.

What is argued here is that this is only one *class* of occurrences in which the sense of *becoming* is intended, not a real conversion but conversion only in a manner of speaking, and that the verb הָיָה standing alone *without* לְ bears the fundamental meaning of *becoming* in the simplest and most complete sense of the word as indicated in Appendix XVIII (page 171 f.).

* * *

APPENDIX XIII

(Reference: p. 55)

The Use of Hayah without the Lamedh Following.

There are 128 occurences of the verb הָיָה as "become" or "became" according to the Authorized Version, of which 39 are without the לְ following. There are numerous additions to this list if other English versions are consulted. The following 39 instances are to be observed in the Authorized Version alone.

Genesis	2.10	I Chronicles	18.2
	3.22		18.6
	19.26		18.13
	21.20	Psalms	69.8
	37.20		79.4
	48.19		83.10
Exodus	7.19		109.25
	8.17 (twice)	Isaiah	7.24
	9.10		29.11
	23.29	Jeremiah	7.11
	36.13		26.18
I Samuel	16.21	Lamentations	1.11
	18.29	Ezekiel	19.3
	28.16		19.6
II Samuel	8.14		23.10
I Kings	11.24	Daniel	2.35
	13.33	Jonah	4.5
II Kings	17.3	Micah	3.12
	24.1		

Added to this list from the Authorized Version, are the following examples from Exodus and Deuteronomy in the Revised Standard Version:

Exodus 16.24; 22.24; 23.29; 40.9.
Deut. 7.26; Jud. 16.7; 16.11; 16.17.
..... and there are many more.

APPENDIX XIV
(Reference: p. 41)

Various Renderings of *waw*, other than *and* or *but*.

Gen. 3. 1:	"*Now* the serpent had...."
Gen. 11. 4:	"A city *with* a tower...." (Driver).
Gen. 15. 2:	"*Seeing* I go childless...."
Gen. 18. 18:	"*Seeing that* Abraham...."
Gen. 24. 31:	"*For* I have prepared...."
Josh. 22. 17:	"*Although* there was a plague...."
Job 2. 1:	"*Again*, there was a day when...."
Job 2. 11:	"*Now when* Job's three friends...."
Job 21. 22:	"*Seeing that* he judges...."
Job 22. 29:	"*When* men are cast down...."
Job 27. 1:	"*Moreover*, Job continued...."
Job 34. 1:	"*Furthermore* Elihu answered... "
Psa. 28. 3·	"*While* mischief is in their hearts" (Driver)
Psa. 44. 17:	"*Yet* have we not forgotten thee...."
Psa. 68. 9:	".... *when* it was weary".
Psa. 124. 3. 4:	"*Then* they had swallowed us up.... *then* the waters had overwhelmed us...."
Ezek. 1. 1:	"*Now* it came to pass...."
Zech. 11. 5:	".... *because* I am rich...."
Zeph. 1. 13:	First *Waw* = *therefore:* second = *and:* third = *but:* and so forth.

* * *

APPENDIX XV

(Reference: p. 73)

Illustrations of Inverted Word Order to Signify a Pluperfect.

Gen.16.1: "Now Sarai, Abram's wife, had borne him no son...." (Driver)
Gen.20.4: "But Abimelech had not come near her...."
Gen.24.62: "Meanwhile Isaac had come from the well...." (RSV).
Gen.31.19: "Meanwhile Laban had gone to shear...." (RSV).
Gen.34.5: "And Jacob had heard...."
Josh.6.22: "But Joshua had said...."
Jud.16.20: ".... the Lord had departed from him...."
Jud.16.31: ".... had ruled Israel for twenty years...."
Jud.17.7: ".... had sojourned there...."
I Sam.9.15: ".... the Lord had told Samuel...."
I Sam. 14.27 (Heb.): "But Jonathan had not heard...." (RSV).
I Sam.16.14: "But the spirit of the Lord had turned...."
I Sam.17.2: "Saul and the men of Israel had gathered...."
I Sam.17.14: "David and his three elder brothers had gone...."
I Sam.25.21: "Now David had said...."
I Sam.28.3: "... Israel had anointed him... Saul had put away."
II Sam.18.18: "Now Absalom had taken...."
I Ki.22.31: "But the king... had commanded..." (RSV).
II Ki.7.17: "Meanwhile the king had appointed.... (RSV).
II Ki.9.16: "For Joram had slept there and Ahaziah, king of Judah, had come down...."
Job 32.4: "Now Elihu had waited till...."
Psa.124.4: "The waters had overwhelmed us, the stream had gone over our soul".
Isa.1.9: ".... had left...."
Jer.2.21: ".... had planted...."
Jer.4.25: ".... had fled...."
Jonah 1.5: "But Jonah had gone down...."

* * *

APPENDIX XVI

(Reference: p. 78)

Meaning of Descriptive Terms Found in Genesis 1.2.

Four descriptive terms are used: *tohu, bohu, ghoshek, and tehom,* translated respectively in the AV as "without form", "void", "darkness", and "deep". The following are the occurrences of *tohu* with their AV, RV, Berkeley, and RSV renderings (in that order).

Deut.32.10:
waste
wilderness
in a .... waste
in a .... waste

I Sam.12.21:
vain things
vain
mere nothings
vain

Job 6.18:
to nothing
into a waste
wastes
the waste

Job 12.24:
a wilderness
wilderness
in a jungle
a pathless waste

Job 26.7:
empty place
empty place
empty place
the void

Psa.107.40:
wilderness
waste
pathless wastes
trackless wastes

Isa.24.10:
confusion
confusion
desolate
chaos

Isa.29.21:
a thing of nought
thing of nought
empty
empty

Isa.34.11:
confusion
confusion
chaos
confusion

Isa.40.17:
vanity
confusion (m.)
worthlessness
as emptiness

Isa.40.23:
vanity
as in a waste
like nothing
as nothing

Isa.41.29:
confusion
confusion
waste
empty

Isa.44.9:
vanity
confusion (m.)
in vain
nothing

Isa.45.18:
not in vain
a waste
in vain
a chaos

Isa.45.19:
not in vain
as in a waste
in vain
in chaos

Isa.49.4:
for nought
for nought
for nothing
for nothing

Isa.59.4:
in vanity
vanity
in confusion
emplty pleas

Jer.4.23:
without form
waste
formless
waste

In the LXX the words *Tohu* and *Bohu* are rendered αόρατος and ἀκατασκευαστος, the first being found also (and only) in Isa.45.3 where it is translated in the AV as "hidden", and in II Macc.9.5 where it is rendered in the RV as "invisible" (an invisible plague!). The second is found only in Gen.1.2 in the LXX and is not again used. In no passage where Hebrew employs the word *tohu* does the Septuagint use the word Chaos (χαος), though the word does appear twice elsewhere in the LXX, ie., in Mic.1.6 and Zech.14.4, in both of which it is clearly employed to indicate a dramatic dis-ordering - not a Chaos in the classical sense of being merely as yet un-ordered. If the idea of something unformed or incomplete were the author's intent in Gen.1.2, it seems that the authors of the LXX could still not appropriately have used the Greek word χαος, since to them, evidently, (on the basis of Mic.1.6 and Zech.14.4) it did not mean what was meant by the term in Classical Greek. It is hard to know what term they could have used to convey the idea of something yet incomplete - if that is what the original means. At any rate they avoided the word χαος as perhaps being ambiguous.

In the New Testament the opposite term κατασκευαζω is used frequently, always with the sense of "furnishing", "making ready", "adorning". Unfortunately, the New Testament does not use the antonym chosen by the LXX for *bohu* so that one cannot be sure in what sense it was employed in Gen.1.2, whether as *un*-formed or *de*-formed. That they did not use the term χαος might be taken as some slight indication that the idea of something un-formed was not considered the meaning of the original. But the evidence is inconclusive in this respect.

By contrast, I do not think that the Hebrew word *tohu* can possibly be viewed as a word *normally* implying something yet incomplete. It is much more frequently, almost overwhelmingly, employed as a term descriptive of something that is, in the view of both men and God, under judgment or in disfavour, worthless or desolated rather than not yet to be made valuable or not yet put in order.

With reference to the word *bohu*, James Strong in his Dictionary gives the meaning (sub entry #922) as "an indistinguishable ruin", though he states that the root (an unused one) means merely "to be empty". The noun occurs only in Gen.1.2 and Jer.4.23. BDB favours the sense of *bohu* as something destroyed, not something being built. Of *tohu* in Gen.1.2, they also support strongly the concept of "land *reduced* to primeval chaos" (my emphasis).

The word "darkness" is in Scripture frequently associated with something under judgment: but it is not *always* so. The word can be used merely for the absence of light, as during the night. Either interpretation of the term in Gen.1.2 would be equally allowable.

Of the term *tehom*, it is difficult to speak without becoming involved also in such words from extra-biblical sources as the Assyrian *Tiamtu*, etc. In the Bible it means "the abyss" or simply, "the deep sea". If one is to argue for a picture of a nebulous first-stage in the process of creation, it is hard to see how a deep sea, an ocean, or at least "waters" (verse 3), could already be in existence. In a number of other passages in Scripture where the word occurs (as for example: Psa.36.7 (Heb.); 71.20; 106.9 , there is a suggestion of judgment or distress, but not always. The "deep" is often an *agent* of destruction, as at the time of the Flood, but in itself it seems to signify no more than the mystery of a great body of water whose depths are unfathomable, as it were. Once again, the evidence is inconclusive. But it does not seem unlikely that deep oceans could be thought of as existing when the earth was still part of a nebula as some have viewed Gen.1.2.

APPENDIX XVII

(Reference: p. 91)

Use of Hayah in a Hebrew Version of the New Testament.

Matt.8.26: וַתְּהִי דְּמָמָה גְדוֹלָה:
ie., "And there became a great calm" (= and it became very calm).

Matt.10.16: עַל־כֵּן הֱיוּ עֲרוּמִים כַּנְּחָשִׁים:
ie., "Wherefore, become as wise as serpents".

Matt.12.45: וְהָיְתָה אַחֲרִית הָאִישׁ הַהוּא רָעָה מֵרֵאשִׁיתוֹ:
ie., "and the latter state of that man shall become worse than the former".

Matt.20.26: כִּיאִם מִי־הֶחָפֵץ לִהְיוֹת גָּדוֹל בָּכֶם יִהְיֶה לָכֶם לִמְשָׁרֵת:
ie., "for if any one desires to become great among you, let him become *as it were* a servant...."

Matt.28.2: וַיְהִי רַעַשׁ גָּדוֹל:
ic., "and there became a great earthquake."

Mark 4.39: וַתְּהִי דְמָמָה גְדוֹלָה:
ie., "and there became a great calm".

Mark 6.14: כִּי נוֹדַע הָיָה שְׁמוֹ בָּאָרֶץ:
ie., "for his name became spread abroad in the land".

Mark 10.43, and 44:
וְלֹא יִהְיֶה כֵן בְּקִרְבְּכֶם כִּי אִם־מִי הֶחָפֵץ לִהְיוֹת
גָּדוֹל בָּכֶם יִהְיֶה לָכֶם לִמְשָׁרֵת: וּמִי מִכֶּם הֶחָפֵץ
לִהְיוֹת לְרֹאשׁ יִהְיֶה עֶבֶד לַכֹּל:

ie., "But it shall not be so among you: but who ever wills to become great among you shall become as your minister: and whoever wills to be chief, shall become as a slave to all".

Lu.1.2: אֵלֶּה אֲשֶׁר הָיוּ עֵדִים:
ie., "these which became witnesses".

Lu.2.42: וּבִהְיוֹתוֹ בֶּן־שְׁתֵּים עֶשְׂרֵה שָׁנָה:
ie., "and (when) in his becoming a son of twelve years".

Lu.4.25: וְרָעָב גָּדוֹל הָיָה בְּכָל־הָאָרֶץ:
ie., "and when a great famine *had* become in all the land".

Lu.10.26: וְעַתָּה מָה־תֹּאמַר מִי מִשְּׁלֹשָׁה אֵלֶּה הָיָה רֵעַ:
ie., "and now, which do you say, who of these three had become neighbour...."

Lu.13.2: הַגְּלִילִים הָהֵם הָיוּ הַטָּאִים מִכָּל־יֹשְׁבֵי הַגָּלִיל:
ie., "(do you suppose that) these Galileans had become more sinful than all the inhabitants of Galilee?"

Jn.9.27: הֲגַם אַתֶּם חֲפֵצִים לִהְיוֹת תַּלְמִידָיו:
ie., "Are you also anxious to become his disciples?"

Jn.12.36: לְמַעַן תִּהְיוּ בְּנֵי־הָאוֹר:
ie., "that ye may become the children of light".

Acts 26.28: כִּי הֱיוֹת אֶהְיֶה מַאֲמִין בִּמְשִׁיחֲךָ כָּמוֹךָ:
ie., "that becoming I should become a believer in your Messiah like you".

Acts 27.36: וַתְּהִי רוּחַ כֻּלָּם:
ie., "then they became of spirit, all of them".

Rom.4.18: כֹּה יִהְיֶה זַרְעֶךָ:
ie., "so shall thy seed become".

Rom.12.16: וְאַל־תִּהְיוּ חֲכָמִים בְּעֵינֵיכֶם:
ie., "And do not become wise in your own eyes".

I Cor.7.23: אַל־תִּהְיוּ עַבְדֵי אָדָם:
ie., "Do not become servants of man".

I Cor.9.29: פֶּן אֶהְיֶה קֹרֵא׃

ie., "Lest I should become one called in question". The modern sense of קרא is not clear to me. It means to summon, to call, read out, select, etc., in biblical Hebrew.

II Cor.8.14: לְמַעַן יִהְיֶה קַו שָׁוֶה׃

ie., "in order that there may come to be a line of equality".

I Tim.5.9: אֲשֶׁר הָיְתָה אֵשֶׁת אִישׁ אֶחָד׃

ie., "who has become the wife of one man (only)". In this, as in many other places, it would seem that the ordinary sense of "been" rather than "become" would be just as (or more) appropriate. Yet the Greek, as in every one of these cases, uses not some verbal form of ειναι but of γινομαι, of *become*, not of *be*.

Heb.2.17: לְמַעַן יְהִי כֹּהֵן גָּדוֹל׃

ie., "that He might become a high priest".

II Pe.2.1: וְגַם נְבִיאֵי שֶׁקֶר הָיוּ בָעָם כַּאֲשֶׁר יִהְיוּ מוֹרִים מַתְעִים גַּם־בָּכֶם׃

ie., "but these became also false prophets among you, even as there shall also come to be false teachers among you".

* * *

APPENDIX XVIII

(Reference: p. 92)

Some Instances where Hayah is Translated "became" in spite of the Absence of Lamedh Following.

Gen. 3.20: "Because she became the mother of every living person" (Berkeley).

Gen. 9.15: "The water shall no more become a flood to destroy the earth" (AV).

Gen. 12.10: "And there became a famine in the Land" (LXX).

Gen. 15.5: "So shall thy seed become" (AV).

Gen. 27.23: "His hands had become hairy like the hands of his brother Esau" (BDB).

Gen. 34.15: "If ye will become as we are" (LXX).

Gen. 38.7: "Judah's firstborn became wicked in the sight of the Lord" (BDB: LXX).

Gen. 47.20: "And the land became Pharaoh's" (LXX).

Gen. 48.19: ".... and his seed shall become a multitude of nations" (AV).

Gen. 49.17: "Dan shall become a serpent in the way" (LXX).

Gen. 50.9: "And it became a very great company (LXX).

Exod. 7.19: "that they may become...." (AV: RSV).

Exod. 23.29: "Lest the earth become desolate...."(AV).

Exod. 36.13: "and so it became one tabernacle" (AV).

Jud. 11.39: "And it became a custom in Israel" (AV).

II Sam. 8.14: ""And all they of Edom became David's servants" (AV).

II Ki. 17.3: "Shalmanezer (came up).... and Hoshea became his servant".

Ezek. 35.4: "Thou shalt become a desolation" (RSV).

Micah 2.11: "He shall become a prophet of this people" (BDB).

The following further references will also be found in the Versions noted.

REVISED
~~Authorized~~ Version.

Gen. 2.20	Exod. 8.17 (2x)
3.20	9.10
19.26	23.29
21.20	36.13
37.20	Jud. 15.14

I Sam.	16.21
	18.29
	28.16
I Ki.	11.24
	13.6, 33
II Ki.	24.1
I Chron.	18.2
	18.6
	18.13
Psa.	69.8
	79.4
	83.10
	109.25
Isa.	7.24
Jer.	26.18
Lam.	1.11
Ezek.	17.6 (2x)
	19.3,6
	23.10
Micah	3.12

Revised Standard Version.

Gen.	39.2 (2x)
Exod.	9.10
Lev.	13.24
Deut.	33.5
Josh.	9.21
Jud.	11.39
	15.14
I Sam.	14.15
	16.21
I Ki.	1.4
	13.16
II Ki.	17.3
I Chron.	18.2
	18.6
	18.13
II Chron.	13.9
Psa.	83.10
Isa.	18.5
Ezek.	19.3,6,11
	23.10
	36.3
Dan.	2.35
Hosea	9.10

Berkeley Version.

Gen.3.20:	"(Eve) *became* the mother of all living".
4.2:	"Abel *became* a herder of flocks".
4.21:	"Jabal *became* father of all tent dwellers".
16.12:	"Jubal *became* the father of all (musicians)".
17.5:	"Your name shall *become* Abraham".
21.19:	".... *became* an expert bowman".
25.27:	"Esau *became* an expert hunter".
28.22:	"(This) pillar shall *become* a house of God".
37.20:	"What *becomes* of his dreams".

All the above are cases where the translation of הָיָה as "became" is not merely *admissible* but virtually mandatory in order to give the true sense of the original: and not one of them is followed by the proposition לְ.

There are times almost without number in the Old Testament where "became" would have been better but was for some reason *not* adopted by translators in the English versions. In Genesis alone there are hundreds of examples. Thus in Gen.4.20 we should have the words "And he became the father of such as dwell in tents", and in verse 21, "And he became the father of such as handle the harp and the organ". The LXX has correctly translated both passages. English versions simply say, "He was the father, etc.", which clearly is not nearly as meaningful, historically speaking. In Gen.5 a recurrent phrase reads, "And all the days of so-and-so came to be (ie., became) such-and-such". The Hebrew has the verb הָיָה in the original, and the LXX correctly renders this ἐγένετο πᾶσαι αἵ ἡμέρα Ἀδαμ", and so forth. The Hebrew scholars in Alexandria had no hesitation in equating הָיָה with ἐγένετο.

Thus if one were to allow all versions to speak with equal voice, it would never again be stated categorically that the translation of הָיָה as "became" is so rare as to be "inadmissible" - as Leupold, for example, holds in his *Exposition of Genesis* at Gen.1.2 (Wartburg Press, Columbus, Ohio, 1942, p.46).

* * *

APPENDIX XIX

(Reference: p. 93)

Meaning of καταβολη in the New Testament.

It is, of course, hardly necessary to say that a noun formed from a verb need not have the same basic meaning and that therefore the verb cannot be used to *prove* anything about the meaning of the noun. In the New Testament there is a recurrent phrase, "the foundation of the world", which many writers, who view Gen. 1.2 as a description of catastrophe, take to be an allusion. On the basis of the verbal root καταβαλλω they argue (as I myself have done) that the noun means "disruption", since the verb means "to cast down". Origen equated the verbal root of καταβολη with the Latin *dejicere*, "to throw down". In this he is essentially correct. And in the LXX the *verb* is similarly used to substitute for the following Hebrew words, all of which are essentially similar in meaning:

הָרַס (Haras)	to tear down, break down, devastate, overthrow, destroy, extirpate.
לָקַח (Laqah)	to take, lay hold of, seize, snatch away, captivate.
נָטַשׁ (Natash)	to stretch or spread out, scatter abroad, reject, let loose, disperse, give up.
נָפַל (Naphal)	to fall, fall away, fall out, fail, hurl down, cast down, fall upon (attack).
נָתַץ (Nathatz)	to break down, destroy, smash down.
פָּרַץ (Paratz)	to break, demolish, scatter, break up, spread abroad.
שָׂטַם (Satam)	to lurk for, way-lay, entrap.
שָׁחַת (Shahath)	to break to pieces, destroy, ruin, lay waste, devastate, violate, injure, corrupt.
שָׁפֵל (Shaphel)	to fall or sink down, to be laid low, humiliate, humble.

This clearly establishes the meaning of the *verb*, but what of the noun formulated from it? In classical Greek it came to have the basic meaning of "foundation" as signifying what has been cast down or thrown down first. It is never found with the meaning of destruction or disruption. In II Macc.2.29 the noun occurs in a context which indicates that the classical sense of "foundation" is intended here also.

In the New Testament there is little doubt that the verbal form has the classical meaning of "casting down" or "casting out", as in II Cor.4.9 and Rev.12.10 for example, or "giving birth to" in Heb. 11.11, ie., "founding" a new line.

On the basis of Heb.6.1 which reads, "Therefore leaving the principles of the doctrine of Christ, let us go on unto perfection, not laying again the foundation of repentance from dead works and of faith towards God", the learned commentator Olshausen argues that we must assume the word is here being used in its most fundamental sense of "casting down", and so of demolishing or destroying. "For", he argues, "the apostle would assuredly not have dissuaded men from laying again the foundation of repentance, in the case of its having been destroyed".

In this passage, moreover, the word for "foundation" is not καταβολη as it might have been in classical Greek, but θεμελιος (*themelios*) as it normally is in the New Testament. Wherever the New Testament is speaking of a true "foundation", this word *themelios* is found. The following references will make this clear:

Luke 6.48-49	I Tim.6.19
Luke 14.29	II Tim.2.19
Acts 12.26	Heb.1.10 (as a verb)
Rom.15.20	Heb.6.1
I Cor.3,10,11,12	Heb.11.10
Eph.2.20	Rev.21.14-19

Thus if there is a word in New Testament Greek, the meaning of which is unequivocably and unambiguously "foundation", it is the word *themelios*. In the recurrent phrase, "the foundation of the world", one might reasonably, therefore, have expected to find this word used, if the meaning really is *the foundation* of the world. On the other hand, to render it, "the disruption of the world", and thereby make it a reference back to a catastrophe implied in Gen,1.2, requires that the noun be given a meaning for which we have no other precedent in Greek literature. Nor did καταβολη, apparently, come by custom to be associated with the word κοσμος ("world"), the word which follows it, as a kind of "accepted formula" for the creation, because elsewhere (when clearly speaking of the creation) the phrase used is ἀπ ἀρχῆς κόσμου , or ἀπ ἀρχῆς κτισεως: ie., "from the beginning of the world" (as in Matt. 24.21) or "from the beginning of the creation" (as in II Pe. 3.4). So also in Mark 10.6 and 13.19. Since the word κοσμος means "order", it would not be surprising if the writers of the New Testament had coined a new phrase to describe the catastrophe, referring to it thereafter as the "disruption of the world order". They may then have used it as a reference point with respect to God's redemptive plans - for this may well have been the first overt rebellion of the created order against the authority of the Creator.

The great majority of Greek scholars would undoubtedly object to any claim that the noun can ever mean "destruction" on the grounds that "there is no evidence for it". But this is circular reasoning. For there is *no evidence* only provided that we refuse to allow καταβολη to be rendered "disruption" in the New Testament. Otherwise, the argument has no force whatever. One cannot disallow something by merely asserting it to be unallowable to start with and saying it cannot be allowed because there is no evidence for it! Classical Greek and New Testament Greek do not always agree. Some words in the New Testament are given meanings which they do not hold in classical Greek, and Heb. 6.1 strongly supports the idea that καταβολη may be one such word.

* * *

APPENDIX XX

(Reference: p. 98)

The Meaning of Exodus 20.11.

It is very frequently argued that the wording of Exod. 20. 11, "For in six days the Lord made heaven and earth, the sea, and all that in them is, and rested on the seventh day....", excludes the possibility of a gap between Gen. 1. 1 and 1. 2 because the whole process of creation was completed within these six days. Those who argue thus assume that the days are literal days - and in this, I think they are quite correct. But it is of tremendous importance in studying the Word of God to observe the precision with which words are used, especially where some important doctrine or institution is involved. What we are told here is that God in six days "made" (עָשָׂה, *'asah*) the heavens and the earth. It does not say that He created (בָּרָא *bara*) them in six days.

I have seen it argued that these verbs are interchangeable because they are used sometimes in successive verses with what appears to be identical meaning. For example, in Gen. 1. 26 it is written, "And God said, Let us *make* man in our image after our likeness....", and in verse 27, "So God *created* man in His image, in the image of God created He him". Superficially, the two verbs do appear to be equated here. But as Origen and other early commentators noted, by carefully observing what is said and what is *NOT* said in these two verses, there is an important lesson to be learned, and the lesson hinges upon the difference in meaning between these two governing verbs, *'asah* and *bara*.

It is often found that light is shed upon the fundamental meaning of a word by noting the way in which it is first used in Scripture. The verb *'asah* appears significantly in this respect in Gen. 1. 16: "And God made two great lights...." It seems unlikely that the sun and the moon were not created until the fourth day since green things would hardly be brought into being before the sun was created. The reference in Gen. 1. 16 seems more likely to refer not to a creation but rather to the *appointment* of the sun and moon as rulers of the Day and Night: they were appointed as markers of time ("signs" - verse 14), precisely as Psa. 104. 19 indicates: "He appointed the moon for seasons". If we allow that the basic meaning of the Hebrew verb *'asah* is not creation but rather the giving of a new role to something already in existence, then we have plenty of illustrations throughout Scripture of the use of this verb in this sense.

In the New Testament we are told that Jesus was *made* a High Priest after the order of Melchizedec (Heb. 6. 20). This illustrates the sense in which "made" means "appointed". In I Ki. 12. 51 we have a quite exact parallel where we are told that Jeroboam appointed (*'asah*) priests of the lowest of the people. In Amos 3. 6 the question is asked, "Is there evil in any city and God hath not appointed (*'asah*) it?"

In the Old Testament where the word *'asah* forms part of a personal name, it is most appropriately rendered by the English "appointed". Thus we have in II Sam. 2. 18 the name Ahasel, meaning "God has appointed". In II Ki. 12. 14 we have the name Asahiah which means "Jah has appointed". In I Chron. 4. 35 we have Asihel, which means "appointed of God".

The word is used of dressing a calf for a meal, ie., preparing it (Gen. 18. 7, 8; Jud. 13. 15). It is used of trimming a beard (II Sam. 19. 25). In Deut. 21. 12 it is used of trimming one's nails! And in Esther 1. 5 it is used of preparing a feast for the court.

Strong's exhaustive *Concordance of the Bible* gives a number of meanings to the verb, including the word "appoint", but never the meaning "to create". The word is employed in speaking of the clothes which God made for man (Gen. 3. 21), and of clothing which man makes for himself (Exod. 28. 2 f.). It always involves working over something which already exists, and usually with a view to changing its form. Sometimes it has more precisely the idea of appointment in the sense that the making is in the future: a multitude of descendants, for example (Gen. 13. 16). And it may have the meaning of appointment in a more abstract sense as when a covenant is made between God and Israel (Gen. 9. 12). At least within biblical usage it never means the creation of something out of nothing.

In Isa. 45. 18 we find a whole series of verbs setting forth God's plan for the earth in which He is said to have created it (*bara*), fashioned it (*yatsar*), appointed it (*'asah*), and established it (*kun*). Each word has a specific meaning, and it is not merely re-iteration.

Allowing the word, then, to bear the sense of appointment rather than assuming that it is a synonym for creation, we may observe in Gen. 1. 26 that God appointed for man that he should bear His image and His likeness: but that when the plan was put into effect and man is spoken of as having been created, reference is made only to the image - and significantly, no reference is made to the likeness. We may gather from this that while both image and likeness were *appointed* (*'asah*), only the image itself was *created* (*bara*) by God, the achievement of the likeness being left as something to be wrought out by experience.

Origen noted, rightly, that while God intended that man should bear both His image and His likeness, He created only the image, whereas the likeness was something which was "appointed", something to be achieved, to be wrought out in life by the individual who therefore has a responsible part to play in the achieving of it. A number of passages indicate that the image has to do with relationship, in fact with sonship, and as a consequence of this relationship involves also in a certain sense ownership. As Jesus said of the coin (Lu. 20. 24), the image which was stamped upon it signified that it belonged to Caesar. The image, when it is stamped upon man, signifies likewise that he belongs to God, and not only that he belongs to God as something possessed but rather that he belongs to God as a son belongs to his father. Hence it is common to find in the New Testament that when a man by new birth becomes a son of God (Jn. 1. 12), he is at the same moment re-created in the image of God, to restore the image lost in the Fall. The image, therefore, is something which God creates, and it gives to the individual his unique relationship with his Creator. God is not the father of His creatures merely because He created them, for He created the cattle also but this does not make Him *their* father. But unlike all other creatures, man was created at first, and is re-created, in the "image of God" and thereby achieves his sonship.

But as to the likeness, it is appointed for man but it is not created, it is something to be achieved through experience but it is not imposed. The force of Satan's initial temptation was that man might achieve this likeness (Gen. 3. 5: "Ye shall become like God") by the wrong means. David said he would only be satisfied when he awoke with His likeness (Psa. 17. 15). When John wrote his first Epistle he said (I Jn. 3. 1, 2): "Behold, what manner of love the Father hath bestowed upon us that we should be called the sons of God.... Beloved, now are we the sons of God, and it doth not yet appear what we shall be: but we know that, when He shall appear, we shall be like Him...." Our assurance is that we are, right now, sons, for by an act of God we have had His image stamped upon us: but we do also have the assurance that the appointed likeness will yet be achieved, being brought to perfection when He comes.

Thus by taking care to distinguish between words which superficially seem to be indistinguishable, Scripture sheds a new light upon the original purposes of God and how they will be fulfilled. The word *'asah* does not mean "to create", but rather "to make" in the English sense of "appointing".

I do not suggest that the meaning of appointment is the only meaning of *'asah*. It has other meanings which come close to the common English word "make" in the sense of doing or working at something. But the fact is that the meaning of appointment, in the sense of working upon something which already exists in order to effect a change in it until it becomes something further is commonly involved. So that when we are told in Exod. 20.11 that God made heaven and earth in six days, we are not called upon to assume that this has reference to the original creation. We may be quite justified in reading this as a reference to the re-working of something which is already in existence, just as the sun and the moon and the stars may very well have been in existence long before they were appointed to mark the times and the seasons for man who was about to be introduced. Exod. 20.11 surely refers to the work of these six days not as a time of creation *ex nihilo* but as a time in which a ruined cosmos was re-ordered as a fit habitation for man. And when this re-ordering was completed, God rested.

* * *

APPENDIX XXI

(Reference: p. 13)

Some Pagan Traditions of a Like Catastrophe.

It is not without significance that people of other cultures whose thinking does not seem to have been influenced by the teaching of Missionaries, have traditions of a catastrophe which overtook the first creation. Not unnaturally, such stories tell of people in this former world, for it is always difficult to conceive of an earth totally devoid of any population. It requires a certain sophistication to conceive a world prior to this one, uninhabited by man.

Thus the Arabians have a strange belief that there were once 40 kings who ruled over a creation prior to Adam, and that they were called "Solimans" (after Solomon, who to them seemed to be the ideal of what a monarch ought to be). They say that their history was recounted by the "Bird of Ages", whom they called the Simorg and who had served them all. Their statues, monstrous pre-adamite forms, were supposed to exist in the mountains of Kaf.[142]

In one of his books, Prof. Franz Cumont remarks that according to the Mithraic teachings;[143]

> "The demoniac confederates of the King of Hell once ascended to the assault of Heaven and attempted to dethrone the successor of Kronos. But, shattered like the Greek giants by the ruler of the gods, these rebel monsters were hurled backwards into the abyss from which they had arisen. They made their escape, however, from that place and wandered about on the face of the earth, there to spread misery and to corrupt the hearts of men, who, in order to ward off the evils that menaced them were obliged to appease them by offering expiatory sacrifices".

There is a Far Eastern tradition in which some further details are provided. Prof. Rawlinson, in one of his Bampton Lectures gave one extract as follows:[144]

> "The Chinese traditions are said to be less clear and decisive than the Babylonian. They speak of a 'first heaven'

> and an age of innocence when 'the whole creation enjoyed a state of happiness'. Then everything was beautiful and everything was good: all things were perfect in their kind. Whereunto succeeded a *second heaven* (his emphasis) *introduced by a great convulsion*, in which the pillars of heaven were broken, the earth shook to its foundations, the heavens sank lower towards the north, the sun, moon, and stars changed their motions, the earth fell apart and the waters enclosed within its bosom burst forth with violence and overflowed."

The Egyptians believed that the earth had suffered more than one destruction and renewal, and certainly the Babylonian traditions held strongly to at least one serious destruction and reconstitution quite apart from their recollections of the great Flood of Noah's time.[145]

Even as we today have found the advantage of animating stories for children, so the early Babylonians turned inanimate forces into spiritual beings, and set much of the early geological history of the earth, as they conceived it, in the form of a titanic struggle between giant forces in personal guise. The great catastrophe of Gen. 1.2 in time became one of the most popular themes of Cuneiform literature.

In a paper titled, "Genesis and Pagan Cosmogonies", Dr. Edward McCrady has given an excellent and concise statement of the matter. He remarks:[146]

> "It is generally conceded that the Dragon, as a personification of the Evil Spirit, is more or less identified with the destructive and rebellious forces of Nature, especially as they bring chaos and suffering to mankind in floods, storms, etc. But it is only in connection with such stories as that of Bel and the Dragon, that we begin to catch a glimpse of the ORIGIN of the original myth: and only again as we compare this Chaldeo-Assyrian legend with the first chapter of Genesis that we begin to realize that this Dragon is but a personification of the watery abyss or chaos mentioned in Genesis. Bel, or Bel-Merodach is a personification of the sun which appearing on the fourth day 'breaks through the watery abyss that envelopes the earth, piercing and tearing asunder the Dragon of the abyss with his glittering sword', and eventually after a long struggle bringing order and law out of chaos. Then we begin to see the explanation of the whole. Similarly, we may see little significance in the Egyptian picture of Kneph

sailing in a boat over the water, and breathing life into its tumultuous depths: or the Phoenician legend of Colpias and his wife Bau - or Bahu, effecting a like organization of the waste of primeval matter: until we remember that Kneph signifies wind, air, living breath, or spirit. And Colpias likewise means 'wind', while Bahu is evidently the Phoenician form of the Hebrew 'bohu', the waste of waters.

"With this discovery, however, it immediately dawns upon us that these legends must obviously refer to the statement of Genesis that 'The Spirit of God moved upon the face of the waters. And God said, Let there be Light; and there was Light'.

"A further careful study of the succession of male and female divinities of the Chaldeo-Assyrian Theogony, Lachmu and Lachamu; An-Sar and Ki-Sar, will also bring to light the fact that they are, respectively, personifications of the Light with his consort Darkness; of the Sky or Heavenly Waters, and the earth waters (divided by the 'expanse'), and occur exactly in order of their appearance in the narrative of Genesis; while the divinities Anos (or Anu), Ilinos (or Enlil), and Aos (or Ea), which follow next, and which are universally identified with the heavens, the earth and the sea, are obviously personifications of these physical phenomena, which as Genesis records, were separated from one another as the next step in the creative process; while as the hero of the next succeeding generation appears, Bel Merodach, easily identified as the sun now appearing for the first time together with the moon and the stars, we have the completion of the fourth day. And these events are still further reflected in the Chaldean myth of the birth of Sin (the Moon), Adar (Saturn), Merodach (Jupiter), Nergal (Mars), Nebo (Mercury), and all the rest of them. The order of the appearance of the corresponding physical phenomena given in Genesis - the Theogony (the 'toledoth of the gods'), of the Chaldeans is simultaneously a cosmogony based on the cosmogony of Genesis."

Subsequently, Dr. McCrady remarks:

"Indeed, the echoes of this primal revelation, transformed and corrupted as we have thus explained, are to be found in nearly all the mythologies, cosmogonies, and theogonies of

> paganism. For besides the Chaldean, Assyrian, Phoenician and other narratives, we find them in Greek and Latin literature also."

In conclusion the author points out what must have occurred to all who study these things in this light, that not only do we find in this the origin of the idea that the world began with a chaos, an idea which found its way almost inevitably into our translations because of the power of habits of thought, but we also find the root of much polytheism and idol worship, for they have exactly done what Paul in his epistle to the Romans reveals, changing "the truth of God into a lie, worshipping and serving the created things more than the Creator, Who is blessed forever" (Rom. 1. 25).

There is, therefore, from the very earliest times, a continuity of tradition that at some remote time in the past, great spiritual powers came under the judgment of God and brought about a disruption of the Cosmos, the record of which is surely reflected in Gen. 1. 1 and 1. 2.

This continuity of tradition from the earliest times to the beginning of the last century is a strong confirmation of the view advocated in this volume. It is a strong confirmation because the individuals who supported it were in an excellent position to know what the original text could mean and at the same time they were quite uninfluenced by modern geological theory and were not, therefore, biased in this respect.

* * *

Index of References.

1. Buswell, J. Oliver, "The Length of the Creative Days", pamphlet published privately, p. 3.
2. Harris, John, "Pre-Adamite Earth", Ward & Co., London, no date, p. 353; (about 1849).
3. Payne, D. F., "Genesis One Reconsidered", Tyndale Press, London, 1964, p. 7 fn.
4. Ginsburg, Louis, "The Legends of the Jews", Jewish Publications Soc. of America, Phila., 1954, Vol. 1, p. 4. In Vol. 5 (the critical notes and documentation) Ginsburg references the following sources for the quotation above; מדרש בראשית רבה: (The Great Midrash on "The Beginning") 3:7; and 9:2. Also Koheleth 3.11; and Tehillim 34, 245.
5. In Luther's Bible, published in Wittenburg, 1557, there is a figure 1 placed against the third verse as indicating that here began the creation of the Mosaic world. Professor E. J. Young remarks upon the pause: "The word הָאָרֶץ (at the end of verse 1) is separated from what follows by means of the disjunctive accent *Rebhîa*, and so we are to let our thoughts dwell upon it before passing on to (what follows)". The fact is also referred to by Jamieson, Fausset and Brown in their "Commentary: Critical, Experimental, and Practical", Collings, Glascow 1871, Vol. 1, Gen. - Deut., p. 3: "In many Hebrew MSS there is the usual mark of a pause".
6. Quoted by Joseph Baylee, Principal of St. Andrews College, Birkenhead, in a paper entitled, "On the Nature of Language" in the Transactions of the Victoria Institute, London, Vol. III, 1868-69, p. 260, 261.
7. Hershon, Paul Isaac, "A Rabbinical Commentary on Genesis", Hodder & Stoughton, London, 1882, p. 2.
8. Thayer, J. H., "A Greek-English Lexicon of the New Testament", Clark, Edinburgh, 4th edition, 1961, p. 336.
9. Origen, on the "casting down" of the world: "De Principiis" in the Ante-Nicene Fathers, Scribner's edition, N.Y., 1917, Vol. IV, Bk. 3, Chap. 5, p. 4.
10. Caedmon, "Genesis: Excursus A", translated from the Old

English by Lawrence Mason, in the "Yale Studies in English" series edited by Albert S. Cook, Henry Holt, N.Y., 1915, lines 14-35, 68, 79, 80, 92 f., 114.

11. King Edgar: according to Erich Sauer, in his "Dawn of World Redemption", Eerdmans, Grand Rapids, 1953, p.36.
12. Hugo, St. Victor, "De Sacramentis Christianae Fidei", Bk.1, Part 1, Chap.VI.
13. Aquinas, Thomas, Second Book of the "Sententiarum" (ie., "Sentences" - a Commentary on the Works of Peter Lombard), Distinct. xiii, Article 3, "Ad Tertium".
14. Petavius, Dionysius, "De Opificio Sex Dierum", Bk. 1, Chap. ii, Section 10.
15. Pererius (or Pereyra, Perera, Pereira), Benedict, philosopher and theologian, born near Valencia and dying at Rome, was one of the most prolific and learned writers of his day. His most comprehensive work, "Commentariorum et disputationum in Genesim" in four volumes, is a mine of information. It was published between 1591 - 99. The reference is Vol.1, chap. 1, vs.4, note 80.
16. Ramm, Bernard, "The Christian View of Science and Scripture", Eerdmans, Grand Rapids, 1954, p.196, fn.26.
17. Alcuin: "The Book of Jasher", edition published by the Rosicrusians.
18. Dathe, J. Auguste, Libre VI, "Ex recensione textus Hebraei et Versionum antiquarum Latine versi, notisque philologicis et criticis illustrati", Halle, 1791, in six volumes.
19. Chalmers concluded (according to Hugh Miller, in his "The Testimony of the Rocks", Nimmo, Edingurgh, 1874, p.108, 109) that "the writings of Moses do not fix the antiquity of the globe".
20. Chalmers, Thomas: Bernard Ramm (*op. cit.* at ref. #16, p. 196, fn.26) gives the following reference to Chalmers: "Works", Vol.1, p.228, and Vol.XII, p.369".
21. Buckland, William, "Geology and Minerology Considered With Reference to Natural Theology", Vol.1, Chap.2, being No.VI of The Bridgewater Treatises, 1836.
22. Harris, John, *op.cit.*, (ref.#2), p.354.
23. Kurtz, J. H., "The Bible and Astronomy", 1853, p.433.
24. Kurtz, J. H., *op.cit*, p.90.
25. Kurtz, J. H., *op.cit*, p.397.
26. Kurtz, J. H., "History of the Old Covenant", T. & T. Clark, Edinburgh, 1859, Introduction, p.iv-lx.

27. Kurtz, J. H., *ibid.*, p.cxxiii.
28. Delitzsch, Franz, "New Commentary on Genesis", Clark, Edinburgh, 1888, Vol.1, p.75 ff.
29. Delitzsch, Franz, *ibid.*, p.79, 80.
30. Delitzsch, Franz, *ibid.*, p.76.
31. Delitzsch, Franz, *ibid.*, p.78.
32. Delitzsch, Franz, *ibid.*, p.79.
33. Deltizsch, Franz, *ibid.*, p.77.
34. Delitzsch, Franz, *ibid.*, p.80.
35. Delitzsch as quoted by Peter Lange in his "Commentary on Genesis", Zondervan, reprint, p.110.
36. Delitzsch as quoted by Fr. H. Reusch, "Nature and the Bible", Clark, Edinburgh, 1886, Vol.1, p.119.
37. Delitzsch, as quoted by E. B. Pusey in his "Daniel the Prophet: Nine Lectures", Innes & Co., London, 1892, p.lxxxiii.
38. Delitzsch, Franz, "A System of Biblical Psychology", reprint (of 1899 edition) by Baker House, Grand Rapids, 1966, p.74,75.
39. Delitzsch, Franz, *ibid.*, p.75.
40, Delitzsch, Franz, *ibid.*, p.76.
41. Delitzsch, Franz, *ibid.*, p.77.
42. Delitzsch, Franz, *op.cit.* (ref.#37), p.lxxxiii.
43. Delitzsch, Franz, *op.cit.* (ref.#37), p. lxxxiii.
44. Reusch, Fr. H., *op.cit.* (ref. #36), p.312.
45. Reusch, Fr. H., *op.cit.* (ref. #36), p.313.
46. Gleig, George, "Annotations on Stackhouse", Bk.1, Chap.1, quoted by W. H. Hoare, "The Veracity of the Book of Genesis", Longman, Green, London, 1860, p.179, 180 fn.
47. Pusey, E. B., *op.cit.* (ref. #37), p.xviii, xix, and xx.
48. Pusey, E. B., *op.cit.* (ref. #37), p.lxxxii and lxxxv.
49. Buswell, J. Oliver, *op.cit.* (ref. #1).
50. Pusey, E. B., *op.cit.* (ref. #37), p.lxxxiii.
51. Dillman, A., "Genesis Critically and Exegetically Expounded", Clark, Edinburgh, 1897 (translated by W. B. Stevenson), Vol.1, p.53.
52. Driver, S. R., "The Book of Genesis", Westminster Commentaries, edited by W. Lock, Methuen, London, 1904, p.22.
53. Skinner, John, "A Critical and Exegetical Commentary on Genesis" in "The International Critical Commentary", Clark, Edinburgh, 1951, p.14 fn.
54. Skinner, John, *ibid.*, p.17.
55. Heward, P. W. and F. F. Bruce, "And the Earth Was Without Form and Void", Transactions of the Victoria Institute, London,

Vol. LXXVIII, p. 13-37.

56. This observation was made by F. A. Filby in his "Creation Revealed", Pickering & Inglis, London, 1964, p. 57, fn.

57. Young, Edward J., "Studies in Genesis One", International Library of Philosophy and Theology; Biblical and Theological Studies, edited by N. M. Kik, Presbyterian & Reformed Publishing Co., Phila., 1964, p. 11.

58. Young, E. J., *ibid.*, p. 11.

59. Young, E. J., *ibid.*, p. 12.

60. Whorf, Benjamin Lee, (a) "Collected Papers on Metalinguistics", Dept. State, Foreign Service Institute, Washington, D. C., 1952. Also (b) "Language, Thought and Reality", Wiley, N. Y., 1956.

61. Gesenius' Hebrew and Chaldee Lexicon, translated by S. P. Tregelles, Wiley & Sons, London, 1889, under הָיָה: p. ccxxii.

62. Davies, Benjamin, "A Compendious and Complete Hebrew and Chaldee Lexicon", founded on Gesenius and Furst, Bradley, Boston, 1890, under הָיָה.

63. Brown, F., S. R. Driver, and C. A. Briggs, "A Hebrew and English Lexicon of the Old Testament Based on Gesenius", Oxford, 1962, under הָיָה.

64. Boman, Thorlief, "Hebrew Thought Compared With Greek", SCM Press, London, 1960, p. 27-51.

65. Boman, T., *ibid.*, p. 42, 43.

66. Boman, T., *ibid.*, p. 38.

67. Barr, James, "The Semantics of Biblical Language", Oxford, 1962, p. 59.

68. Boman, T., *op. cit.* (ref. #64), p. 38.

69. Boman, T., *op. cit.* (ref. #64), p. 38 (iii).

70. Boman, T., *op. cit.* (ref. #64), p. 38.

71. Boman, T., *op. cit.* (ref. #64), p. 39.

72. On Ratschow, see Boman, *op. cit.* (ref. #64), p. 39. ff.

73. Whorf, Benjamin Lee, *op. cit.* (ref. #60 (a)), p. 3-7.

74. Boman, T., *op. cit.* (ref. #64), p. 36.

75. Boman, T., *op. cit.* (ref. #64), p. 38.

76. Boman, T., *op. cit.* (ref. #64), p. 38.

77. Boman, T., *op. cit.* (ref. #64), p. 39, i, ii, iii.

78. Basson, H. H., and O. J. O'Connor, "Language and Philosophy" in *Philosophy*, the Journal of the Royal Institute of Philosophy (London), 1947, Vol. 22, p. 49-65.

79. Leo, Christopher, translation of: "A Hebrew Lexicon of the Old Testament", by D. W. Gesenius, Cambridge, 1825.

80. Tregelles: see ref. #61 above.
81. Davies: see ref. #62 above.
82. Whitcomb, John C., "The Creation of the Heavens and the Earth", *Creation Research Society Quarterly*, 4:1967, p.71.
83. Young, Robert, "A Literal Translation of the Bible", Pickering & Inglis, London, no date, at Song of Songs 1.5.
84. Driver, S. R., "A Treatise on the Tenses in Hebrew", Oxford, 3rd. edition, 1892, xvi and 306 pp.
85. Driver, S. R., *ibid*., p.84.
86. Driver, S. R., *ibid*., p.84, fn.
87. Driver, S. R., *ibid*., p.84.
88. Blake, Frank R., "A Resurvey of Hebrew Tenses", Pontificum Institutum Biblicum, Rome, 1951, section 10, p.18, 19.
89. Driver, S. R., *op. cit.* (ref. #84), p.84,85.
90. Driver, S. R., *op. cit.* (ref. #84), p.85.
91. Driver, S. R., *op. cit.* (ref. #84), p.84.
92. Driver, S. R., *op. cit.* (ref. #84), p.85-87.
93. Driver, S. R., *op. cit.* (ref. #84), p.88.
94. Driver, S. R., *op. cit.* (ref. #84), p.88.
95. Driver, S. R., *op. cit.* (ref. #84), p.196.
96. Young, Edward J., *op. cit.* (ref. #57), p.11.
97. Thayer, J. H., *op. cit.* (ref. #8), sub δε, p.125.
98. Barr, James, *op. cit.*(ref. #67), p.59.
99. Pusey, E. B., *op. cit.* (ref. #37), p.xviii, xviv
100. Pusey, E. B., *op. cit.* (ref. #37), p.lxxxiv.
101. Pusey, E. B., *op. cit.* (ref. #37), p.lxxxvi.
102. Young, Edward J., *op. cit.* (ref. #57), p.12.
103. Pember, G. H., "Earth's Earliest Ages", Hodder & Stoughton, London, 9th edition, p.19-21.
104. Thayer, J. H., *op.cit.*, (ref. #8), p.179, V, 2.
105. Thayer, J. H., *op. cit.* (ref. #8), p.117.
106. Heward, P. W., *op. cit.* (ref. #55), p.14.
107. Lamsda, George M., "The Four Gospels According to the Eastern Version", translated from the Aramaic, Holman, Phila., 1933.
108. Heward, P. W, and F. F. Bruce, *op. cit.* (ref. #55),
109. Dillman, A., *op.cit.* (ref. #51), Vol.1, p.53.
110. Filby, F. A., *op.cit.* (ref. #56), p.57.
111. Filby, F. A., *op.cit.* (ref. #56), p.57.
112. Filby, F. A., *op.cit.* (ref. #56), p.58.
113. Buswell, J. Oliver, *op.cit.* (ref. #1), p.8.
114. Whitcomb, John C., "The Ruin-Reconstruction Theory of Gen.

1.2", *Creation Research Annual*, 2:1965, p.3.
115. Whitcomb, John C., *ibid*., p.3.
116. Kalisch, M. M., "A Historical and Critical Commentary on the Old Testament with a New Translation", Longman, Brown, and Green, London, 1858, p.48.
117. Kalisch, M. M., *ibid*., p.48.
118. Morris, Henry, "Science, Scripture, and Salvation: The Genesis Record", an excellent handbook for Bible Study leaders prepared by Baptist Publ. Inc., Denver, 1965, p.8 (margin).
119. Driver, S. R.: quoted by L. M. Davies in discussion of the paper by F. F. Bruce (see ref. #55, p.29).
120. Skinner, John, *op.cit.* (ref. #53), p.14 fn.
121. Bruce, F. F., *op.cit.* (ref. #55), p.22.
122. Skinner, John, *op.cit.* (ref. #55), p.16.17.
123. Boman, T., *op.cit.* (ref. #64), p.36.
124. Boman, T., *op.cit.* (ref. #64), p.36.
125. Boman, T., *op.cit.* (ref.#64), p.36.
126. Barr, James, *op.cit.* (ref. #67), p.59.
127. Surburg, Raymond, "In the Beginning God Created" in "Darwin, Evolution, and Creation", ed. by Paul Zimmerman, Concordia Publ., St. Louis, 1959, p.53.
128. Ramm, Bernard, *op.cit.* (ref. #16), p.202.
129, Ramm, Bernard, *op.cit.* (ref. #16), p.202.
130. Ramm, Bernard, *op.cit.* (ref. #16), p.202.
131. Thayer, J. H., *op.cit.* (ref. #8), p.117.
132. Ramm, Bernard, *op.cit.* (ref. #16), p.202.
133. Ramm, Bernard, *op.cit.* (ref. #16), p.202 fn.
134. Howitt, John R., "A Brief Note on the Translation of the Word 'Day' in Genesis 1", *Journal of the American Scientific Affiliation*, 5:1953, p.14.
135. Ramm, Bernard, *op.cit.* (ref. #16), p.213.
136. Ramm, Bernard, *op.cit.* (ref. #16), p.220.
137. Surburg, Raymond, *op.cit.* (ref. #127), p.53.
138. Young, Robert, "The Holy Bible: Translated According to the Letter and Idioms of the Original Languages", Pickering and Inglis, London, no date.
139. Driver, S. R., *op.cit.* (ref. #84), p.vi.
140. Driver, S. R., *op.cit.* (ref. #84), p.vi.
141. Skinner, John, *op.cit.* (ref. #53), p.14.
142. Mountains of Kaf: see D'Herbelot's "Soliman ben David" in Stanley's "History of the Jewish Church", Scribners, N.Y., Vol.2, Lect.26, p.144.

143. Cumont, Franz, "Mysteries of Mithra", Open Court, Chicago, 1903, p.112.
144. Rawlinson: quoted by Lord Arundell, "Tradition: Mythology and the Law of Nations", Burns & Oates, London, 1872, p.328.
145. Egyptian beliefs: W. J. Dawson, "The Origin of the World", Dawson, Montreal, 1877, p.148.
146. McCrady, Edward, Transactions of the Victoria Institute, London, Vol. LXXII, 1940, p.46, 47, and 59.

* * *

Index of Names.

* * *

Index of Biblical References.

* * *

General Bibliography.

Alcuin, Book of Jasher, edition published by the Rosicrucians.

Allis, O. T., "The Time Element in Gen. 1. 2", Torch and Trumpet, Vol. III, No. 3, 1958, pp. 16-19.

Anstey, Martin, "The Romance of Bible Chronology", Marshall Bros., London, 1913.

Aquinas, Thomas, "Sententiarum" (ie., "Sentences - A Commentary on the Works of Peter Lombard"), 3nd Book, Distinct. xiii, article 3, "Ad Tertium".

Barr, James, "The Semantics of Biblical Language", Oxford, 1962.

Basson, H. H., "Language and Philosophy" in Philosophy, Journal of Roy. Inst. Phil. (London), Vol. 22, pp. 49-65.

Baylee, Joseph, "On the Nature of Language", Transactions of the Victoria Institute, London, Vol. III, 1868-69.

Blake, Frank R., "A Resurvey of Hebrew Tenses", Pontificum Institutum Biblicum, Rome, 1951.

Boman, Thorlief, "Hebrew Though Compared With Greek", SCM Press, London, 1960.

Brown, F., S. R. Driver, and C. A. Briggs, "A Hebrew and English Lexicon of the Old Testament Based on Gesenius", Oxford, 1962.

Browne, E. Harold, "Genesis: or the First Book of Moses", Scribners, N.Y., 1873.

Bruce, F. F., "And the Earth Was Without Form and Void", Transactions of the Victoria Institute, London, Vol. 78, 1946.

Buckland, William, "Geology and Mineralogy Considered With Reference to Natural Theology", Bridgewater Treatises, Vol. 1, No. VI, Chap. 2.

Bush, George, "Notes, Critical and Practical, on the Book of Genesis", Ward, London, 3rd edition, 1838, in two volumes.

Buswell, J. Oliver, "The Length of the Creative Days", pamphlet published privately.

Butler, I. G., "The Bible-Work: Old Testament", Gen. - Exod. XIII, Vol. 1, Funk & Wagnalls, N.Y., 1887.

Caedmon: "Genesis: Excursus A", translated by Lawrence Mason in "Yale Studies in English", series edited by Albert S. Cook, Henry Holt, N.Y., 1915.

Chalmers, Thomas, "Works", Vol. 1 and XII particularly, and also "An Examination of Cuvier's Theory of the Earth", 1814.

Dathe, J. Auguste, Libre VI, "Ex recensione textus Hebraei et Versionum antiquarum Latine versi, notisque philologicis et criticis illustrati", Halle, 1791, in 6 volumes.

Davies, Benjamin, "A Compendious and Complete Hebrew and Chaldee Lexicon" (based on Gesenius and Furst), Bradley, Boston, 1890.

Delitzsch, Franz, "Commentary on Genesis", 3rd. edition, and "A New Commentary on Genesis", 5th ed., Vol. 1 & II, Clark, Edinburgh, 1888, also "A System of Biblical Psychology", 2nd. edition, T. & T. Clark, Edinburgh, 1899 (reprinted by Baker Book House, Grand Rapids, 1966).

Dillman, A., "Genesis Critically and Exegetically Expounded" translated by W. B. Stevenson, Clark, Edinburgh, 1897.

Driver, S. R., "A Treatise on the Tenses in Hebrew", Oxford, 3rd. ed., 1892; "The Book of Genesis", Westminster Commentaries, ed. by W. Lock, Methuen, London, 1904.

Edersheim, Alfred, "The World Before the Flood and the History of the Patriarchs", Religious Tract Society, London, no date.

Exell, J. S., "Pulpit Commentary on Genesis", Kegan Paul, Trench and Trubner, London, 1897.

Filby, F. A., "Creation Revealed", Pickering & Inglis, London, 1964.

Garland, D. V., "Genesis With Notes", Rivingtons, London, 1878.

Ginsberg, Louis, "The Legends of the Jews", Jewish Publ. Soc. of Amer., Phila., 1954, in seven volumes.

Green, W. H., "The Unity of the Book of Genesis", N.Y., 1895, pp. 7-20 for an excellent discussion of Gen. 1.2.

Harris, John, "The Pre-Adamite Earth: Contributions to Theological Science", Ward & Co., London, n.d. (circa 1849); and "Primeval Man", Ward & Co., London, 1849.

Heidel, A., "The Babylonian Genesis", Univ. of Chicago Press, 1942

Hershon, Paul Isaac, "A Rabbinical Commentary on Genesis", Hodder & Stoughton, London, 1882.

Heward, P. W., "And the Earth was Without Form and Void", Transactions of the Victoria Institute, London, Vol. 78, 1946, pp. 13 to 37.

Hoare, William H., "The Veracity of the Book of Genesis", Longman, Green, London, 1860.

Howitt, John R., "A Brief Note on the Translation of the Word 'Day' in Genesis 1", Journal American Scientific Affiliation, 5:1953.

Hugo, St. Victor, "De Sacramentis Christianae Fidei", Bk. 1, Pt. 1 Chap. VI.

Jameison, Fausset, and Brown, "Commentary: Critical, Experimental and Practical", Collins, Edinburgh, 1871.

Jones, J. C., "Primeval Revelation", Hodder & Stoughton, London, 1897.

Kalisch, M. M., "A Historical and Critical Commentary on the Old Testament with a New Translation", Longman, Brown, and Green, London, 1858.

Keil, C. F. and F. Delitzsch, "Biblical Commentary on the Pentateuch", T. & T. Clark, Edinburgh, 1864.

Kline, Meredith G., "Because It Had Not Rained", Westminster Theological Journal, Vol. XX, No. 2, 1958, pp. 146-157.

Kurtz, J. H., "The Bible and Astronomy", 1853; and "A History of the Old Covenant", Clark, Edinburgh, 1859,

Lamsda, George M., "The Four Gospels According to the Eastern Versions", translated from Aramaic, Holman, Phila., 1933.

Lange, Peter, "Commentary on Genesis", Zondervan, Grand Rapids, (reprinted from the 1864 edition).

Leo, Christopher, translation of "A Hebrew Lexicon of the Old Testament by D. W. Gesenius", Cambridge, 1825.

Lewis, Taylor, "Divine Human in the Scriptures", Carter, N.Y., no date (probably around 1860).

McCaul, A. I., "Biblical Interpretation in Connection With Science", Transactions of the Victoria Institute, London, Vol. IX, 1875-76, pp. 147-175.

Orlinsky, Harry M., "The Plain Meaning of Ru'ah in Gen. 1.2", Jewish Quarterly Review, Vol. XLVIII, 1957-58, valuable for reference to relevant literature.

Origen, "De Principiis" in Ante-Nicene Fathers, Scribners, N.Y., 1917.

Payne, D. F., "Genesis One Reconsidered", Tyndale Press, London, 1964.

Pearson, Anton T., "An Exegetical Study of Gen. 1.1-3", Bethel Seminary Quarterly, Nov., 1953, pp. 14-33.

Pember, G. H., "Earth's Earliest Ages", Hodder & Stoughton, London, 1901.

Pererius, Benedict, "Commentariorum et disputationum in Genesim", in 4 volumes, published between 1591-99.

Petavius, Dionysius, "De Opificio Sex Deierum", Bk. 1, Chap. ii, Section 10.

Pratt, H., "Scripture and Science NOT at Variance", Churchill, London, no date.

Pusey, E. B., "Daniel the Prophet: Nine Lectures", Innes & Co., London, 1892.

Ramm, Bernard, "The Christian View of Science and Scripture", Eerdman's, Grand Rapids, 1954.

Ratschow, C. H., "Werden und Wirken", Bernefte zur ZAW, 70, Alfred Topelmann, 1941.

Reusch, Fr. H., "Nature and the Bible: Lectures on the Mosaic History of Creation in Its Relation to Natural Science", translated by Kathleen Lyttleton from 4th ed., Clark, Edinburgh, 1886.

Ridderbos, N. H., "The Meaning of Genesis One", Free University Quarterly, Vol. IV, 1955-57, p. 222 f.

Rosenmuller, J. G., "Antiquissima Telluris Historia", Ulm, 1776.

Suer, Erich, "Dawn of World Redemption", Eerdman's, Grand Rapids, 1953.

Sedgewick, Adam, "Discourses on the Studies of the Universe", Cambridge, (circa 1860).

Skinner, John, "A Critical and Exegetical Commentary on Genesis" in The International Critical Commentary, Clark, Edinburgh, 1951.

Smith, J. Pye, "Scripture and Geology", London, 4th ed., (5th ed. in 1854).

Stoner, Peter W., "The Reconstruction or Catacysmic Theory", Journal American Scientific Affiliation, Sept., 1954, p.9-13.

Surburg, Raymond, "In the Beginning God Created" in "Darwin,

Evolution, and Creation", ed. by Paul A. Zimmerman, Concordia Publ., St. Louis, 1959.

Thayer, J. H., "A Greek-English Lexicon of the New Testament", Clark, Edinburgh, 4th ed., 1961.

Tregelles, S. P., translated "Gesenius' Hebrew and Chaldee Lexicon", Wiley & Sons, London, 1889.

Whitcomb, John C., "The Creation of the Heavens and the Earth", Creation Research Society Annual, Sept., 1967, pp.69-74; and "The Ruin-Reconstruction Theory of Gen.1.2", CRS Annual, 2:1965.

Whorf, Benjamin Lee, "Collected Papers on Metalinguistics", Dept. of State, Foreign Service Inst., Washington, D.C., 1952; "Language, Thought and Reality", Wiley & Co., N.Y., 1956.

Wiseman, Cardinal, "Lectures on the Connexion Between Science and Revealed Religion", 2 volumes, London, 1849.

Young, Edward J., "Studies in Genesis One", in "International Library of Philosophy and Theology: Biblical and Theological Studies", ed. by J. M. Kik, Presbyterian & Reformed Publ. Co., Phila., 1964; "Genesis One and Natural Science", Torch and Trumpet, 7, No.4; "The Relation of the First Verse of Genesis to verses 2 and 3:, Westminster Theological Journal, Vol.21, 1959, pp.133-146; "The Interpretation of Genesis 1.2", Westminster Theological Journal, Vol.23, 1961, pp.151-178.

Young, Robert, "A Literal Translation of the Bible", Pickering & Inglis, London, (n,d.); "The Holy Bible: A Translation According to the Letter and Idioms of the Original Languages", Pickering & Inglis, London, n.d.

* * *